lonely planet

FRENCH

Travel Phrasebook & Dictionary

Credits

Production Editor Megan Graieg

Language Writers Michael Janes, Jean-Pierre Masclef, Jean-Bernard Carillet

---

Thanks

Sofie Andersen, Marc Backwell, Fergal Condon, Gwen Cotter, Kellie Langdon, Vicky Smith, Saralinda Turner, Clifton Wilkinson

---

Published by Lonely Planet Global Limited
CRN 554153

Digital Depot, Roe Lane off Thomas Street, Dublin D08 TCV4, Ireland (EU authorised representative)

9th Edition – Sep 2026
ISBN 978 1 83758 463 5

Cover Image Croissant. Prophoto42/Shutterstock
Printed in China 10 9 8 7 6 5 4 3 2 1

Contact lonelyplanet.com/contact

Look out for the following icons throughout the book:

'Shortcut' Phrase
Easy-to-remember alternative to the full phrase

Q&A Pair
'Question-and-answer' pair – we suggest a response to the question asked

Look for
Phrases you may see on signs, menus etc

Listen for
Phrases you may hear from officials, locals etc

LANGUAGE TIP

An insight into the French language

CULTURE TIP

An insight into the local culture

How to read the phrases:

- Coloured words and phrases throughout the book are phonetic guides to help you pronounce the French.
- Lists of phrases with tinted background are options you can choose to complete the phrase above them.

These abbreviations will help you choose the right words and phrases in this book:

f	feminine	m	masculine	sg	singular
inf	informal	pl	plural		
lit	literal	pol	polite		

CONTENTS

INTRO

French

FRANÇAIS/FRON·SAY

Who speaks French?

Widely Understood Algeria – Andorra – Egypt Lebanon – Mauritania – Mauritius – Morocco – Tunisia

Why Bother

You may be told of a cosy vineyard way off the tourist track, or discover that there's little merit in the stereotype about the French being rude.

Distinctive Sounds

Throaty r, silent h, nasal vowels (pronounced as if you're trying to force the sound 'through the nose').

French in the World

French is the official language of a number of international organisations (including the UN and the International Olympic Committee). French films are internationally

112 MILLION speak French as their first language

312 MILLION speak French as a first or second language

renowned, and France has won the Nobel Prize in Literature more times than any other country.

French in France

Speaking a language other than their own is an emotional affair for the French, as attested by the online Musée des Horreurs (Museum of Horrors) of the Paris-based Défense de la Langue Française (DLF; Defence of the French Language; langue-francaise.org, in French).

False Friends

Warning: many French words look like English words but have a different meaning altogether, eg *menu* me·new is a set lunch, not a menu (which is *carte* kart in French).

Language Family

Romance (developed from the Latin spoken by the Romans during their conquest of the 1st century BCE). Close relatives include Italian, Spanish, Portuguese and Romanian.

Must-Know Grammar

French has a formal and informal word for 'you' (*vous* voo and *tu* tew respectively); it distinguishes between masculine and feminine forms of words, eg *beau/belle* bo/bel m/f (beautiful).

Donations to English

Numerous – thanks to the Norman invasion of England in the 11th century, some estimate that three-fifths of everyday English vocabulary arrived via French. You may recognise *café, déjà vu, bon vivant, cliché...*

5 Phrases TO LEARN BEFORE YOU GO

01 What are the opening hours?

Quelles sont les heures d'ouverture?

kel son lay zer doo·vair·tewr

French business hours are governed by a maze of regulations, so it's a good idea to check before you make plans.

02 I'd like the set menu, please.

Je voudrais le menu, s'il vous plaît.

zher voo·dray ler mer·new seel voo play

The best-value dining in France is the two- or three-course meal at a fixed price. Most restaurants have one on the chalkboard.

03 Which wine would you recommend?

Quel vin conseillez-vous?

kel vun kon·say·yay voo

Who better to ask for advice on wine than the French?

04 Can I address you with 'tu'?

Est-ce que je peux vous tutoyer?

es ker zher per voo tew·twa·yay

Before you start addressing someone with the informal 'you' form, it's polite to ask permission first.

05 Do you have plans for tonight/tomorrow?

Vous avez prévu quelque chose ce soir/demain?

voo za·vay pray·vew kel·ker shoz ser swar/der·mun

To arrange to meet up without sounding pushy, ask friends if they're available rather than inviting them directly.

10 Phrases TO SOUND LIKE A LOCAL

Cool!	**Génial!**	zhay·nyal
No worries.	**Pas de soucis.**	pa der soo·see
Sure.	**D'accord.**	da·kor
No way!	**Pas question!**	pa kay·styon
Just joking!	**Je plaisante!**	zher play·zont
Too bad.	**Tant pis.**	tom pee
What a shame.	**Quel dommage.**	kel do·mazh
What's up?	**Qu'est-ce qu'il y a?**	kes keel ya
Well done!	**Bien joué!**	byun zhoo·ay
Not bad.	**Pas mal.**	pa mal

FRENCH
Pronunciation

The sounds used in spoken French can almost all be found in English. There are a few exceptions: nasal vowels, the 'funny' u sound and that deep-in-the-throat r, but throwing caution to the wind and mimicking every French accent you've heard can be surprisingly effective.

VOWEL SOUNDS

Generally, French vowel sounds are short and don't glide into other vowels. As you order another coffee, listen to fellow patrons and note some of the differences in their pronunciation, like the ay in *café*. It's close to the English sound, but it's shorter and sharper.

SYMBOL	ENGLISH EQUIVALENT	FRENCH EXAMPLE	TRANSLITERATION
a	run	tasse	tas
ai	aisle	travail	tra·vai
air	fair	faire	fair
ay	say	musée	mew·zay
e	red	sept	set
ee	bee	lit	lee
er	her	deux	der
ew	ew with rounded lips	tu	tew
o	pot	pomme	pom
oo	moon	chou	shoo

NASAL VOWEL SOUNDS

Nasal vowels are pronounced as if you're trying to force the sound out of your nose rather than your mouth. It's easier than it sounds! English also has nasal vowels to some extent – when you say 'sing' in English, the 'i' is nasalised by the 'ng'. In French, though, nasal vowels cause the nasal consonant sound that follows them to be omitted, but a 'hint' of what the implied consonant is can sometimes be heard. We've used nasal consonant sounds (m, n, ng) with the nasal vowel to help you produce the sound with more confidence. Although there are four nasal vowels in French, our pronunciation guides use only two: o and u. These approximate the actual sounds. The four nasal sounds can be quite close, so to get you out there speaking, we've simplified it in the following way:

SYMBOL	ENGLISH EQUIVALENT	FRENCH EXAMPLE	TRANSLITERATION
om on ong	like 'pot' + nasal consonant sound	mouton	moo·ton
um un ung	similar to 'bat' + nasal consonant sound	magasin	ma·ga·zun

CONSONANT SOUNDS

Swallow deeply and prepare for just one sticking point when it comes to pronouncing French consonants: the r sound. It's made in the back of the throat, a little like a growl. Using an English 'r' sound will get you by, but it's one of the French sounds that will really help you sound natural – it's well worth working on. The other consonant sounds can all be found in English.

SYMBOL	ENGLISH EQUIVALENT	FRENCH EXAMPLE	TRANSLITERATION
b	big	billet	bee·yay
d	din	date	dat
f	fun	femme	fum
g	go	grand	gron
k	kick	carte	kart
l	loud	livre	leev·rer
m	man	merci	mair·see
n	no	non	nong
ng	sang	cinquante	sung·kont
ny	canyon	signe	see·nyer
p	pig	parc	park
r	run	rue	rew
s	so	si	see
sh	show	changer	shon·zhay
t	tin	tout	too
v	van	verre	vair
w	win	oui	wee
y	yes	payer, billet	pay·yay, bee·yay
z	is	vous avez	voo za·vay
zh	pleasure	je	zher

WORD STRESS & RHYTHM

Syllables in French words are, for the most part, equally stressed. English speakers tend to stress the first syllable, which is definitely unusual in French, so try adding a light stress on the final syllable to compensate.

The rhythm of a French sentence is based on breaking the phrase into meaningful sections, then stressing the final syllable in each. The stress at these points is characterised by a slight rise in intonation. The 'beat' of the sentence is quite regular because of these stressed syllables (in italics in the example following).

French pronunciation, unlike that of English, is quite easy.

La prononciation du français, à la différence de l'anglais, est assez facile.
la pro·non·see·a·syon dew fron·*say* a la dee·fair·rons der long·*glay* ay ta·say fa·*seel*

INTONATION

A rising intonation in French is used when asking a question. There is also a rise in intonation when listing items: your voice goes up after each item until you say the final item in the list, at which point your voice falls.

READING & WRITING

Writing French is a little more complicated than speaking it. The spelling of verb endings is a great example: sometimes an ending might consist of up to five letters and sound the same as a two-letter ending (eg both *-aient* and *-ai* sound like ay). Take heart though: the French themselves have difficulty with spelling – the annual national spelling competition attests to that.

If you try to compare the written French and the pronunciation guides in this book, you'll start to notice some of the relationships between sound and writing.

FRENCH ALPHABET

A a a	**B b** bay	**C c** say
D d day	**E e** er	**F f** ef
G g zhay	**H h** ash	**I i** ee
J j zhee	**K k** ka	**L l** el
M m em	**N n** en	**O o** o
P p pay	**Q q** kew	**R r** air
S s es	**T t** tay	**U u** ew
V v vay	**W w** doo·bler·vay	**X x** iks
Y y ee·grek	**Z z** zed	

FRENCH
Grammar

This chapter is designed to explain the main grammatical structures you need in order to make your own sentences. Look under each heading – listed in alphabetical order – for information on functions which these grammatical categories express in a sentence. For example, demonstratives are used for giving instructions, so you'll need them to tell the taxi driver where your hotel is. A glossary of grammatical terms is included at the end of the chapter to help you.

ADJECTIVES & ADVERBS

Describing People/Things • Doing Things

As a rule, adjectives come after the noun in French. There are exceptions, however, such as *grand* gron (big) and *petit* per·tee (small), which come before the noun.

an expensive hotel	un hôtel cher (lit: a hotel expensive-m-sg) un o·tel shair

In French, adjectives agree with the noun in gender (see also **gender**, p17). Generally, for the feminine form of an adjective just add an *-e* to the end. Note though that this ending usually causes the consonant before it to be pronounced, or it may change the final vowel sound or the preceding consonant.

	MASCULINE		FEMININE	
small	petit	per·tee	petite	per·teet
next	prochain	pro·shun	prochaine	pro·shen
white	blanc	blong	blanche	blonsh

Adjectives whose masculine form ends in *-e* don't change form for gender, eg *jeune* zhern (young) or *riche* reesh (rich). Other adjectives differ more significantly in their masculine and feminine form, eg *beau/belle* m/f bo/bel (beautiful).

Adjectives also agree with the noun in number. In general, to make an adjective plural, add *-s* to the end (see also **plurals**, p20).

gay venue	boîte gaie	bwat gay
gay venues	boîtes gaies	bwat gay

To form adverbs in French, you generally add the ending *-ment* mon (just like you add '-ly' in English) to the feminine form of the adjective, or to the masculine form if it ends in a vowel. Adverbs are placed after the verb they modify (see also **verbs**, p24).

slow	lent(e) m/f	lon(t)
to speak slowly	parler lentement	par·lay lon·ter·mon

ARTICLES

Naming People/Things

French has three words for the definite article (ie 'the' in English), depending on the noun's gender and number (see **gender**, p17; and **plurals**, p20). Both *le* and *la* become *l'* before a word beginning with a vowel or *h*, eg *l'hôtel* lo·tel (hotel) or *l'eau* lo (water).

DEFINITE ARTICLES

m sg	le	ler	**the steak**	le biftek	ler beef·tek
f sg	la	la	**the tart**	la tarte	la tart
pl	les	lay	**the snails**	les escargots	lay zes·kar·go

Similarly, there are three words for the indefinite article (ie 'a' or 'an' in English) to match the gender and number of the noun.

INDEFINITE ARTICLES

m	un	un	**a ticket**	un ticket	un tee·kay
f	une	ewn	**a postcard**	une carte postale	ewn kart pos·tal
pl	des	day	**some apples**	des pommes	day pom

BE

Describing People/Things • Making Statements

The verb *être* e·trer (be) changes form depending on the subject, just as in English. For information on negative forms, see **negatives**, p18.

ÊTRE (BE) – PRESENT TENSE

I am	je suis	zher swee
you are sg inf	tu es	tew ay
you are sg pol	vous êtes	voo zet
he/she is	il/elle est	eel/el ay
we are	nous sommes	noo som
you are pl	vous êtes	voo zet
they are	ils/elles sont m/f	eel/el son m/f

DEMONSTRATIVES

Giving Instructions • Indicating Location • Pointing Things Out

The easiest way to point something out in French is to use the phrase *c'est* say (lit: it-is).

That's the right train.	C'est le bon train. (lit: it-is the-m-sg good-m-sg train) say ler bon trun

The demonstrative adjectives 'this' and 'that' are translated with the same word in French – *ce* ser for masculine singular nouns and *cette* set for feminine singular nous. The plural form of both words is *ces* say (these/those). See also **gender** and **plurals** (p20).

this/that group	ce groupe	ser groop
this/that woman	cette femme	set tam
these/those people	ces gens	say zhon

GENDER

Naming People/Things

In French, all nouns (words which denote a thing, person or idea) have either masculine or feminine gender. You can recognise the noun's gender by the article, demonstrative, possessive or any other adjective accompanying the noun, as they change form to agree with the noun's gender (see **adjectives & adverbs**, p14; **articles**, p15; **demonstratives**, **possessives**, p21). The gender of words is also indicated in the dictionary, but here are some general rules:

- A word is masculine/feminine if it refers to a man/woman.
- Words ending in a consonant, *-acle*, *-age*, *-ème* or *-isme* are generally masculine.
- Words ending in *-e*, *-ion* or *-aison* are usually feminine.

The masculine and feminine forms of words are indicated with m and f throughout this phrasebook where relevant. See also the boxed text, p129.

HAVE

Possessing

Possession can be indicated in various ways in French (see also **possessives**, p21). One way is by using the verb *avoir* a·vwar (have). For information on negative forms, see **negatives**.

AVOIR (HAVE) – PRESENT TENSE

I have	j'ai	zhay
you have sg inf	tu as	tew a
you have sg pol	vous avez	voo za·vay
he/she has	il/elle a	eel/el a
we have	nous avons	noo za·von
you have	vous avez	voo za·vay
they have	ils/elles ont m/f	eel/el zon m/f

NEGATIVES

Negating

To make a sentence negative, French uses two words – *ne* ner and *pas* pa, both meaning 'not' – around the verb:

I don't know.	Je ne sais pas. (lit: I not know not) zher ner say pa

If there are two verbs or two words that make up the verb, the *ne* ... *pas* goes around the first verb or first part of the verb:

I don't want to go.	Je ne veux pas aller. (lit: I not want not go) zher ner ver pa za·lay

With another negative word in the sentence, *pas* is omitted:

I have nothing to declare.	Je n'ai rien à déclarer. (lit: I not-have nothing to declare) zher nay ryun a day·kla·ray

The word *pas* pa (not) is used alone when there is no verb:

Not yet.	Pas encore.	pa ong·kor
Not bad.	Pas mal.	pa mal

PERSONAL PRONOUNS

Making Statements • Naming People/Things

Personal pronouns ('I', 'you' etc) change form in French depending on whether they're the subject or the object in a sentence, just like English has 'I' and 'me' as the subject and object pronouns (eg 'I see her' and 'She sees me'). The subject pronoun *on* on (one) is often used to refer to a nonspecific subject:

French is spoken here.	On parle français ici. (lit: one speaks French here) on parl fron·say ee·see

SUBJECT PRONOUNS

I	je	zher	**we**	nous	noo
you sg inf	tu	tew	**you** pl	vous	voo
you sg pol	vous	voo			
he/it	il	eel	**they**	ils m	eel m
she/it	elle	el		elles f	el f

When talking to someone familiar or younger than you, use the informal form of 'you', *tu* tew, rather than the polite form, *vous* voo. Phrases in this book use the form of 'you' that is appropriate to the situation. Where both forms are used, they are indicated by pol and inf. See also the boxed text, p99.

OBJECT PRONOUNS

me	me	mer	**us**	nous	noo
you sg inf	te	ter	**you** pl	vous	voo
you sg pol	vous	voo			
him/it	le/lui	ler/lwee	**them**	les/leur	lay/ler
her/it	la/lui	la/lwee			

In the table above, the French forms separated by a slash are direct/indirect object pronouns.

The direct and indirect object pronouns differ only for the third person ('he', 'she', 'it', 'they').

I see him.	Je le vois. (lit: I him see) zher ler vwa
I gave him the ticket.	Je lui ai donné le billet. (lit: I to-him have given the-m-sg ticket) zher lwee ay do·nay ler bee·yay

The object pronouns are placed before the verb. The direct object pronoun comes before the indirect object pronoun.

I gave it to him.	Je le lui ai donné. (lit: I it-m-sg to-him have given) zher ler lwee ay do·nay

PLURALS

Naming People/Things

To form the plural of a noun in French, an *-s* is added to the noun in writing (though there are exceptions), but it's often not pronounced. In spoken language, the easiest way to indicate plural is to use words like *beaucoup de* bo·koo der (a lot of), numbers or the plural articles *les* lay and *des* day (see **articles**, p15).

I'd like two tickets.	Je voudrais deux billets. (lit: I would-like two tickets) zher voo·dray der bee·yay

POSSESSIVES

Possessing

A common way of indicating possession is by using possessive adjectives before the noun they refer to. Like other adjectives, they agree with the noun in number, and sometimes also in gender (see also **gender**, p17, and **plurals**).

POSSESSIVE ADJECTIVES

my	mon/mes m ma/mes f	mon/may m ma/may f	**our**	notre/nos	no·trer/no
your sg inf	ton/tes m ta/tes f	ton/tay m ta/tay f	**your** pl	votre/vos	vo·trer/vo
your sg pol	votre/vos	vo·trer/vo			
his/her/its	son/ses m sa/ses f	son/say m sa/say f	**their**	leur/leurs	ler/ler

In the table above, the French forms separated by a slash are used with a singular/plural noun.

When a singular noun begins with 'h' or a vowel, *mon, ton* and *son* are used, regardless of the noun's gender:

my team	mon équipe (lit: my team-f-sg) mon ay·keep

Another way to indicate possession is by using possessive pronouns, which also agree in number and sometimes gender with the noun. The corresponding definite article is used before the possessive pronoun (see **articles**, p15).

That bag is mine.	Ce sac est le mien. (lit: that-m-sg bag is the-m-sg mine-m-sg) ser sak ay ler myun

POSSESSIVE PRONOUNS

mine	mien/miens m mienne/miennes f	myun/myun m myen/myen f	**ours**	nôtre/nôtres	no·trer/no·trer
yours sg inf	tien/tiens m tienne/tiennes f	tyun/tyun m tyen/tyen f	**yours** pl	vôtre/vôtres	vo·trer/vo·trer
yours sg pol	vôtre/vôtres	vo·trer/vo·trer			
his/hers/its	sien/siens m sienne/siennes f	syun/syun m syen/syen f	**theirs**	leur/leurs	ler/ler

In the table above, the French forms separated by a slash are used with a singular/plural noun.

You can also indicate ownership by using the verb *avoir* a·vwar (see **have**, p18) or with '*de* der (of) + noun', just as in English:

Marie's bag	le sac de Marie (lit: the-m-sg bag of Marie) ler sak der ma·ree

PREPOSITIONS

Giving Instructions • Indicating Location • Pointing Things Out

Like English, French uses prepositions to explain where things are in time or space. Common prepositions are listed in the table below; for more prepositions, see the **dictionary**, p196.

PREPOSITIONS

after	après	a·pray	**from**	de	der
at (time)	à	a	**in (place)**	dans	don
before	avant	a·von	**to**	à	a

QUESTIONS

Asking Questions • Negating

The easiest way to ask a 'yes/no' question in French is to make a statement and add a rise in your intonation as you speak. Alternatively, you can use *est-ce que* es ker (lit: is-it that) in front of a statement.

Is this the right train?	Est-ce que c'est le bon train? (lit: is-it that it-is the-m-sg good-m-sg train) es ker say ler bon trun

Another way to ask a 'yes/no' question is to put the verb before the subject of the sentence, as in English, and link them with a hyphen.

Do you have a car?	As-tu une voiture? (lit: have-you-sg-inf a-f-sg car) a·tew ewn vwa·tewr

Just as in English, there are also question words for asking more specific questions. These words are used at the start of the sentence in French.

QUESTION WORDS

how	comment	ko·mon	**where**	où	oo
what	qu'est-ce que	kes ker	**who**	qui	kee
when	quand	kon	**why**	pourquoi	poor·kwa

To answer 'yes' after a question in the affirmative, use *oui* wee, and to answer 'yes (I do)' after a question in the negative, use *si* see. The negative answer is *non* non (no).

ABOUT FRENCH GRAMMAR

VERBS

Doing Things

There are three verb categories in French – those whose infinitive (dictionary form) ends in *-ir, -er* or *-re,* eg *finir* fee·neer (finish), *parler* par·lay (speak), *vendre* von·drer (sell). Tenses are formed by adding various endings for each person to the verb stem (the part of the verb that remains after removing *-ir, -er* or *-re*), and for most verbs these endings follow regular patterns according to the verb category. The verb endings for the present and future tenses are shown in the following tables. For negative forms of verbs, see **negatives**, p18.

PRESENT TENSE

		finir	parler	vendre
I	je	finis	parle	vends
you sg inf	tu	finis	parles	vends
you sg pol	vous	finissez	parlez	vendez
he/she	il/elle	finit	parle	vend
we	nous	finissons	parlons	vendons
you pl	vous	finissez	parlez	vendez
they	ils/elles m/f	finissent	parlent	vendent

The main past tense in French, used for a completed action, is a compound tense, which means it is made up of an auxiliary verb – either *être* e·trer (be) or *avoir* a·vwar (have) – in the present tense, plus a form of the main verb, called 'past participle' (see also **be**, p16, and **have**, p18). The past participle is formed by replacing the infinitive endings *-ir, -er* or *-re* with *-i, -é* or *-u* respectively (some past participles are irregular). Past participles of the verbs taking *être* must agree with the subject in gender and number, while past participles of the verbs taking *avoir* don't change form.

We arrived. Nous sommes arrivées. (lit: we are arrived-f-pl)
noo som za·ree·vay

They saw. Elles ont vu. (lit: they-f have seen)
el zon vew

	INFINITIVE		PAST PARTICIPLE	
finish	finir	fee·neer	fini	fee·nee
speak	parler	par·lay	parlé	par·lay
sell	vendre	von·drer	vendu	von·dew

In the future tense, the endings follow the same pattern for all three verb categories, and they are simply added to the infinitive (dictionary form of the verb), not the verb stem. For verbs ending in *-re* the final *e* is dropped before adding the new endings.

FUTURE TENSE

		finir	**parler**	**vendre**
I	je	finirai	parlerai	vendrai
you sg inf	tu	finiras	parleras	vendras
you sg pol	vous	finirez	parlerez	vendrez
he/she	il/elle	finira	parlera	vendra
we	nous	finirons	parlerons	vendrons
you pl	vous	finirez	parlerez	vendrez
they	ils/elles m/f	finiront	parleront	vendront

WORD ORDER

Making Statements

The basic word order in French is subject-verb-object, just as in English. See also **negatives**, p18, and **questions**, p23.

I speak French. Je parle français. (lit: I speak French)
zher parl fron·say

GRAMMAR GLOSSARY

adjective	a word that describes something – 'there are five **basic** types of cheese in France'
adverb	a word that explains how an action is done – 'that are **usually** displayed in cheese shops'
article	the words 'a', 'an' and 'the'
demonstrative	a word that means 'this' or 'that'
direct object	the thing or person in the sentence that has the action directed to it – 'you can sample **them**'
gender	classification of *nouns* into classes (like masculine and feminine), requiring other words (eg *adjectives*) to belong to the same class
indirect object	the person or thing in the sentence that is the recipient of the action – 'and the merchants will often give **you** advice'
infinitive	dictionary form of a *verb* – 'on what **to choose**'
noun	a thing, person or idea – 'it's a **matter** of **taste**'
number	whether a word is singular or plural – 'and the **choices** on offer can be overwhelming'
personal pronoun	a word that means 'I', 'you' etc
possessive adjective	a word that means 'my', 'your' etc
possessive pronoun	a word that means 'mine', 'yours' etc
preposition	a word like 'for' or 'before'
subject	the thing or person in the sentence that does the action – '**you** should also consider'
tense	form of a *verb* that tells you whether the action is in the present, past or future – eg 'eat' (present), 'ate' (past), 'will eat' (future)
verb	a word that tells you what action happened – 'which wine **goes** best with each type of cheese'
verb stem	part of a *verb* that doesn't change – eg '**sampl**' in '**sampling**' and '**sampled**'

BASICS

Understanding

KEY PHRASES

Do you speak English?	Parlez-vous anglais?	par·lay·voo ong·glay
I don't understand.	Je ne comprends pas.	zher ner kom·pron pa
What does ... mean?	Que veut dire ...?	ker ver deer ...

Q **Do you speak English?**	Parlez-vous anglais? par·lay·voo ong·glay
A **I speak a little.**	Je parle un peu. zher parl um per
Q **Do you understand?**	Comprenez-vous? kom·prer·nay·voo
A **I understand.**	Je comprends. zher kom·pron
A **I don't understand.**	Je ne comprends pas. zher ner kom·pron pa
I need an interpreter who speaks English.	J'ai besoin d'un interprète de langue anglaise. zhay ber·zwun dun nun·tair·pret der long ong·glayz
I'd like to practise French.	Je voudrais parler en français. zher voo·dray par·lay on fron·say
What does ... mean?	Que veut dire ...? ker ver deer ...

LANGUAGE TIP: FALSE FRIENDS

Many French words look like English words but have a different meaning altogether – beware!

Here are a few:

car	kar coach/bus (not 'car', which is *voiture* vwa·tewr)
information	un·for·ma·syon news (not 'information', which is *renseignement* ron·sen·yer·mon)
introduire	un·tro·dweer insert (not 'introduce', which is *présenter* pray·zon·tay)
librairie	lee·bray·ree bookshop (not 'library', which is *bibliothèque* bee·blee·o·tek)
menu	me·new set menu (not 'menu', which is *carte* kart)
prune	prewn plum (not 'prune', which is *pruneau* prew·no)
vacance	va·kons holidays (not 'vacancy', which is *poste vacant* post va·kon)

How do you pronounce this?	Comment le prononcez-vous? ko·mon ler pro·non·say voo
How do you write ...?	Comment est-ce qu'on écrit ...? ko·mon es kon ay·kree ...
Could you please repeat that?	Pourriez-vous répéter, s'il vous plaît? poo·ree·yay·voo ray·pay·tay seel voo play

LANGUAGE TIP: READING FRENCH

In written French, you'll often see an *l'* in front of a word beginning with a vowel or a silent *h:* this replaces a *le* or a *la* (the) and is pronounced as a single word starting with an *l*, eg, *l'orange* lo·ronzh.

Generally, you don't pronounce a consonant at the end of a word, eg *faux* fo. There's one exception – final 'c', eg *sec* sek. Also, you do pronounce a final consonant if the next word starts with a vowel or an *h*, eg *faux ami* fo zami.

Could you please write it down?	Pourriez-vous l'écrire, s'il vous plaît?	poo·ree·yay·voo lay·kreer seel voo play
Could you please speak more slowly?	Pourriez-vous parler plus lentement, s'il vous plaît?	poo·ree·yay·voo par·lay plew lon·ter·mon seel voo play
Slowly, please!	Lentement, s'il vous plaît!	lon·ter·mon seel voo play

Numbers & Amounts

KEY PHRASES

How many/much?	Combien?	kom·byun
a few/some	quelques	kel·ker
a lot/many	beaucoup de	bo·koo der

CARDINAL NUMBERS

0	zéro	zay·ro
1	un	un
2	deux	der
3	trois	trwa
4	quatre	ka·trer
5	cinq	sungk
6	six	sees
7	sept	set
8	huit	weet
9	neuf	nerf
10	dix	dees
11	onze	onz
12	douze	dooz
13	treize	trez
14	quatorze	ka·torz
15	quinze	kunz
16	seize	sez
17	dix-sept	dee·set
18	dix-huit	dee·zweet

19	dix-neuf	deez·nerf
20	vingt	vung
21	vingt et un	vung tay un
22	vingt-deux	vung·der
30	trente	tront
40	quarante	ka·ront
50	cinquante	sung·kont
60	soixante	swa·sont
70	soixante-dix	swa·son·dees
80	quatre-vingts	ka·trer·vung
90	quatre-vingt-dix	ka·trer·vung·dees
100	cent	son
1000	mille	meel
1,000,000	un million	um meel·yon

ORDINAL NUMBERS

1st	premier/première m/f	prer·myay/prer·myair
2nd	deuxième	der·zyem
3rd	troisième	trwa·zyem

USEFUL AMOUNTS

How many/ much?	Combien?	kom·byun
a quarter	un quart	ung kar
a third	un tiers	un tyair
a half	un demi	un der·mee
all	tout	too
none	rien	ryun

For other useful amounts, see **self-catering** (p169).

Time & Dates

KEY PHRASES

What time is it?	Quelle heure est-il?	kel er ay·teel
At what time?	À quelle heure?	a kel er
What date?	Quelle date?	kel dat

TELLING THE TIME

The 24-hour clock is usually used when telling the time in French. After the half hour, use the next hour minus (*moins* mwun) the minutes until that hour arrives.

Q **What time is it?**	Quelle heure est-il? kel er ay·teel
A **It's one o'clock.**	Il est une heure. ee lay ewn er
A **It's (10) o'clock.**	Il est (dix) heures. ee lay (deez) er
Quarter past (10).	Il est (dix) heures et quart. ee lay (deez) er ay kar
Twenty past (10).	Il est (dix) heures vingt. ee lay (deez) er vung
Half past (10).	Il est (dix) heures et demie. ee lay (deez) er ay der·mee
Twenty to (10).	Il est (dix) heures moins vingt. ee lay (deez) er mwun vung
Quarter to (10).	Il est (dix) heures moins le quart. ee lay (deez) er mwun ler kar

At what time?	À quelle heure? a kel er	
At ...	À ... a ...	

morning	matin m	ma·tun
day	jour m	zhoor
midday	midi m	mee·dee
afternoon	après-midi m	a·pray·mee·dee
evening	soir m	swar
night	nuit f	nwee
midnight	minuit m	mee·nwee

THE CALENDAR

Monday	lundi m	lun·dee
Tuesday	mardi m	mar·dee
Wednesday	mercredi m	mair·krer·dee
Thursday	jeudi m	zher·dee
Friday	vendredi m	von·drer·dee
Saturday	samedi m	sam·dee
Sunday	dimanche m	dee·monsh

January	janvier m	zhon·vyay
February	février m	fayv·ryay
March	mars m	mars
April	avril m	a·vreel
May	mai m	may
June	juin m	zhwun
July	juillet m	zhwee·yay
August	août m	oot
September	septembre m	sep·tom·brer
October	octobre m	ok·to·brer

November	novembre m	no·vom·brer
December	décembre m	day·som·brer
summer	été m	ay·tay
autumn	automne m	o·ton
winter	hiver m	ee·vair
spring	printemps m	prun·tom

What date?	Quelle date? kel dat
Q **What's today's date?**	C'est quel jour aujourd'hui? say kel zhoor o·zhoor·dwee
A **It's (18 October).**	C'est le (dix-huit octobre). say ler (dee·zwee tok·to·brer)

PRESENT

today	aujourd'hui	o·zhoor·dwee
this morning	ce matin	ser ma·tun
this afternoon	cet après-midi	say ta·pray·mee·dee
tonight	ce soir	ser swar
this week	cette semaine	set ser·men
this month	ce mois	ser mwa
this year	cette année	set a·nay

PAST

half an hour ago	une demi-heure avant ewn de·mee·er a·von
(three) days ago	il y a (trois) jours eel ya (trwa) zhoor
(five) years ago	il y a (cinq) ans eel ya (sungk) on
day before yesterday	avant-hier a·von·tyair

yesterday morning	hier matin ee·yair ma·tun
yesterday afternoon	hier après-midi ee·yair a·pray·mee·dee
yesterday evening	hier soir ee·yair swar
last week	la semaine dernière la ser·men dair·nyair
last month	le mois dernier ler mwa dair·nyay
last year	l'année dernière la·nay dair·nyair

FUTURE

in (five) minutes	dans (cinq) minutes don (sungk) mee·newt
within an hour	d'ici une heure dee·see ewn er
in (six) days	dans (six) jours don (see) zhoor
tomorrow morning	demain matin der·mun ma·tun
tomorrow afternoon	demain après-midi der·mun a·pray·mee·dee
tomorrow evening	demain soir der·mun swar
day after tomorrow	après-demain a·pray·der·mun
next week	la semaine prochaine la se·men pro·shen
next month	le mois prochain ler mwa pro·shun
next year	l'année prochaine la·nay pro·shen

PRACTICAL

Transport

KEY PHRASES

When's the next bus?	Le prochain bus passe à quelle heure?	ler pro·shun bews pas a kel er
One ticket to ..., please.	Un billet pour ..., s'il vous plaît.	um bee·yay poor ... seel voo play
Can you tell me when we get to ...?	Pouvez-vous me dire quand nous arrivons à ...?	poo·vay·voo mer deer kon noo za·ree·von a ...
Please take me to this address.	Conduisez-moi à cette adresse, s'il vous plaît.	kon·dwee·zay·mwa a set a·dres seel voo play
I'd like to hire a car.	Je voudrais louer une voiture.	zher voo·dray loo·way ewn vwa·tewr

GETTING AROUND

What time does the ... leave? À quelle heure part ...?
a kel er par ...

boat	le bateau	ler ba·to
bus	le bus	ler bews
plane	l'avion	la·vyon
train	le train	ler trun
tram	le tramway	ler tram·way

What time's the first bus? Le premier bus passe à quelle heure?
ler prer·myay bews pas a kel er

What time's the last bus?	Le dernier bus passe à quelle heure?	ler dair·nyay bews pas a kel er
What time's the next bus?	Le prochain bus passe à quelle heure?	ler pro·shun bews pas a kel er
What time does it arrive?	À quelle heure est-ce qu'il arrive?	a kel er es keel a·ree·ve
Which platform does it depart from?	Il part de quel quai?	eel par der kel kay
Which bus goes to (Bordeaux)?	Quel bus va à (Bordeaux)?	kel bews va a (bor·do)
That's my seat.	C'est ma place.	say ma plas
Is this seat taken?	Est-ce que cette place est occupée?	es ker set plas ay to·kew·pay

Is it taken? C'est occupée? say to·kew·pay

For bus numbers, see **numbers & amounts** (p31).

Can we get there by public transport?	Peux-t-on s'y rendre en transport publique?	per·ton see ron·dre on trons·por pewb·leek
I'd prefer to walk there.	Je préfère y marcher.	zhe pray·fair ee mar·shay
Can I take my car on the boat?	Je peux transporter ma voiture sur ce bateau?	zher per trons·por·tay ma vwa·tewr sewr ser ba·to
Can I take my bike?	Je peux amener mon vélo?	zher per am·nay mon vay·lo

Can you tell me when we get to (Nice)?	Pouvez-vous me dire quand nous arrivons à (Nice)? poo·vay·voo mer deer kon noo za·ree·von a (nees)
I want to get off at (Nantes).	Je veux descendre à (Nantes). zher ver day·son·drer a (nont)
I want to get off here.	Je veux descendre ici. zher ver day·son·drer ee·see

For phrases for getting through customs and immigration, see **border crossing** (p50). For phrases on disabled access, see **seniors & travellers with disabilities** (p93).

BUYING TICKETS

Where can I buy a ticket?	Où peut-on acheter un billet? oo per·ton ash·tay um bee·yay
Do I need to book?	Est-ce qu'il faut réserver une place? es keel fo ray·zer·vay ewn plas
I'd like to ... my ticket, please.	Je voudrais ... mon billet, s'il vous plaît. zher voo·dray ... mom bee·yay seel voo play

cancel	annuler	a·new·lay
change	changer	shon·zhay
collect	retirer	re·tee·ray
confirm	confirmer	kon·feer·may

How much is it?	C'est combien? say kom·byun
It's full.	C'est complet. say kom·play

Buying a Ticket

WHAT TIME IS THE NEXT ...?
À quelle heure part le prochain ...?
a kel er par ler pro·shun ...

BOAT
bateau
ba·to

BUS
bus
bews

TRAIN
train
trun

ONE ... TICKET, PLEASE.
Un billet ..., s'il vous plaît.
um bee·yay ... seel voo play

ONE-WAY
simple
sum·pler

RETURN
aller et retour
a·lay ay rer·toor

I'D LIKE A/AN ... SEAT.
Je voudrais une place ...
zher voo·dray ewn plas ...

AISLE
côté couloir
ko·tay koo·lwar

WINDOW
côté fenêtre
ko·tay fe·ne·trer

WHICH PLATFORM DOES IT DEPART FROM?
Il part de quel quai?
eel par der kel kay

One ... ticket (to Paris), please.	Un billet ... (pour Paris), s'il vous plaît. um bee·yay ... (poor pa·ree) seel voo play

1st-class	de première classe	der prem·yair klas
2nd-class	de seconde classe	der sgond klas
child's	au tarif enfant	o ta·reef on·fon
one-way	simple	sum·pler
return	aller et retour	a·lay ay rer·toor
student's	au tarif étudiant	o ta·reef ay·tew·dyon

I'd like a/an ... seat.	Je voudrais une place ... zher voo·dray ewn plas ...

aisle	côté couloir	ko·tay koo·lwar
nonsmoking	non-fumeur	non few·mer
smoking	fumeur	few·mer
window	côté fenêtre	ko·tay fe·ne·trer

Is there air-conditioning?	Est-qu'il y a la climatisation? es·keel ya la klee·ma·tee·za·syon
Is there a toilet?	Est-qu'il y a des toilettes? es·keel ya day twa·let
How long does the trip take?	Le trajet dure combien de temps? ler tra·zhay dewr kom·byun der tom
Is it a direct route?	Est-ce que c'est direct? es ker say dee·rekt

LUGGAGE

Where's the baggage claim?	Où est la livraison des bagages? oo ay la lee·vray·zon day ba·gazh
My luggage has been damaged/stolen.	Mes bagages ont été endommagés/volés. may ba·gazh on tay·tay on·do·ma·zhay/vo·lay
My luggage hasn't arrived.	Mes bagages ne sont pas arrivés. may ba·gazh ner son pa za·ree·vay
I'd like a luggage locker.	Je voudrais une consigne automatique. zher voo·dray ewn kon·see·nyer o·to·ma·teek

C'est quelle gare?
say kel gar
What station is this?

TRAIN

What station is this?	C'est quelle gare? say kel gar
What's the next station?	Quelle est la prochaine gare? kel ay la pro·shen gar
Does this train stop at (Amboise)?	Est-ce que ce train s'arrête à (Amboise)? es ker se trun sa·ret a (om·bwaz)
Do I need to change trains?	Est-ce qu'il faut changer de train? es keel fo shon·zhay der trun
Which carriage is for (Bordeaux)?	C'est quelle voiture pour (Bordeaux)? say kel vwa·tewr poor (bor·do)
Which is the dining car?	Où est le wagon-restaurant? oo ay ler va·gon·res·to·ron

BOAT

Are there life jackets?	Est-ce qu'il y a des gilets de sauvetage? es keel ya day zhee·lay der sov·tazh
What's the sea like today?	L'état de la mer est bon? lay·ta der la mair ay bon
I feel seasick.	J'ai le mal de mer. zhay ler mal der mair

TAXI

I'd like a taxi (at nine o'clock).	Je voudrais un taxi (à neuf heures). zher voo·dray un tak·see (a nerf er)

I'd like a taxi tomorrow.	Je voudrais un taxi demain. zher voo·dray un tak·see der·mun
Where's the taxi stand?	Où est la station de taxis? oo ay la sta·syon der tak·see
Is this taxi available?	Vous êtes libre? voo zet lee·brer
Please put the meter on.	Mettez le compteur, s'il vous plaît. me·tay ler kon·ter seel voo play
How much is it to (the Eiffel Tower)?	C'est combien pour aller à (la Tour Eiffel)? say kom·byun poor a·lay a (la toor ee·fel)
Please take me to (this address).	Conduisez-moi à (cette adresse), s'il vous plaît. kon·dwee·zay·mwa a (set a·dres) seel voo play
To ...	À ... a ...
How much is the final fare?	C'est combien en tout? say kom·byun on too
Please slow down.	Roulez plus lentement, s'il vous plaît. roo·lay plew lont·mon seel voo play
Please wait here.	Attendez ici, s'il vous plaît. a·ton·day ee·see seel voo play
Stop at the corner.	Arrêtez-vous au coin de la rue. a·ray·tay·voo o kwun der la rew
Stop here.	Arrêtez-vous ici. a·ray·tay·voo ee·see

For other useful phrases, see **directions** (p52), and **money & banking** (p83).

CAR & MOTORBIKE

I'd like to hire a/an ...	Je voudrais louer ... zher voo·dray loo·way ...

4WD	un quatre-quatre	ung kat·kat
automatic	une automatique	ewn o·to·ma·teek
(small/large) car	une (petite/ grosse) voiture	ewn (per·teet/ gros) vwa·tewr
manual	une manuel	ewn ma·nwel
motorbike	une moto	ewn mo·to

How much for daily hire?	Quel est le tarif par jour? kel ay ler ta·reef par zhoor
How much for weekly hire?	Quel est le tarif par semaine? kel ay ler ta·reef par ser·men
Does that include mileage?	Est-ce que le kilométrage est compris? es ker ler kee·lo·may·trazh ay kom·pree

LOOK FOR

Cédez la Priorité	say·day la pree·o·ree·tay	Give Way
Entrée	on·tray	Entrance
Péage	pay·azh	Toll
Sens Interdit	sons un·ter·dee	No Entry
Sens Unique	sons ew·neek	One-Way
Sortie	sor·tee	Exit
Stop	stop	Stop

Does that include insurance?	Est-ce que l'assurance est comprise? es ker la·sew·rons ay kom·preez
Can I return it in another city?	Je peux la rendre dans une autre ville? zher per la ron·drer don zewn o·trer veel
What's the speed limit?	Quelle est la vitesse maximale permise? kel ay la vee·tes mak·see·mal per·meez
Is this the road to (Toulouse)?	C'est la route pour (Toulouse)? say la root poor (too·looz)
(How long) Can I park here?	(Combien de temps) Est-ce que je peux stationner ici? (kom·byun der tom) es ker zher per sta·syo·nay ee·see

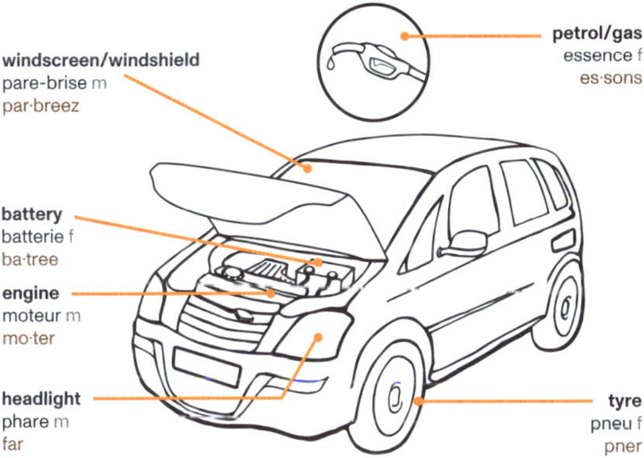

LOOK FOR

diesel m	dyay·zel	diesel
au plomb	o plom	leaded
essence f	es·sons	petrol/gas
ordinaire	or·dee·nair	regular

Where's a petrol station?	Où est-ce qu'il y a une station-service? oo es keel ya ewn sta·syon·ser·vees
Please fill it up.	Le plein, s'il vous plaît. ler plun seel voo play
I'd like (20) litres.	Je voudrais (vingt) litres. zher voo·dray (vung) lee·trer
Where do I pay?	Où est-ce que je paie? oo es ker zher pay
Please check the oil/water.	Contrôlez l'huile/l'eau, s'il vous plaît. kon·tro·lay lweel/lo seel voo play
Please check the tyre pressure.	Contrôlez la pression des pneus, s'il vous plaît. kon·tro·lay la pre·syon day pner seel voo play
I need a mechanic.	J'ai besoin d'un mécanicien. zhay ber·zwun dun may·ka·nee·syun
The car/motorbike has broken down (at Amboise).	La voiture/moto est tombée en panne (à Amboise). la vwa·tewr/mo·to ay tom·bay on pan (a om·bwaz)
I had an accident.	J'ai eu un accident. zhay ew un ak·see·don

BICYCLE

Where can I ...?

Où est-ce que je peux ...?
oo es ker zher per ...

have my bike repaired	faire réparer mon vélo	fair ray·pa·ray mon vay·lo
hire a bicycle	louer un vélo	loo·way un vay·lo
leave my bike	laisser mon vélo	lay·say mon vay·lo

Are there any bicycle paths?
Est-ce qu'il y a des pistes cyclables?
es keel ya day peest see·kla·bler

Can I take my bike on the train?
Est-ce que ce train accepte les vélos à bord?
es ker ser trun ak·sept lay vay·lo a bor

Can we get there by bike?
Peut-on s'y rendre en vélo?
pe·ton see ron·dre on vay·lo

Do I have to wear a helmet?
Il faut porter un casque?
eel fo por·tay ung kask

Is it within cycling distance?
On peut y aller à vélo?
on per ee a·lay a vay·lo

Is there bicycle parking?
Y a-t'il une zone de stationnement pour bicyclettes?
ya·teel ewn zon der sta·syon·mon poor bee·see·klet

☑ CULTURE TIP: BIKE BAG

Travelling with a bicycle in France can be made a great deal easier if you have *une housse* ewn hoos – a bike bag. In such a bag, your bike can be transported on any train or bus, including the TGV (high-speed train).

Border Crossing

KEY PHRASES

I'm here for ... days.	Je suis ici pour ... jours.	zher swee zee·see poor ... zhoor
I'm staying at ...	Je loge à ...	zher lozh a ...
I have nothing to declare.	Je n'ai rien à déclarer.	zher nay ryun a day·kla·ray

PASSPORT CONTROL

I'm here on business.	Je suis ici pour le travail. zher swee zee·see poor ler tra·vai
I'm here on holiday.	Je suis ici pour les vacances. zher swee zee·see poor lay va·kons
I'm here for study.	Je suis ici pour les études. zher swee zee·see poor lay zay·tewd
I'm here for (two) days.	Je suis ici pour (deux) jours. zher swee zee·see poor (der) zhoor
I'm here for (two) months.	Je suis ici pour (deux) mois. zher swee zee·see poor (der) mwa
I'm here for (two) weeks.	Je suis ici pour (deux) semaines. zher swee zee·see poor (der) ser·men
I'm in transit.	Je suis ici de passage. zher swee zee·see der pa·sazh

LISTEN FOR

Votre passeport/visa, s'il vous plaît.	vo·trer pas·por/vee·za seel voo play Your passport/visa, please.
Vous voyagez en famille/groupe?	voo vwa·ya·zhay on fa·mee/groop Are you travelling with a family/group?
Vous voyagez seul?	voo vwa·ya·zhay serl Are you travelling on your own?

I'm going to (Paris).	Je vais à (Paris). zher vay a (pa·ree)
I'm staying at the ...	Je loge à ... zher lozh a ...

AT CUSTOMS

I have nothing to declare.	Je n'ai rien à déclarer. zher nay ryun a day·kla·ray
I have something to declare.	J'ai quelque chose à déclarer. zhay kel·ker·shoz a day·kla·ray
That's not mine.	Ce n'est pas à moi. ser nay pa a mwa
I didn't know I had to declare it.	Je ne savais pas que je devais déclarer cela. zher ner sa·vay pa ker zher der·vay day·kla·ray ser·la

For phrases on payments and receipts, see **money & banking** (p83).

Directions

KEY PHRASES

Where's ...?	Où est ...?	oo es ...
What's the address?	Quelle est l'adresse?	kel ay la·dres
How far is it?	C'est loin?	say lwun

Where's a (bank)?	Où est-ce qu'il ya (une banque)? oo es keel ya (ewn bongk)
I'm looking for (a hotel).	Je cherche (un hôtel). zher shairsh (un o·tel)
Can you show me (on the map)?	Pouvez-vous m'indiquer (sur la carte)? poo·vay·voo mun·dee·kay (sewr la kart)
What's the address?	Quelle est l'adresse? kel ay la·dres
How do I get there?	Comment faire pour y aller? ko·mon fair poor ee a·lay
How far is it?	C'est loin? say lwun
by bus	en bus om bews
by taxi	en taxi on tak·see
by train	en train on trun

on foot	à pied a pyay
Turn at the corner.	Tournez au coin. toor·nay o kwun
Turn at the traffic lights.	Tournez aux feux. toor·nay o fer
It's ...	C'est ... say ...

(10) minutes	(dix) minutes	(dee) mee·newt
(100) metres	(cent) mètres	(son) me·trer
left	à gauche	a gosh
right	à droite	a drwat

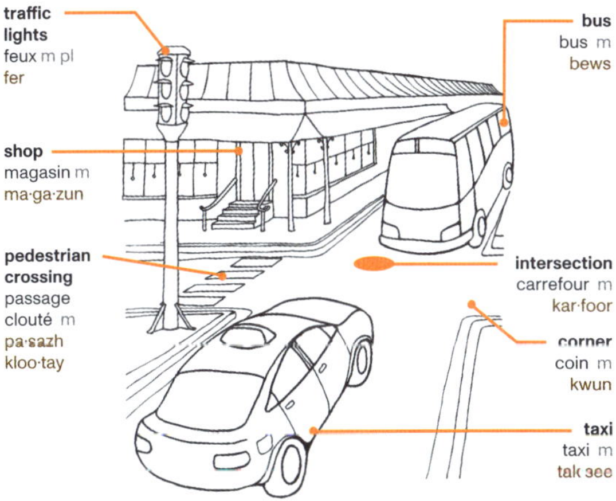

It's ... C'est ...
say ...

east	à l'est	a lest
west	à l'ouest	a lwest
behind ...	derrière ...	dair·yair ...
beside ...	à côté de ...	a ko·tay der ...
in front of ...	devant ...	der·von ...
here	ici	ee·see
there	là	la
far away	loin d'ici	lwun dee·see
on the corner	au coin	o kwun
north	au nord	o nor
south	au sud	o sewd
opposite ...	en face de ...	on fas der ...
near here	près d'ici	pray dee·see
straight ahead	tout droit	too drwa

Accommodation

KEY PHRASES

Where's a hotel?	Où est-ce qu'on peut trouver un hôtel?	oo es kon per troo·vay un o·tel
Do you have a double room?	Avez-vous une chambre double?	a.vay.voo ewn shom.brer dew.bler
How much is it per night?	Quel est le prix par nuit?	kel ay ler pree par nwee
Is breakfast included?	Le petit déjeuner est-il inclus?	ler per·tee day·zher·nay ay·teel un·klew
What time is checkout?	Quand faut-il régler?	kon fo·teel ray·glay

FINDING ACCOMMODATION

Where's a ...? Où est-ce qu'on peut trouver ...? oo es kon per troo·vay ...

camping ground	un terrain de camping	un tay·run der kom·peeng
guesthouse	une pension	ewn pon·syon
hotel	un hôtel	un o·tel
mountain hut	un refuge	un rer·fewzh
youth hostel	une auberge de jeunesse	ewn o·bairzh der zher·nes

Can you recommend somewhere (cheap)?	Est-ce que vous pouvez recommander un logement (pas cher)? es ker voo poo·vay rer·ko·mon·day un lozh·mon (pa shair)
Can you recommend somewhere (nearby)?	Est-ce que vous pouvez recommander un logement (près d'ici)? es ker voo poo·vay rer·ko·mon·day un lozh·mon (pray dee·see)

For responses, see **directions** (p52).

BOOKING AHEAD & CHECKING IN

I'd like to book a room, please.	Je voudrais réserver une chambre, s'il vous plaît. zher voo·dray ray·zair·vay ewn shom·brer seel voo play

Are there rooms?	Y a t'il des chambres?	ya teel day shom·brer

I have a reservation.	J'ai une réservation. zhay ewn ray·zair·va·syon
There are (three) of us.	Nous sommes (trois). noo som (trwa)
I'd like to stay for (two) nights.	Je voudrais rester pour (deux) nuits. zher voo·dray res·tay poor (der) nwee
From (2 July) to (6 July).	Du (deux juillet) au (six juillet). dew (der zhwee·yay) o (see zhwee·yay)

Finding a Room

DO YOU HAVE A ... ROOM?
Avez-vous une chambre ...?
a·vay·voo ewn shom·brer ...

DOUBLE
avec un double
a·vek ung dew·bler

SINGLE
simple
sum·pler

HOW MUCH IS IT PER ...?
Quel est le prix par ...?
kel ay ler pree par ...

NIGHT
nuit
nwee

PERSON
personne
per·son

IS BREAKFAST INCLUDED?
Le petit déjeuner est-il inclus?
ler per·tee day·zher·nay ay·teel un·klew

CAN I SEE THE ROOM?
Est-ce que je peux voir la chambre?
es ker zher per vwar la shom·rer

I'LL TAKE IT.
Je la prends.
zher la prond

I WON'T TAKE IT.
Je ne la prends pas.
zher ner la prond pa

LISTEN FOR

Désolé, c'est complet.	day·zo·lay say kom·play I'm sorry, we're full.
Combien de nuits?	kom·byun der nwee For how many nights?
Votre passeport, s'il vous plaît.	vo·trer pas·por seel voo play Your passport, please.

Is breakfast included?	Le petit déjeuner est-il inclus? ler per·tee day·zher·nay ay·teel un·klew
Is there parking?	Y a-t'il un parking? ya·teel um par·keeng
Do you have a double room?	Avez-vous une chambre double? a·vay·voo ewn shom·brer dew·bler
Do you have a single room?	Avez-vous une chambre simple? a·vay·voo ewn shom·brer sump·ler
Do you have a twin room?	Avez-vous une chambre avec des lits jumeaux? a·vay·voo ewn shom·brer a·vek day lee zhew·mo
Can I see the room?	Est-ce que je peux voir la chambre? es ker zher per vwar la shom·brer
How much is it per night?	Quel est le prix par nuit? kel ay ler pree par nwee
How much is it per person?	Quel est le prix par personne? kel ay ler pree par per·son

Do I need to pay upfront?	Est-ce qu'il faut payer par avance? es keel fo pay·yay par a·vons
Can I pay by credit card?	Est-ce qu'on peut payer avec une carte de crédit? es kom per pay·yay a·vek ewn kart der kray·dee

For other methods of payment, see **money & banking** (p83).

REQUESTS & QUERIES

When/Where is breakfast served?	Quand/Où le petit déjeuner est-il servi? kon/oo ler per·tee day·zher·nay ay·teel sair·vee
Please wake me at (seven).	Réveillez-moi à (sept) heures, s'il vous plaît. ray·vay·yay·mwa a (set) er seel voo play
Can I use the ...?	Est-ce que je peux utiliser ...? es ker zher per ew·tee·lee·zay ...

internet	l'Internet	lun·tair·net
kitchen	la cuisine	la kwee·zeen
laundry	la blanchisserie	la blon·shees·ree
telephone	le téléphone	ler tay·lay·fon

Do you have a/an...?	Avez-vous ...? a·vay·voo ...

elevator	un ascenseur	un a·son·ser
laundry service	un service de blanchisserie	un sair·vees der blon·shees·ree
safe	un coffre-fort	ung ko·frer·for
swimming pool	une piscine	ewn pee·seen

Do you change money here?	Echangez-vous l'argent ici? ay·shon·zhay·voo lar·zhon ee·see
Do you arrange tours here?	Organisez-vous des excursions ici? or·ga·nee·zay·voo day zeks·kewr·syon ee·see
Is there a message for me?	Vous avez un message pour moi? voo za·vay um me·sazh poor mwa
There's no hot water.	Il n'y a pas d'eau chaude. eel nya pa do shod
I'm locked out of my room.	Je me suis enfermé(e) dehors. m/f zher mer swee zon·fair·may der·or
The (bathroom) door is locked.	La porte (de la salle de bain) est verrouillée. la port (der la sal der bun) ay ver·roo·yay
There's no need to change my sheets.	Il n'y a pas besoin de changer mes draps. eel nee·ya pa be·zwun de shon·zhay may dra
Can I get another blanket?	Est-ce que je peux avoir une autre couverture? es ker zher per a·vwar ewn o·trer koo·vair·tewr
It's too ...	C'est trop ... say tro ...

cold	froid	frwa
dark	sombre	som·brer
expensive	cher	shair
noisy	bruyant	brew·yon
small	petit	per·tee

The ... doesn't work.	... ne fonctionne pas.	... ner fong·syon pa
air-conditioning	la climatisation	la klee·ma·tee·za·syon
fan	Le ventilateur	ler von·tee·la·ter
heater	L'appareil de chauffage	la·pa·ray der sho·fazh
toilet	Les toilettes	lay twa·let
window	La fenêtre	la fer·ne·trer

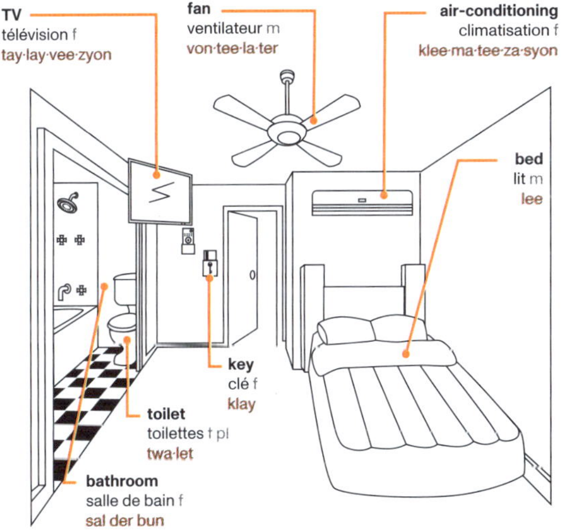

ANSWERING THE DOOR

Who is it?	Qui est-ce? kee es
Just a moment.	Un instant. un uns·ton
Come in.	Entrez. on·tray
Come back later, please.	Veuillez repasser plus tard, s'il vous plaît. ver·yay rer·pa·say plew tar seel voo play

CHECKING OUT

What time is checkout?	Quand faut-il régler? kon fo·teel ray·glay
Can I have a late checkout?	Pourrai-je régler plus tard? poo·rezh ray·glay plew tar
I'm leaving now.	Je pars maintenant. zher par mun·ter·non
Can you call a taxi for me (for 11 o'clock)?	Pouvez-vous appeler un taxi pour moi (pour onze heures)? poo·vay·voo a·play un tak·see poor mwa (poor on zer)
Can I leave my luggage here until (Wednesday)?	Puis-je laisser mes bagages jusqu'à (mercredi)? pweezh lay·say may ba·gazh zhews·ka (mair·krer·dee)
I'll be back in (three) days.	Je retournerai dans (trois) jours. zher rer·toor·ner·ray don (trwa) zhur
Could I have my deposit, please?	Est-ce que je pourrais avoir ma caution, s'il vous plaît? es ker zher poo·ray a·vwar ma ko·syon seel voo play

Could I have my passport, please?	Est-ce que je pourrais avoir mon passeport, s'il vous plaît? es ker zher poo·ray a·vwar mon pas·por seel voo play
Could I have my valuables, please?	Est-ce que je pourrais avoir mes biens précieux, s'il vous plaît? es ker zher poo·ray a·vwar may byun pray·syer seel voo play
I had a great stay, thank you.	J'ai fait un séjour magnifique, merci. zhay fay un say·zhoor ma·nyee·feek mair·see
I'll recommend it to my friends.	Je le recommanderai à mes amis. zher ler rer·ko·mon·dray a may za·mee
I'll be back on (Tuesday).	Je retournerai (mardi). zher rer·toor·ner·ray (mar·dee)

CAMPING

Where's the nearest ...?	Où est le ... le plus proche? oo ay ler ... ler plew prosh

campsite	terrain de camping	tay·run der kom·peeng
shop	magasin	ma·ga·zun
shower facility	bloc sanitaire	blok sa·nee·tair
toilet block	bloc toilettes	blok twa·let

How much is it per ...?	C'est combien pour chaque ...? say kom·bee·un poor shak ...

caravan	caravane	ka·ra·van
person	personne	pair·son
tent	tente	tont
vehicle	véhicule	vay·ee·kewl

Do you have ...?	Avez-vous ...? a·vay·voo ...	
electricity	l'électricité	lay·lek·tree·see·tay
shower facilities	un bloc sanitaire	um blok sa·nee·tair
a site	un emplacement	un om·plas·mon
tents for hire	des tentes à louer	day tont a loo·ay

Is the water drinkable?	L'eau est-elle potable? lo ay·tel po·ta·bler
Can I camp here?	Est-ce que je peux camper ici? es ker zher per kom·pay ee·see
Who do I ask to stay here?	Je m'adresse où pour rester ici? zher ma·dres oo poor res·tay ee·see
Could I borrow a spade?	Est-ce que je pourrais emprunter une pelle? es ker zher poo·ray um·prun·tay ewn pel
Could I borrow a torch/flashlight?	Est-ce que je pourrais emprunter une lampe de poche? es ker zher poo·ray um·prun·tay ewn lomp der posh

RENTING

Do you have ... for rent?	Avez-vous ... à louer? a·vay·voo ... a loo·ay	
an apartment	un appartement	un a·par·ter·mon
a house	une maison	ewn may·zon
a room	une chambre	ewn shom·brer
a villa	une villa	ewn vee·la

I'm here about the ... for rent.	Je suis ici au sujet de ... à louer. zher swee zee·see o sew·zhay der ... a loo·ay
How much is it for (one) week?	C'est combien pour (une) semaine? say kom·byun poor (ewn) ser·men
How much is it for (two) months?	C'est combien pour (deux) mois? say kom·byun poor (der) mwa
Is there a deposit/bond?	Faut-il verser une caution? fo·teel vair·say ewn ko·syon

Avez-vous un appartement à louer?

a·vay·voo un a·par·ter·mon a loo·ay

Do you have an apartment for rent?

STAYING WITH LOCALS

Can I stay at your place?	Est-ce que je peux rester chez vous? es ker zher per ray·stay shay voo
I have my own sleeping bag.	J'ai un sac de couchage. zhay un sak der koo·shazh
Is there anything I can do to help?	Y a-t-il quelque chose que je peux faire pour aider? ya·teel kel·ker shoz ker zher per fair poor ay·day
Thanks for your hospitality.	Merci pour votre hospitalité. mair·see poor vo·trer os·pee·ta·lee·tay
Can I ...?	Puis-je ...? pwee·zher ...

bring anything for the meal	apporter quelque chose pour le repas	a·por·tay kel·ker shoz poor ler rer·pa
do the dishes	faire la vaisselle	fair la vay·sel
set the table	mettre la table	me·trer la ta·bler
take out the rubbish	sortir les poubelles	sor·teer lay poo·bel

To compliment your hosts' cooking, see **eating out** (p156). See also **making conversation** (p101).

Shopping

KEY PHRASES

I'd like to buy ...	Je voudrais acheter ...	zher voo·dray ash·tay ...
Can I look at it?	Est-ce que je peux le voir?	es ker zher per ler vwar
Can I try it on?	Puis-je l'essayer?	pwee·zher lay·say·yay
How much is it?	C'est combien?	say kom·byun
That's too expensive.	C'est trop cher.	say tro shair

LOOKING FOR ...

Where's (a supermarket)?	Où est-ce qu'il y a (un supermarché)? oo es keel ya (un sew·pair·mar·shay)
Where can I buy (locally produced goods/souvenirs)?	Où puis-je acheter (des marchandises/souvenirs produits localement)? oo pweezh ash·tay (day mar·shon·deez/soov·neer pro·dwee lo·kal·mon)

For additional shops and services, see the **dictionary** (p196).

MAKING A PURCHASE

How much is it?	C'est combien? say kom·byun

How much?	Combien?	kom·byun

LISTEN FOR

Non, nous n'en avons pas.	non noo non a·vom pa	No, we don't have any.
Autre chose?	o·trer shoz	Anything else?
Vous désirez?	voo day·zee·ray	Can I help you?
Vous en désirez combien?	voo zon day·zee·ray kom·byun	How much/many do you want?
Je vous l'emballe?	zher voo lom·bal	Would you like it wrapped?

I'd like to buy ...	Je voudrais acheter ... zher voo·dray ash·tay ...
What is this made of?	C'est fabriqué avec quoi? say fa·bree·kay a·vek kwa
I'm just looking.	Je regarde. zher rer·gard
Can you write down the price?	Pouvez-vous écrire le prix? poo·vay·voo ay·kreer ler pree
Do you have any others?	Vous en avez d'autres? voo zon a·vay do·trer
Can I look at it?	Est-ce que je peux le voir? es ker zher per ler vwar
I don't need a bag, thanks.	Je n'ai pas besoin de sac, merci. zher nay pa ber·zwun der sak mair·see
Do you accept credit cards?	Est-ce que je peux payer avec une carte de crédit? es ker zher per pay·yay a·vek ewn kart der kray·dee
Do you accept debit cards?	Est-ce que je peux payer avec une carte de débit? es ker zher per pay·yay a·vek ewn kart der day·bee

laking a Purchase

I'D LIKE TO BUY ...
Je voudrais acheter ...
zher voo·dray ash·tay ...

HOW MUCH IS IT?
C'est combien?
say kom·byun

OR

CAN YOU WRITE THE PRICE?
Pouvez-vous écrire le prix?
poo·vay·voo ay·kreer ler pree

DO YOU ACCEPT CREDIT CARDS?
Est-ce que je peux payer avec une carte de crédit?
es ker zher per pay·yay a·vek ewn kart der kray·dee

COULD I HAVE A ..., PLEASE?
Puis-je avoir un ..., s'il vous plaît?
pweezh a·vwar un ... seel voo play

RECEIPT
reçu
rer·sew

BAG
sac
sak

Could I have a bag/ receipt, please?	Puis-je avoir un sac/reçu, s'il vous plaît? pweezh a·vwar un sak/rer·sew seel voo play

Receipt, please.	Un reçu, s'il vous plaît.	un rer·sew seel voo play

Could I have it wrapped?	Pouvez-vous l'emballer? poo·vay·voo lom·bal·ay
Does it have a guarantee?	Est-ce qu'il y a une garantie? es keel ya ewn ga·ron·tee
Can I have it sent overseas?	Pouvez-vous me l'envoyer à l'étranger? poo·vay·voo mer lon·vwa·yay a lay·tron·zhay
Can I pick it up later?	Je peux passer le prendre plus tard? zher per pa·say ler pron·drer plew tar
It's faulty/broken.	C'est défectueux/cassé. say day·fek·twer/ka·say
I'd like my change, please.	Je voudrais ma monnaie, s'il vous plaît. zher voo·dray ma mo·nay seel voo play

LISTEN FOR

occasion f	o·ka·zyon	bargain
chercheur/ chercheuse m/f **d'occasions**	shair·sher/ shair·sherz do·ka·zyon	bargain hunter
arnaque f	ar·nak	rip-off
soldes m pl	sold	sales
promotions f pl	pro·mo·syon	specials

C'est combien?
say kom·byun
How much is it?

I'd like my money back, please.	Je voudrais un remboursement, s'il vous plaît. zher voo·dray un rom·boors·mon seel voo play
I'd like to return this, please.	Je voudrais rapporter ceci, s'il vous plaît. zher voo·dray ra·por·tay ser·see seel voo play

BARGAINING

That's too expensive.	C'est trop cher. say tro shair
Can you lower the price?	Vous pouvez baisser le prix? voo poo·vay bay·say ler pree

I'll give you ...	Je vous donnerai ... zher voo don·ray ...
Do you have something cheaper?	Avez-vous quelque chose de moins cher? a·vay·voo kel·ker shoz der mwun shair

REPAIRS

Can I have my camera repaired here?	Puis-je faire réparer mon appareil photo ici? pwee·zher fair ray·pa·ray mon a·pa·ray fo·to ee·see
Can I have my (sun)glasses repaired here?	Puis-je faire réparer mes lunettes (de soleil) ici? pwee·zher fair ray·pa·ray may lew·net (der so·lay) ee·see
When will it be ready?	Quand est-ce que ce sera prêt? kon tes ker ser ser·ra pray

CLOTHES

I'm looking for shoes/ underwear.	Je cherche des chaussures/ sous-vêtements. zher shairsh day sho·sewr/ soo·vet·mon
Can I try it on?	Puis-je l'essayer? pwee·zher lay·say·yay
My size is (medium).	Je fais du (moyen). zher fay dew (mwa·yen)
It doesn't fit.	Ce n'est pas la bonne taille. ser nay pa la bon tai
It's too big/small.	C'est trop grand/petit. say tro gron/per·tee

For items of clothing, see the **dictionary**. For sizes, see **numbers & amounts** (p31).

BOOKS & READING

Is there an English-language section?	Y a-t-il un rayon anglais? ya·teel un ray·yon ong·glay
I'd like a dictionary/ newspaper.	Je voudrais un dictionnaire/ journal. zher voo·dray un deek·syo·nair/ zhoor·nal
Can you recommend a book for me?	Pouvez-vous me conseiller un roman? poo·vay·voo mer kon·say·yay un ro·mon
I'm looking for something by (Albert Camus).	Je cherche quelque chose de (Albert Camus). zher shairsh kel·ker shoz der (al·bair ka·mew)

For more on books and reading, see **interests** (p111).

MUSIC

I'd like headphones.	Je voudrais un casque. zher voo·dray ung kask
What's his/her best recording?	Quel est son meilleur enregistrement? kel ay som may·yer on·rer·zhees·trer·mon

PHOTOGRAPHY

I need a cable to connect my camera to a computer.	J'ai besoin d'un câble pour connecter mon appareil photo à un ordinateur. zhay ber·zwun dung ka·bler poor ko·nek·tay mong na·pa·ray fo·to a un nor·dee·na·ter
I need a cable to recharge this battery.	J'ai besoin d'un câble pour recharger cette pile. zhay ber·zwun dung ka·bler poor rer·shar·zhay set peel
Can you recharge the battery for my digital camera?	Pourriez-vous recharger les piles de mon appareil numérique? poo·ree·yay·voo rer·shar·zhay lay peel der mon na·pa·ray new·may·reek
Can you print digital photos?	Pourriez-vous imprimer des photos numériques? poo·ree·yay·voo um·pree·may day fo·to new·may·reek
I need a passport photo taken.	J'ai besoin d'une photo d'identité. zhay ber·zwun dewn fo·to dee·don·tee·tay

Do you have (a) ... for this camera?	Avez-vous ... pour cet appareil? a·vay·voo ... poor set ta·pa·ray	
batteries	des piles	day peel
memory cards	des cartes mémoire	day kart may·mwar
zoom (lens)	un objectif	un nop·zhek·teef

I'm not happy with these photos.

Je ne suis pas content(e) de ces photos. m/f
zher ner swee pa kon·ton(t) der say fo·to

Communications

KEY PHRASES

I'd like to check my email.	Je voudrais consulter mon courrier électronique.	zher voo·dray kon·sewl·tay mong koor·yay ay·lek·tro·neek
I'd like a SIM card.	Je voudrais une carte SIM.	zher voo·dray ewn kart seem

POST OFFICE

I want to send a letter.	Je voudrais envoyer une lettre. zher voo·dray on·vwa·yay ewn le·trer
I want to send a parcel.	Je voudrais envoyer un colis. zher voo·dray on·vwa·yay ung ko·lee
I want to buy an envelope.	Je voudrais acheter une enveloppe. zher voo·dray ash·tay ewn on·vlop
I want to buy a stamp.	Je voudrais acheter un timbre. zher voo·dray ash·tay un tum·brer
Where's the poste restante section?	Où est le service de poste restante? oo ay ler sair·vees der post res·tont
Is there any mail for me?	Y a-t-il du courrier pour moi? ya·teel dew koor·yay poor mwa

LISTEN FOR

déclaration en douane f	day·kla·ra·syon on doo·wan	customs declaration
national(e) m/f	na·syo·nal	domestic
fragile	fra·zheel	fragile
international(e) m/f	un·tair·na·syo·nal	international
boîte aux lettres f	bwat o lay·trer	mailbox
adresse postale f	a·dres pos·tal	postal address
code postal m	kod pos·tal	postcode

Please send it (to Australia) by ...
Envoyez-le (en Australie) ..., s'il vous plaît.
on·vwa·yay·ler (on os·tra·lee) ... seel voo play

airmail	par avion	par a·vyon
express post	en exprès	on neks·pres
registered mail	en recommandé	on rer·ko·mon·day
sea mail	voie maritime	vwa ma·ree·teem

It contains ...
Cela contient ...
ser·la kon·tyun ...

PHONE

Q What's your phone number?
Quel est votre numéro de téléphone?
kel ay vo·trer new·may·ro der tay·lay·fon

A The number is ...
Le numéro est ...
ler new·may·ro ay ...

LISTEN FOR

À qui voulez-vous parler?	a kee voo·lay·voo par·lay	Who do you want to speak to?
Désolé, vous vous trompez de numéro.	day·zo·lay voo voo trom·pay der new·may·ro	Sorry, wrong number.
Qui est-ce?	kee es	Who's calling?
Non, il/elle n'est pas là.	non eel/el nay pa la	No, he/she is not here.
Je peux prendre un message?	zher per pron·drer um may·sazh	Can I take a message?

I'd like to know the number for ...	Je voudrais connaître le numéro de ... zher voo·dray ko·nay·trer ler new·may·ro der ...

I want to make a local call.	Je veux passer un appel téléphonique local. zher ver pa·say un na·pel tay·lay·fo·neek lo·kal
I want to make a call to (Singapore).	Je veux téléphoner à (Singapour). zher ver tay·lay·fo·nay a (sung·ga·poor)
I want to make a reverse-charge/collect call.	Je veux téléphoner en PCV. zher ver tay·lay·fo·nay om pay·say·vay
What's the area/country code for ...?	Quel est l'indicatif pour ...? kel ay lun·dee·ka·teef poor ...

Quel est votre numéro de téléphone?

kel ay vo·trer new·may·ro der tay·lay·fon

What's your phone number?

It's busy.	La ligne est occupée. la lee·nyer ay to·kew·pay
I've been cut off.	J'ai été coupé(e). m/f zhay ay·tay koo·pay
The connection is bad.	La ligne est mauvaise. la lee·nyer ay mo·vayz
Can I leave a message?	Je peux laisser un message? zher per lay·say um may·sazh
I'll call back later.	Je rappellerai plus tard. zher ra·pel·ray plew tar
My number is ...	Mon numéro est ... mon new·may·ro ay ...

For telephone numbers, see **numbers & amounts** (p31).

MOBILE/CELL PHONE

I'd like a/an ...	Je voudrais ... zher voo·dray ...

adaptor plug	une prise multiple	ewn preez mewl·tee·pler
charger for my phone	un chargeur pour mon portable	un shar·zher poor mom por·ta·bler
SIM card for the network	une carte SIM pour le réseau	ewn kart seem poor ler ray·zo

What are the rates?	Quels sont les tarifs? kel son lay ta·reef

THE INTERNET

Do you have public internet access here?	Avez-vous une connexion Internet ici? a·vay·voo ewn ko·nek·syon un·tair·net ee·see
Is there wireless internet access here?	Avez-vous le wifi ici? a·vay·voo ler wee·fee ee·see
Can I connect my laptop here?	Est-ce que je peux utiliser mon ordinateur portable ici? es ker zher per ew·tee·lee·zay mong or·dee·na·ter por·ta·bler ee·see
Do you have headphones (with a microphone)?	Avez-vous un casque (avec un micro)? a·vay·voo ung kask (a·vek un mee·kro)
I'd like to ...	Je voudrais ... zher voo·dray ...

check my email	consulter mon courrier électronique	kon·sewl·tay mong koor·yay ay·lek·tro·neek
download my photos	télécharger mes photos	tay·lay·shar·zhay may fo·to
use a printer	utiliser une imprimante	ew·tee·lee·zay ewn um·pree·mont
use a scanner	utiliser un scanner	ew·tee·lee·zay un ska·nair

How much per page?	C'est combien la page? say kom·byun la pazh
How do I log on?	Comment faire pour me con-necter? ko·mon fair poor mer ko·nek·tay
Can you help me change to English-language preference?	Pouvez-vous m'aider à choisir l'anglais comme langue de préférence? poo·vay·voo may·day a shwa·zeer long·glay kom long der pray·fay·rons
It's crashed.	C'est tombé en panne. say tom·bay om pan
I've finished.	J'ai terminé. zhay tair·mee·nay
Can I connect my ... to this computer?	Est-ce que je peux brancher ... sur cet ordinateur? es ker zher per bron·shay ... sewr set or·dee·na·ter

camera	mon appareil photo	mon na·pa·ray fo·to
iPhone/ iPad	mon iPhone/ iPad	mon nai·fon/ nai·pet
portable hard drive	mon disque dur portable	mon disk dewr por·ta·bler
memory stick	ma clé USB	ma klay ew·es·bay

Money & Banking

KEY PHRASES

How much is it?	Ça fait combien?	sa fay kom·byun
What's the exchange rate?	Quel est le taux de change?	kel ay ler to der shonzh
Where's the nearest ATM?	Où est le guichet automatique le plus proche?	oo ay ler gee·shay o·to·ma·teek ler plew prosh

PAYING THE BILL

Q **How much is it?**	Ça fait combien? sa fay kom·byun
A **It's free.**	C'est gratuit. say gra·twee
A **It's (12) euros.**	C'est (douze) euros. say (dooz) er·ro
Can you write down the price?	Pouvez-vous écrire le prix? poo·vay·voo ay·kreer ler pree
There's a mistake in the bill.	Il y a une erreur dans la note. eel ya ewn ay·rer don la not
Do you want to sign or use your PIN?	Vous préférez signer ou utiliser votre code? voo pray·fay·ray see·nyay oo ew·tee·lee·zay vo·trer kod
Do you accept credit/ debit cards?	Est-ce que je peux payer avec une carte de crédit/débit? es ker zher per pay·yay a·vek ewn kart der kray·dee/day·bee

I'd like my change, please.	Je voudrais ma monnaie, s'il vous plaît. zher voo·dray ma mo·nay seel voo play
I'd like a receipt, please.	Je voudrais un reçu, s'il vous plaît. zher voo·dray un rer·sew seel voo play

AT THE BANK

Where can I ...?	Où est-ce que je peux ...? oo es ker zher per ...
I'd like to ...	Je voudrais ... zher voo·dray ...

arrange a transfer	faire un virement	fair un veer·mon
change money	changer de l'argent	shon·zhay der lar·zhon
get a cash advance	une avance de crédit	ewn a·vons der kray·dee
get change for this note	faire de la monnaie avec ce billet	fair der la mo·nay a·vek ser bee·yay
withdraw money	retirer de l'argent	rer·tee·ray der lar·zhon

LISTEN FOR

Dans quatre jours ouvrables.	don ka·trer zhoor oo·vra·bler	In four working days.
Il ne vous reste plus d'argent.	eel ner voo rest plew dar·zhon	You have no funds left.
Notez-le.	no·tay·ler	Write it down.
papiers d'identité	pa·pyay dee·don·tee·tay	ID
Signez ici.	see·nyay ee·see	Sign here.

Where's the nearest ATM?	Où est le guichet automatique le plus proche? oo ay ler gee·shay o·to·ma·teek ler plew prosh
Where's the nearest foreign exchange office?	Où est le bureau de change le plus proche? oo ay ler bew·ro der shonzh ler plew prosh
The ATM took my card.	Le guichet automatique a avalé ma carte de crédit. ler gee·shay o·to·ma·teek a a·va·lay ma kart der kray·dee
I've forgotten my PIN.	J'ai oublié mon code confidentiel. zhay oo·blee·yay mong kod kon·fee·don·syel
What's the exchange rate?	Quel est le taux de change? kel ay ler to der shonzh
What's the charge for that?	Quel est le tarif pour cela? kel ay ler ta·reef poor ser·la
Has my money arrived yet?	Est-ce que mon argent est arrivé? es ker mon ar·zhon ay ta·ree·vay

Business

KEY PHRASES

I'm attending a conference.	Je participe à une conférence.	zhe par·tee·seep a ewn kon·fay·rons
I have an appointment with ...	J'ai rendez-vous avec ...	zhay ron·day·voo a·vek ...
Can I have your business card?	Pourriez-vous me laisser votre carte de visite?	poo·ree·yay·voo mer lay·say vo·trer kart der vee·zeet

As you'd expect, doing business in France could be the topic of a whole book. As a starting point though, remember to use polite forms when speaking to clients and colleagues (until invited to use the familiar form – see p99) and it's probably best to save cheek-kisses for *very* successful meetings...

I'm attending a ...	Je participe à un/une ... m/f zhe par·tee·seep un/ewn ...
Where's the ...?	Où est le/la ...? m/f oo ay ler/la...

conference	conférence f	kon·fay·rons
course	stage m	stazh
meeting	réunion f	ray·ew·nyon
trade fair	foire commerciale f	fwar ko·mair·syal

I'm with my colleague(s).	Je suis avec mon/mes collègue(s). sg/pl zher swee a·vek mong/may ko·leg

I'm alone.	Je suis seul(e). m/f zher swee serl
I'm with (two) others.	Je suis avec (deux) autres. zher swee a·vek (der) o·trer
I need an interpreter.	J'ai besoin d'un interprète. zhay ber·zwun dun un·tair·pret
Q **Can I have your business card?**	Pourriez-vous me laisser votre carte de visite? poo·ree·yay·voo mer lay·say vo·trer kart der vee·zeet
A **Here's my business card.**	Voici ma carte. vwa·see ma kart
I have an appointment with ...	J'ai rendez-vous avec ... zhay ron·day·voo a·vek ...
I'm expecting a call.	Je attends un appel. zha·ton un a·pel
I'd like to connect to the internet.	Je voudrais me connecter à l'Internet. zher voo·dray mer ko·nek·tay a lun·tair·net
I'd like to use a computer.	Je voudrais utiliser un ordinateur. zher voo·dray ew·tee·lee·zay un or·dee·na·ter
Is there a data projector?	Y a-t-il un projecteur data? ya·teel um pro·zhek·ter da·ta
Is there a laser pointer?	Y a-t-il un pointeur laser? ya·teel un pwun·ter la·zair
That went very well.	Ça c'est très bien passé. sa say tray byun pa·say
Thank you for your time/interest.	Merci pour votre temps/attention. mair·see poor vo·trer tom/a·ton·syon

Sightseeing

KEY PHRASES

I'd like a guide.	Je voudrais un guide.	zher voo·dray ung geed
Can I take photographs?	Je peux prendre des photos?	zher per pron·drer day fo·to
When's the museum open?	Le musée ouvre à quelle heure?	ler mew·zay oo·vrer a kel er

I'd like to see ...
J'aimerais voir ...
zhem·ray vwar ...

Do you have information on ... sights?
Avez-vous des renseignements sur les sites ... à visiter?
a·vay·voo day ron·sen·yer·mon sewr lay seet ... a vee·zee·tay

free	gratuits	gra·twee
historical	historiques	ees·to·reek
local	locaux	lo·ko
natural	naturels	na·tew·rel

I'd like to hire a guide.
Je voudrais faire appel aux services d'un guide.
zher voo·dray fair a·pel o sair·vees dung geed

What's that?
Qu'est-ce que c'est?
kes ker say

How old is it?	Ça date de quand? sa dat der kon
Can I take photographs?	Je peux prendre des photos? zher per pron·drer day fo·to
I'll send you the photograph.	Je vous enverrai la photo. zher voo zon·vay·ray la fo·to
I'd like a/an ...	Je voudrais ... zher voo·dray ...

audio set	un écouteur	un ay·koo·ter
city map	un plan de la ville	um plon der la veel
guide	un guide	ung geed
local map	une carte de la région	ewn kart der la ray·zhyon

GETTING IN

What's the admission charge?	Quel est le prix d'admission? kel ay ler pree dad·mee·syon
What time does it open?	Quelle est l'heure d'ouverture? kel ay ler doo·vair·tewr
What time does it close?	Quelle est l'heure de fermeture? kel ay ler der fer·mer·tewr
Is there a discount for ...?	Il y a une réduction pour les ...? eel ya ewn ray·dewk·syon poor lay ...

children	enfants	zon·fon
families	familles	fa·mee
groups	groupes	groop
older people	seniors	say·nyor
students	étudiants	zay·tew·dyon

GALLERIES & MUSEUMS

When's the gallery open?	La galerie ouvre à quelle heure? la gal·ree oo·vrer a kel er
When's the museum open?	Le musée ouvre à quelle heure? ler mew·zay oo·vrer a kel er
Q **What's in the collection?**	Qu'est-ce qu'il y a dans la collection? kes keel·ya don la ko·lek·syon
A **It's a/an ... exhibition.**	C'est une exposition ... set ewn ek·spo·zee·syon ...
I like the works of ...	J'aime l'œuvre de ... zhem ler·vrer der ...
It reminds me of ...	Cela me rappelle ... ser·la mer ra·pel ...
... art	l'art ... lar ...

contemporary	contemporain	kon·tom·po·run
impressionist	impressionniste	um·pray·syo·neest
modernist	moderniste	mo·dair·neest
Renaissance	de la Renaissance	der la rer·nay·sons

TOURS

Are there (organised) walking tours?	Y a-t'il des visites guidées (organisées) à pied? ya·teel day vee·zeet gee·day (or·ga·nee·zay) a pyay

I'd like to do cooking/ language classes.	Je voudrais suivre des cours de cuisine/langue. zher voo·dray swee·vrer day koor der kwee·zeen/long
Can you recommend a tour?	Pouvez-vous me recommander une excursion? poo·vay·voo mer rer·ko·mon·day ewn eks·kewr·syon
When's the next (day) trip?	C'est quand la prochaine excursion (d'une journée)? say kon la pro·shen eks·kewr·syon (dewn zhoor·nay)

Je peux prendre des photos?
zher per pron·drer day fo·to
Can I take photographs?

LISTEN FOR

Il y a (pas) beaucoup à voir.	eel ya (pa) bo·koo a vwar There is (not) a lot to see .
des escrocs	day zes·kro rip-off merchants
trop de touristes	tro der too·reest too many tourists
Le meilleur moment pour partir c'est en (décembre).	ler may·yer mo·mon poor par·teer se ton (day·som·brer) The best time to go is (December).

Is accommodation included?	Est-ce que le logement est inclus? es ker ler lozh·mon ay tung·klew
Is food included?	Est-ce que la nourriture est incluse? es ker la noo·ree·tewr ay tung·klewz
Is transport included?	Est-ce que le transport est inclus? es ker ler trons·por ay tung·klew
How long is the tour?	L'excursion dure combien de temps? leks·kewr·syon dewr kom·byun der tom
What time should we be back?	On doit rentrer pour quelle heure? on dwa ron·tray poor kel er
I've lost my group.	J'ai perdu mon groupe. zhay pair·dew mon groop

Seniors & Travellers with Disabilities

KEY PHRASES

I need assistance.	J'ai besoin d'aide.	zhay ber·zwun ded
Is there wheelchair access?	Y a-t-il un accès pour fauteuil roulant?	ya·teel un ak·say poor fo·ter·yer roo·lon
Are there toilets for people with a disability?	Est-ce qu'il y a des toilettes pour handicapés?	es keel ya day twa·let poor on·dee·ka·pay

I have a disability.	Je suis en situation de handicap. zher swee zon sit·chu·a·syon de on·dee·kap
I need assistance.	J'ai besoin d'aide. zhay ber·zwun ded
Is there wheelchair access?	Y a-t-il un accès pour fauteuil roulant? ya·teel un ak·say poor fo·ter·yer roo·lon
How many steps are there?	Il y a combien de marches? eel ya kom·byun der marsh
Is there a lift/elevator?	Est-ce qu'il y a un ascenseur? es keel ya un a·son·ser
Are guide dogs permitted?	Est-ce que les chiens d'aveugle sont permis? es ker lay shyun da·ver·gler son pair·mee

Is there somewhere I can sit down?	Est-ce qu'il y a un endroit où on peut s'asseoir? es keel ya un on·drwa oo on per sa·swar
Are there any toilets for people with a disability?	Est-ce qu'il y a des toilettes pour handicapés? es keel ya day twa·let poor on·dee·ka·pay
Are there rails in the bathroom?	Est-ce qu'il y a des barres dans la salle de bain? es keel ya day bar don la sal der bun
Are there parking spaces for people with a disability?	Est-ce qu'il y a des emplacements pour handicapés? es keel ya day zom·plas·mon poor on·dee·ka·pay
Could you call me an accessible taxi?	Pouvez-vous appeler un taxi pour personne handicapée? poo·vay·voo a·play un tak·see poor pair·son on·dee·ka·pay
Could you help me cross this street?	Pouvez-vous m'aider à traverser cette rue? poo·vay·voo may·day a tra·vair·say set rew
crutches	béquilles f pl bay·kee·yer
guide dog	chien d'aveugle m shyun da·ver·gler
ramp	rampe f romp
walking frame	déambulateur m day·om·bew·la·ter
walking stick	canne f kan
wheelchair	fauteuil roulant m fo·ter·yee roo·lon

Travel with Children

KEY PHRASES

Are children allowed?	Les enfants sont permis?	lay zon·fon son pair·mee
Is there a child discount?	Y a-t-il un tarif réduit pour les enfants?	ya teel un ta·reef ray·dwee poor lay zon·fon
Is there a baby change room?	Y a-t-il un endroit pour changer le bébé?	ya teel un on·drwa poor shon·zhay ler bay·bay

I need a ... J'ai besoin ...
zhay ber·zwun ...

child seat	d'un siège-enfant	dun syezh·on·fon
cot	d'un lit pour bébé	dun lee poor bay·bay
potty	d'un pot de bébé	dum po der bay·bay
stroller	d'une poussette	dewn poo·set

Do you sell ...? Avez-vous ...?
a·vay·voo ...

baby wipes	des lingettes pour bébé	day lun·zhet poor bay·bay
disposable nappies/ diapers	des couches jetables	day koosh zher·ta·bler
milk formula	du lait maternisé	dew lay ma·tair·nee·say

Is there a/an ...?	Y a-t-il ...? ya teel ...

baby change room	un endroit pour changer le bébé	un on·drwa poor shon·zhay ler bay·bay
child discount	un tarif réduit pour les enfants	un ta·reef ray·dwee poor lay zon·fon
child-minding service	une garderie	ewn gar·dree
children's menu	un menu pour enfant	un mer·new poor on·fon
creche	une crèche	ewn kresh
high chair	une chaise haute	ewn shay zot

Can I breastfeed here?	Je peux allaiter mon bébé ici? zher per a·lay·tay mon bay·bay ee·see
Are children allowed?	Les enfants sont permis? lay zon·fon son pair·mee
Is this suitable for (six)-year-old children?	Cela convient-il aux enfants de (six) ans? ser·la kon·vyun·teel o zon·fon der (seez) on

If your child is sick, see **health** (p146).

SOCIAL

Meeting People

KEY PHRASES

My name is ...	Je m'appelle ...	zher ma·pel ...
I'm from ...	Je viens de ...	zher vyun der ...
I work in ...	Je travaille dans ...	zher tra·vai don ...
I'm ... years old.	J'ai ... ans.	zhay ... on
And you?	Et vous/toi? pol/inf	ay voo/twa

BASICS

Yes.	Oui. wee
No.	Non. non
Please.	S'il vous plaît. seel voo play
Thank you (very much).	Merci (beaucoup). mair·see (bo·koo)
You're welcome.	Je vous en prie. pol zher voo zon pree
Excuse me.	Excusez-moi. ek·skew·zay·mwa
Sorry.	Pardon. par·don

GREETINGS

A kiss on each cheek remains a common greeting in France, though between men (and when meeting a man or a woman for the first time) a handshake is more usual.

Hello.	Bonjour. bon·zhoor
Hi.	Salut. sa·lew
Good morning/afternoon.	Bonjour. bon·zhoor
Good evening/night.	Bonsoir. bon·swar
See you later.	À bientôt. a byun·to
Goodbye.	Au revoir. o rer·vwar

LANGUAGE TIP: ADDRESSING PEOPLE

When talking to people familiar to you, or to children, it's usual to use the informal form of you, *tu* tew, rather than the plural or polite form, *vous* voo. The verb ending also changes. Phrases in this book are generally in the polite form, but where you see inf, you have a casual option to use where appropriate. If you feel you've become familiar enough to start using the informal form, you can ask if it's OK to use it:

Est-ce que je peux vous tutoyer?	es ker zher per voo tew·twa·yay

See also **personal pronouns** (p19) in the **grammar** chapter.

Ⓠ **How are you?**	Comment allez-vous? pol ko·mon ta·lay·voo Ça va? inf sa va
Ⓐ **Fine. And you?**	Bien, merci. Et vous/toi? pol/inf byun mair·see ay voo/twa
Ⓠ **What's your name?**	Comment vous appelez-vous? pol ko·mon voo za·play·voo Comment tu t'appelles? inf ko·mon tew ta·pel
Ⓐ **My name is ...**	Je m'appelle ... zher ma·pel ...
I'm pleased to meet you.	Enchanté(e). m/f on·shon·tay
I'd like to introduce you to ...	Je vous présente ... pol zher voo pray·zont ...

This is ...	Voici ...	vwa·see ...

The French can seem very formal about addressing people they don't know. They use *Monsieur* (M), *Madame* (Mme) or *Mademoiselle* (Mlle; used mainly for girls and teens) where English speakers would use no term of address at all.

Mr/Sir	Monsieur mer·syer
Ms/Mrs	Madame ma·dam
Miss	Mademoiselle mad·mwa·zel
Doctor	Docteur dok·ter

MAKING CONVERSATION

Sport and culture are safe areas of conversation and food is a sure way to get a French person speaking, but money talk (prices, income, etc) is best avoided.

Do you speak English?	Parlez-vous anglais? pol par·lay·voo ong·glay
Do you live here?	Vous habitez ici? pol voo za·bee·tay ee·see
Q **Do you like it here?**	Ça vous plaît ici? pol sa voo play ee·see
A **I love it here.**	Ça me plaît beaucoup ici. sa mer play bo·koo ee·see
Where are you going?	Où allez-vous? pol oo a·lay·voo
What are you doing?	Que faites-vous? pol ker fet·voo
Can I take a photo (of you)?	Je peux (vous) prendre en photo? pol zher per (voo) pron·drer on fo·to
That's (beautiful), isn't it?	C'est (beau), non? say (bo) non

LISTEN FOR

Ça ira mieux la prochaine fois.	sa ee·ra myer la pro·shen fwa	Better luck next time.
Quelle chance.	kel shons	How lucky!
C'est marrant.	say ma·ron	It's strange.
Pas de problème.	pa der pro·blem	No problem.
Tant pis.	tom pee	Too bad.
Quel dommage.	kel do·mazh	What a shame.
Qu'est-ce qu'il ya?	kes keel ya	What's up?

LISTEN FOR

Hé!	ay	Hey!
Formidable!	for·mee·da·bler	Great!
D'accord.	da·kor	Sure.
Peut-être.	per·te·trer	Maybe.
Pas question!	pa kay·styon	No way!
(C'est) bien.	(say) byun	(It's) OK.

Q **Are you here on holiday?**	Vous êtes ici pour les vacances? pol voo zet ee·see poor lay va·kons
A **I'm here for a holiday.**	Je suis ici pour les vacances. zher swee zee·see poor lay va·kons
A **I'm here on business.**	Je suis ici pour le travail. zher swee zee·see poor ler tra·vai
A **I'm here to study.**	Je suis ici pour les études. zher swee zee·see poor lay zay·tewd
This is my first trip (to France).	C'est la première fois que je viens (en France). say la prer·myair fwa ker zher vyun (on frons)
I'm here for ... days/ weeks.	Je reste ici ... jours/semaines. zher rest ee·see ... zhoor/ser·men
How long have been here?	Vous êtes ici depuis quand? pol voo zet ee·see der·pwee kon
Have you ever been (to England)?	Est-ce-que vous êtes déjà allé(e) (en Angleterre)? m/f pol es ker voo zet day·zha a·lay (on ong·gler·tair)
Do you want to come out with me?	Voulez-vous sortir avec moi? pol voo·lay·voo sor·teer a·vek mwa

NATIONALITIES

What part of ... do you come from?	D'où est-ce que vous venez en ...? pol doo es ker voo ver·nay on ... D'où est-ce que tu viens en ...? inf doo es ker tew vyun on ...
Q **Where are you from?**	Vous venez d'où? pol voo ver·nay doo Tu viens d'où? inf tew vyun doo
A **I'm from ...**	Je viens ... zher vyun ...

Australia	d'Australie	dos·tra·lee
Canada	du Canada	dew ka·na·da
the UK	du Royaume-Uni	doo rwa·yom·oo·ni
New Zealand	de la Nouvelle-Zélande	der la noo·vel·zay·lond
the USA	des USA	day zew·es·a

For more countries, see the **dictionary** (p196).

AGE

Q **How old are you?**	Quel âge avez-vous? pol kel azh a·vay·voo Quel âge as-tu? inf kel azh a·tew
A **I'm ... years old.**	J'ai ... ans. zhay ... on
A **Too old!**	Trop vieux/vieille! m/f tro vyer/vyay
A **I'm younger than I look.**	Je ne fais pas mon âge. zher ner fay pa mon azh

Q **How old is your son/ daughter?**	Quel âge a votre fils/fille? pol kel azh a vo·trer fees/fee·yer
A **He/She is ... years old.**	Il/Elle a ... ans. m/f eel/el a ... on

For your age, see **numbers & amounts** (p31).

OCCUPATIONS & STUDY

Q **What's your occupation?**	Vous faites quoi comme métier? pol voo fet kwa kom may·tyay Tu fais quoi comme métier? inf tew fay kwa kom may·tyay
A **I'm a chef.**	Je suis un(e) cuisinier/cuisinière. m/f zher swee zun/zewn kwee·zee·nyay/kwee·zee·nyair
A **I'm a student.**	Je suis un(e) étudiant(e). m/f zher swee zun/zewn ay·tew·dyon(t)
A **I work in education.**	Je travaille dans l'enseignement. zher tra·vai don lon·sen·yer·mon
A **I work in health.**	Je travaille dans la santé. zher tra·vai don la son·tay
A **I'm retired.**	Je suis retraité(e). m/f zher swee rer·tray·tay
A **I'm self-employed.**	Je suis indépendant(e). m/f zher swee un·day·pon·don(t)
A **I'm unemployed.**	Je suis chômeur/chômeuse. m/f zher swee sho·mer/sho·merz

Q **What are you studying?**	Que faites-vous comme études? pol ker fet·voo kom ay·tewd Que fais-tu comme études? inf ker fay·tew kom ay·tewd
A **I'm studying engineering.**	Je fais des études d'ingénieur. zher fay day zay·tewd dun·zhay·nyer
A **I'm studying French.**	Je fais des études de français. zher fay day zay·tewd der fron·say

For more occupations and fields of study, see the **dictionary** (p196).

FAMILY

Q **Do you have a ...?**	Vous avez ...? pol voo·za·vay ... Tu as ...? inf tew a ...
A **I have a ...**	J'ai ... zhay ...
A **I don't have a ...**	Je n'ai pas ... zher nay pa ...

boyfriend	un petit ami	um per·tee ta·mee
brother	un frère	un frair
child	un/une enfant m/f	un/ewn on·fon
family	une famille	ewn fa·mee·yer
father	un père	um pair
girlfriend	une petite amie	ewn per·tee ta·mee
husband	un mari	um ma·ree
mother	une mère	ewn mair
partner	un/une partenaire m/f	um/ewn par·ter·nair
sister	une sœur	ewn ser
wife	une femme	ewn fam

Ⓠ **Are you married?**	Est-ce que vous êtes marié(e)? **m/f pol** es ker voo zet mar·yay Est-ce que tu es marié(e)? **m/f inf** es ker tew ay mar·yay
Ⓐ **I'm single.**	Je suis célibataire. zher swee say·lee·ba·tair
Ⓐ **I'm married.**	Je suis marié(e). **m/f** zher swee mar·yay
Ⓐ **I live with my ...**	J'habite avec mon/ma/mes ... **m/f/pl** zha·beet a·vek mon/ma/may ...
Ⓐ **I live with someone.**	Je vis avec quelqu'un. zher vee a·vek kel·kun

TALKING WITH CHILDREN

What's your name?	Comment tu t'appelles? ko·mon tew ta·pel
How old are you?	Quel âge as-tu? kel azh a·tew
Do you like school?	L'école te plaît? lay·kol ter play
Do you learn English?	Tu apprends l'anglais? tew a·pron long·glay

FAREWELLS

Let's swap addresses.	Échangeons nos adresses. ay·zhon·zhon no za·dres
Are you on social media/Do you use social media?	Es-tu sur les réseaux sociaux? inf ay·tew sewr lay rez·o so·syo

Ⓠ **What's your ...?** | Quel est votre ... ? pol
kel ay vo·trer ...
Quel est ton ...? inf
kel ay ton ...

Ⓐ **Here's my ...** | Voici mon ...
vwa·see mon ...

address	adresse	a·dress
email	e-mail	ay·mel
mobile/cell number	numéro de portable	new·may·ro der por·ta·bler
phone number	numéro de téléphone	new·may·ro der tay·lay·fon

If you ever visit (Laos), come and visit us. | Si vous voyagez au (Laos), il faut nous rendre visite. pol
see voo vwa·ya·zhay o (low) eel fo noo ron·drer vee·zeet

Keep in touch! | Reste en contact! inf
rest ong kon·takt

It's been great meeting you! | Ravi d'avoir fait ta connaissance! inf
ra·vee da·vwar fay ta ko·nay·sons

WELL-WISHING

Congratulations! | Félicitations!
fay·lee·see·ta·syon

Happy birthday! | Joyeux anniversaire!
zhwa·yer za·nee·ver·sair

Merry Christmas! | Joyeux Nöel!
zhwa·yer no·el

Happy Easter! | Joyeuses Pâques!
zhwa·yerz pak

Interests

KEY PHRASES

What do you do in your spare time?	Que fais-tu pendant tes loisirs?	ker fay·tew pon·don tay lwa·zeer
Do you like ...?	Aimes-tu ...?	em·tew ...
I (don't) like ...	J'aime .../Je n'aime pas ...	zhem .../zher nem pa ...

In this section, phrases are given in an informal form. If you're unsure about what this means, see the box, p99.

COMMON INTERESTS

What do you do in your spare time?	Que fais-tu pendant tes loisirs? ker fay·tew pon·don tay lwa·zeer
Q **Do you like (art)?**	Aimes-tu (l'art)? em·tew (lar)
A **I like (hiking).**	J'aime (la randonnée). zhem (la ron·do·nay)
A **I don't like (cooking).**	Je n'aime pas (cuisiner). zher nem pa (kwee·zee·nay)

For sporting interests, see **sports** (p132) and the **dictionary** (p196).

MUSIC

Do you like to go to concerts?	Aimes-tu aller aux concerts? em·tew a·lay o kon·sair

Do you like to listen to music?	Aimes-tu écouter de la musique? em·tew ay·koo·tay der la mew·zeek
Do you like to play an instrument?	Aimes-tu jouer d'un instrument? em·tew zhoo·ay dun uns·trew·mon
Have you heard the latest album by ...?	As-tu entendu le dernier album de ...? a tew on·ton·dew ler dair·nyay al·bom der ...
Which bands do you like?	Quels groupes aimes-tu? kel groop em·tew
Which music do you like?	Quels genres de musique aimes-tu? kel zhon·rer der mew·zeek em·tew
Where can I buy this music?	Où puis-je trouver ce type de musique? oo pweezh troo·vay ser teep der mew·zeek

See also **going out** (p117).

CINEMA & THEATRE

I feel like going to a movie.	J'aimerais bien voir un film. zhem·ray byun vwar un feelm
I feel like going to a play.	J'aimerais bien voir une pièce de théâtre. zhem·ray byun vwar ewn pyes der tay·a·trer
What's showing at the cinema tonight?	Qu'est-ce qui passe au cinéma ce soir? kes kee pas o see·nay·ma ser swar

Does it have subtitles?	C'est sous-titré? say soo·tee·tray
Is it dubbed in English/ French?	Ce film est-il doublé en anglais/français? ser feelm ay·teel doo·blay on ong·glay/fron·say
Is there a cloakroom?	Y a-t-il un vestiaire? ya·teel un vest·yair
Is there an intermission?	Y a-t-il un entracte? ya·teel un on·trakt
Is there a programme?	Y a-t-il un programme? ya·teel un pro·gram
Where can I get a cinema/ theatre guide?	Où pourrais-je trouver un programme de cinéma/ théâtre? oo poo·rezh troo·vay um pro·gram der see·nay·ma/ tay·atrer
Are those seats taken?	Est-ce que ces places sont prises? es ker say plas son preez
Have you seen ...?	As-tu vu ...? a·tew vew ...
Q **Who's in it?**	Qui joue dans ce film? kee zhoo don ser feelm
A **It stars ...**	... est la vedette du film. ... ay la ver·det dew feelm
Q **Did you like the film?**	As-tu aimé le film? a·tew ay·may ler feelm
Q **Did you like the play?**	As-tu aimé la pièce? a·tew ay·may la pyes

(A) **I thought it was excellent.**	Je l'ai trouvé excellent. zher lay troo·vay ek·say·lon
(A) **I thought it was long.**	Je l'ai trouvé long. zher lay troo·vay long
I don't like (action movies).	Je n'aime pas les (films d'action). zher nem pa lay (feelm dak·syon)
I like (French films).	J'aime (les films français). zhem (lay feelm fron·say)

READING

(Q) **What kind of books do you read?**	Quel genre de livres lis-tu? kel zhon·rer der lee·vrer lee·tew
(Q) **Have you read ...?**	As-tu lu ...? a·tew lew ...
(A) **I read ...**	Je lis ... zher lee ...
(Q) **Who's your favourite author?**	Quel est ton auteur préféré? kel ay ton o·ter pray·fay·ray
(Q) **Which (French) author do you recommend?**	Quel auteur (français) peux-tu recommander? kel o·ter (fron·say) per·tew rer·ko·mon·day
(A) **I recommend ...**	Je peux recommander ... zher per rer·ko·mon·day ...
Where can I exchange books?	Où puis-je échanger des livres? oo pweezh ay·shon·zhay day lee·vrer

For more on books and reading, see **shopping** (p67).

Feelings & Opinions

KEY PHRASES

Are you ...?	Êtes-vous ...?/ Es-tu ...? pol/inf	et voo .../ ay·tew ...
I'm (not) ...	Je suis .../ Je ne suis pas ...	zher swee .../ zher ner swee pa ...
What did you think of it?	Qu'est-ce que vous en avez pensé? pol	kes ker voo zon na·vay pon·say
I thought it was OK.	Je l'ai trouvé bien.	zher lay troo·vay byun
Did you hear about ...?	Vous avez entendu parler de ...? pol	voo za·vay on·ton·dew par·lay der ...

FEELINGS

Feelings are described with either nouns or adjectives: the nouns use 'have' in French (eg 'I have hunger') and the adjectives use 'be' (like in English).

Q **Are you (sleepy)?**	Avez-vous (sommeil)? pol a·vay voo (so·may) As-tu (sommeil)? inf a·tew (so·may)
A **I'm (hot).**	J'ai (chaud). zhay (sho)
A **I'm not (hungry).**	Je n'ai pas (faim). zher nay pa (fum)

Q **Are you ...?**	Êtes-vous ...? pol et voo ... Es-tu ...? inf ay·tew ...
A **I'm ...**	Je suis ... zher swee ...
A **I'm not ...**	Je ne suis pas ... zher ner swee pa ...

disappointed	déçu(e) m/f	day·sew
happy	heureux/ heureuse m/f	er·reu/ er·reuz
sad	triste	treest
satisfied	satisfait(e) m/f	sa·tees·fay(t)

If you're not feeling well, see **health** (p146).

C'est beau!
say bo
It's beautiful!

LISTEN FOR

un peu	um per	a little
Je suis un peu triste.	zher swee zum per treest	I'm a little sad.
vraiment	vray·mon	really
Je suis vraiment navré.	zher swee vray·mon na·vray	I'm really sorry.
très	tray	very
Je me sens très vulnérable.	zher mer son tray vewl·nay·ra·bler	I feel very vulnerable.

OPINIONS

Q **What did you think of it?**	Qu'est-ce que vous en avez pensé? pol kes ker voo zon na·vay pon·say
Q **Did you like it?**	Cela vous a plu? pol ser·la voo za plew
A **I thought it was ...**	Je l'ai trouvé ... zher lay troo·vay ...
A **It's ...**	C'est ... say ...

beautiful	beau	bo
better	mieux	myer
great	formidable	for·mee·da·bler
horrible	horrible	o·ree·bler
OK	bien	byun
strange	étrange	ay·tronzh
weird	bizarre	bee·zar
worse	pire	peer

POLITICS & SOCIAL ISSUES

Q **Who do you vote for?**	Pour qui votez-vous? pol poor kee vo·tay·voo
A **I support the ... party.**	Je soutiens le parti ... zher soo·tyun ler par·tee ...

communist	communiste	ko·mew·neest
conservative	conservateur	kon·sair·va·ter
democratic	démocrate	day·mo·krat
green	écologiste	ay·ko·lo·zheest
labour	travailliste	tra·va·yeest
republican	républicain	ray·pew·blee·kun
social democratic	social démocrate	so·syal day·mo·krat
socialist	socialiste	so·sya·leest

Did you hear about ...?	Vous avez entendu parler de ...? pol voo za·vay on·ton·dew par·lay der ...
How do people feel about ...?	Qu'est-ce qu'on pense de ...? kes kom pons der ...
Q **Do you agree with it?**	Êtes-vous d'accord avec cela? pol et·voo da·kor a·vek ser·la
A **I (don't) agree with ...**	Je (ne) suis (pas) pour .... zher (ner) swee (pa) poor ...
Q **Are you in favour of (it)?**	Êtes-vous pour (cela)? pol et·voo poor (ser·la)
A **I'm against (it).**	Je suis contre (cela). zher swee kon·trer (ser·la)
economy	économie f ay·ko·no·mee
environment	environnement m on·vee·ron·mon

CULTURE TIP: FAMOUS QUOTES

'Comment est-il possible de gouverner un pays qui produit plus de trois cent soixante-dix fromages différents?' (Charles de Gaulle)
ko·mon ay·teel po·see·bler der goo·vair·nay un pay·ee kee pro·dwee plews der trwa·son swa·son·dees fro·mazh dee·fay·ron
'How is it possible to govern a country that produces more than 370 different cheeses?'

immigration	immigration f ee·mee·gra·syon
the war in ...	la guerre f en ... la gair on ...

THE ENVIRONMENT

Is there an environmental problem here?	Y a-t-il un problème d'environnement ici? ya·teel un pro·blem don·vee·ron·mon ee·see
Is this a protected forest/species?	C'est une forêt/espèce protégée? set ewn fo·ray/es·pes pro·tay·zhay
Where can I recycle this?	Où est-ce que je peux recycler ceci? oo es ker zhe per re·see·klay se·see
climate change	changement climatique m shon·zhe·mon klee·ma·teek
pollution	pollution f po·lew·syon
recycling	recyclage m rer·see·klazh

Going Out

KEY PHRASES

What's on tonight?	Qu'est-ce qu'on joue ce soir?	kes kon zhoo ser swar
When shall we meet?	On se retrouve à quelle heure?	on ser rer·troov a kel er
Where will we meet?	On se retrouve où?	on ser rer·troov oo

In this section, phrases are given in an informal form. If you're unsure about what this means, see the box, p99.

WHERE TO GO

What's on today?	Qu'est-ce qu'on joue aujourd'hui? kes kon zhoo o·zhoor·dwee
What's on tonight?	Qu'est-ce qu'on joue ce soir? kes kon zhoo ser swar
What's on this weekend?	Qu'est-ce qu'on joue ce week-end? kes kon zhoo ser week·end
Where are the ...?	Où sont les ...? oo son lay ...

clubs	clubs	klerb
discos	discothèques	dees·ko·tek
gay venues	boîtes gaies	bwat gay
places to eat	restaurants	res·to·ron
pubs	pubs	perb

Is there a local entertainment/film guide?	Y a-t-il un programme des spectacles/films? ya·teel un pro·gram day spek·ta·kler/feelm
Is there a local gay guide?	Y a-t-il un guide des endroits gais? ya·teel un geed day zon·drwa gay
What's there to do in the evenings?	Qu'est-ce qu'on peut faire le soir? kes kon per fair ler swar
I'd like to go to a/the ...	Je voudrais aller ... zher voo·dray a·lay ...

ballet	au ballet	o ba·lay
bar	au bar	o bar
cafe	au café	o ka·fay
cinema	au cinéma	o see·nay·ma
concert	à un concert	a ung kon·sair
nightclub	en boîte	on bwat
opera	à l'opéra	a lo·pay·ra
pub	au pub	o perb
restaurant	au restaurant	o res·to·ron
theatre	au théâtre	o tay·a·trer

INVITATIONS

What are you doing right now?	Que fais-tu maintenant? ker fay·tew mun·ter·non
What are you doing this evening?	Que fais-tu ce soir? ker fay·tew ser swar
What are you doing this weekend?	Que fais-tu ce week-end? ker fay·tew ser week·end

Would you like to go?	Tu voudrais aller? tew voo·dray a·lay
Would you like to go for a coffee?	Tu voudrais aller boire un café? tew voo·dray a·lay bwar ung ka·fay
My round.	C'est ma tournée. say ma toor·nay
Do you know a good restaurant?	Tu connais un bon restaurant? tew ko·nay un bon res·to·ron
Do you want to come to the concert with me?	Tu veux aller au concert avec moi? tew ver a·lay o kon·sair a·vek mwa
We're having a party.	Nous allons faire une fête. noo za·lon fair ewn fet
You should come.	Tu dois venir. tew dwa ver·neer

RESPONDING TO INVITATIONS

Sure!	D'accord! da·kor
Yes, I'd love to.	Je viendrai avec plaisir. zher vyun·dray a·vek play·zeer
Where shall we go?	Où aller? oo a·lay
No, I'm afraid I can't.	Non, désolé, je ne peux pas. non day·zo·lay zher ner per pa
What about tomorrow?	Et demain? ay der·mun

ARRANGING TO MEET

Q **What time shall we meet?**	On se retrouve à quelle heure? on ser rer·troov a kel er
A **Let's meet at (eight o'clock).**	On peut se retrouver à (huit heures). on per ser rer·troo·vay a (wee ter)
Q **Where will we meet?**	On se retrouve où? on ser rer·troov oo
A **Let's meet at the (entrance).**	On peut se retrouver devant (l'entrée). on per ser rer·troo·vay der·von (lon·tray)
I'll pick you up (at seven).	Je viendrai te chercher (à sept heures). zher vyun·dray ter shair·shay (a set er)
If I'm not there by (nine), don't wait for me.	Si je ne suis pas là avant (neuf heures), ne m'attends pas. see zher ner swee pa la a·von (ner ver) ner ma·ton pa
I'm looking forward to our meeting.	J'attends notre rendez-vous avec impatience. zha·ton no·trer ron·day·voo a·vek um·pa·syons
Agreed/OK!	D'accord! da·kor
I'll see you then.	À bientôt. ah byun·to
See you later.	À plus tard. a plew tar
See you tomorrow.	À demain. a der·mun

Sorry I'm late.	Désolé d'être en retard. day·zo·lay de·trer on rer·tar
Never mind.	Ce n'est pas grave. ser nay pa grav

NIGHTCLUBS & BARS

Are there any nightclubs here?	Est-ce qu'il y a des boîtes de nuit ici? es keel ya day bwat der nwee ee·see
Where can we go (salsa) dancing?	Où est-ce qu'on peut danser (la salsa)? oo es kom per don·say (la sal·sa)

Je m'amuse bien!
zher ma·mewz byun
I'm having a great time!

What time does the show start?	Le spectacle commence à quelle heure? ler spek·ta·kler ko·mons a kel er
How do I get there?	Comment y aller? ko·mon ee a·lay
What's the cover charge?	C'est combien le couvert? say kom·byun ler koo·vair
Come on!	Allez! a·lay
Q **What type of music do you like?**	Quel genre de musique aimes-tu? kel zhon·rer der mew·zeek em·tew
A **I like (reggae).**	J'aime (le reggae). zhem (ler ray·gay)
This place is great!	C'est formidable ici! say for·mee·da·bler ee·see
I'm having a great time!	Je m'amuse bien! zher ma·mewz byun
I don't like the music here.	Je n'aime pas la musique ici. zher nem pa la mew·zeek ee·see
Let's go somewhere else.	Allons ailleurs. a·lon za·yer
Do you want to go closer to the stage?	Tu veux bien t'approcher de la scène? tew ver byun ta·pro·shay der la sen
Do you want to sit at the front?	Tu veux bien t'asseoir au premier rang? tew ver byun ta·swar o prer·myay rong

Do you want to sit at the back?	Tu veux bien t'asseoir au dernier rang? tew ver byun ta·swar o dair·nyay rong
What a fantastic concert/group!	Quel concert/groupe fantastique! kel kon·sair/groop fon·ta·steek
What a great singer!	Quel(le) chanteur/chanteuse formidable! m/f kel shon·ter/shon·terz for·mee·da·bler

For more on bars, drinks and partying, see **eating out** (p156).

DRUGS

I don't take drugs.	Je ne touche pas à la drogue. zher ner toosh pa a la drog
I take ... occasionally.	Je prends du ... occasionnellement. zher pron dew ... o·ka·zyo·nel·mon
Do you want to have a smoke?	Tu veux fumer? tew ver few·may
Do you have a light?	Vous avez du feu? voo za·vay dew fer

If the police are talking to you about drugs, see **police** (p144), for useful phrases.

Romance

KEY PHRASES

Do you want to go out with me?	Veux-tu sortir avec moi?	ver·tew sor·teer a·vek mwa
I love you.	Je t'aime.	zher tem
Leave me alone, please.	Laissez-moi tranquille, s'il vous plaît.	lay·say·mwa trong·keel seel voo play

In this section, phrases are given in an informal form – if you're unsure about what this means, see the box, p99.

ASKING SOMEONE OUT

Q **Would you like to do something?**	Est-ce que tu aimerais faire quelque chose? es ker tew em·ray fair kel·ker shoz
A **Yes, I'd love to.**	Oui, j'aimerais bien. wee zhem·ray byun
A **I'm sorry, I can't.**	Non, je suis désolé(e), je ne peux pas. m/f non zher swee day·zo·lay zher ner per pa
A **No chance!**	Jamais de la vie! zha·may der la vee

PICK-UP LINES

You look like someone I know.	Tu me fais penser à quelqu'un que je connais. tew mer fay pon·say a kel·kun ker zher ko·nay
Would you like a drink?	Si on buvait quelque chose? see on bew·vay kel·ker shoz
What star sign are you?	Tu es de quel signe? tew ay der kel see·nyer
Shall we get some fresh air?	Nous allons prendre l'air? noo za·lon pron·drer lair
You're a fantastic dancer.	Tu danses vraiment bien. tew dons vray·mom byun
Do you come here often?	Tu viens ici souvent? tew vyun ee·see soo·von
Can I ...?	Puis-je ...? pweezh ...

dance with you	danser avec toi	don·say a·vek twa
see you again	te revoir	ter rer·vwar
sit here	m'asseoir ici	ma·swar ee·see
take you home	te raccompagner	ter ra·kom·pa·nyay

Do you have a boyfriend?	Est-ce que tu as un petit ami? es ker tew a um per·tee ta·mee
Do you have a girlfriend?	Est-ce que tu as une petite amie? es ker tew a ewn per·teet a·mee
Do you have a light?	Est-ce que tu as du feu? es ker tew a dew fer

SOCIAL ROMANCE

You have (a) beautiful ...	Tu as ... tew a ...

body	un beau corps	um bo kor
eyes	de beaux yeux	der bo zyer
hands	de belles mains	der bel mun
smile	un beau sourire	um bo soo·reer
personality	une belle personnalité	ewn bel pair·so·na·lee·tay

Will you take me home?	Tu veux bien me ramener à la maison? tew ver byun mer ram·nay a la may·zon
Do you want to come inside for a while?	Tu veux entrer un instant? tu ver on·tray un un·ston

REJECTIONS

Excuse me, I have to go now.	Excusez-moi, je dois partir maintenant. ek·skyew·zay·mwa zher dwa par·teer mun·ter·non
No, thank you.	Non, merci. non mair·see
I'd rather not.	Je n'ai pas très envie. zher nay pa tray zon·vee
Your ego is out of control!	Tu es complètement imbu(e) de toi-même! **m/f** tew ay kom·plet·mon um·bew der twa·mem
Leave me alone!	Laissez-moi tranquille! lay·say·mwa trong·keel
Don't touch me!	Ne me touchez pas! ner mer too·shay pa

LANGUAGE TIP: SWEAR WORD WARNING

The word for 'a kiss' in French is *un baiser* un bay·zay, but the *un* word is the key here – without it, the word becomes a certain strong swear word beginning with 'f'. The verb 'kiss' is *embrasser* om·bra·say.

I'm not interested.	Ça ne m'intéresse pas. sa ner mun·tay·res pa
Go to hell!	Va te faire voir! va ter fair vwar
You're disturbing me.	Tu me gênes. tew mer zhen

GETTING CLOSER

Q **Do you like me too?**	Tu m'aimes aussi? tew mem o·see
A **I like you very much.**	Je t'aime beaucoup. zher tem bo·koo
You're very attractive.	Tu es très beau/belle. m/f tew ay tray bo/bel
I'm interested in you.	Je m'intéresse vraiment à toi. zher mun·tay·res vray·mon a twa
You're great.	Tu es formidable. tew ay for·mee·da·bler
Can I kiss you?	Je peux t'embrasser? zher per tom·bra·say

SEX

I want to make love to you.	Je veux faire l'amour avec toi. zher ver fair la·moor a·vek twa
Let's use (a condom).	On va utiliser (un préservatif). on va ew·tee·lee·zay (um pray·zair·va·teef)
I think we should stop now.	Il faut arrêter maintenant. eel fo a·ray·tay mun·ter·non
Let's go to bed!	On va se coucher. on va ser koo·shay
Kiss me.	Embrasse-moi. om·bras·mwa
I want you.	Je te veux. zher ter ver
Q **Do you like this?**	Ça te plaît? sa ter play
A **I like that.**	J'aime ça. zhem sa
A **I don't like that.**	Je n'aime pas ça. zher nem pa sa
Easy tiger!	Vas-y mollo! va·zee mo·lo
Stop!	Arrête! a·ret
Don't stop!	N'arrête pas! na·ret pa

LANGUAGE TIP: MASCULINE & FEMININE

In this book, masculine forms appear before the feminine forms. If a letter has been added to denote the feminine form (often an *-e*), it will appear in parentheses. If the change involves more than the addition of a letter, two words are given, separated by a slash. For more information, see **gender** in the **grammar** chapter (p17).

LOVE

Q **Do you love me?**	Tu m'aimes? tew mem
A **I love you.**	Je t'aime. zher tem
Do you want to go out with me?	Veux-tu sortir avec moi? ver·tew sor·teer a·vek mwa
Let's move in together!	Vivons ensemble! vee·von on·som·bler
Will you marry me?	Veux-tu m'épouser? ver·tew may·poo·zay

Beliefs & Culture

KEY PHRASES

What's your religion?	Quelle est votre/ta religion? pol/inf	kel ay vo·trer/ta rer·lee·zhyon
I'm ...	Je suis ...	zher swee ...
I'm sorry, it's against my beliefs.	Je m'excuse, c'est contraire à ma religion.	zher mek·skewz say kon·trair a ma rer·lee·zhyon

RELIGION

Q **What's your religion?**	Quelle est votre/ta religion? pol/inf kel ay vo·trer/ta·ray·lee·zhyon
A **I'm ...**	Je suis ... zher swee ...
A **I'm not ...**	Je ne suis pas ... zher ner swee pa ...

agnostic	agnostique	ag·no·steek
atheist	athée	a·tay
practising	pratiquant(e) m/f	pra·tee·kon(t)
religious	croyant(e) m/f	krwa·yon(t)

For religions, see the **dictionary** (p196).

I (don't) believe in God.	Je (ne) crois (pas) en Dieu. zher (ner) krwa (pa) on dyer

Where can I attend mass?	Où est-ce qu'on peut aller à la messe? oo es kom per a·lay a la mes
Where can I attend a service?	Où est-ce qu'on peut aller à l'office? oo es kom per a·lay a lo·fees
Where can I pray?	Où est-ce qu'on peut faire ses dévotions? oo es kom per fair say day·vo·syon

CULTURAL DIFFERENCES

Is this a local custom?	Est-ce que c'est une coutume locale? esk ker say·tewn koo·tewm lo·kal
I didn't mean to say anything wrong.	Mes propos n'avaient rien de blessant. may pro·po na·vay ryun der blay·son
I'll try it.	Je vais essayer ça. zher vay ay·say·yay sa
I'd rather not join in.	Je ne veux pas participer. zher ner ver pa par·tee·see·pay
I'm sorry, it's against my culture/religion.	Je m'excuse, c'est contraire à ma culture/religion. zher mek·skewz say kon·trair a ma kewl·tewr/rer·lee·zhyon
This is very different/interesting.	Ceci est très différent/intéressant. ser·see ay tray dee·fay·ron/zun·tay·ray·son

For phrases relating to cultural differences and food, see **vegetarian & special meals** (p174).

Sports

KEY PHRASES

Which sport do you play?	Quel sport faites-vous? pol	kel spor fet·voo
Who's your favourite team?	Quelle est votre équipe favorite? pol	kel ay vo·trer ay·keep fa·vo·reet
What's the score?	Quel est le score?	kel ay ler skor

SPORTING INTERESTS

Do you like sport?	Vous aimez le sport? voo zay·may ler spor
I prefer watching sport.	Je préfère regarder le sport. zher pray·fair rer·gar·day le spor
Which sport do you play?	Quel sport faites-vous? pol kel spor fet·voo
Q **Which sports do you like?**	Quels sports aimez-vous? pol kel spor ay·may·voo
A **I like (football/soccer).**	J'aime (le football). zhem (ler foot·bol)
Who's your favourite sportsperson?	Quel(le) est votre sportif/sportive favori(te)? m/f pol kel ay vo·trer spor·teef/spor·teev fa·vo·ree(t)
Who's your favourite team?	Quelle est votre équipe favorite? pol kel ay vo·trer ay·keep fa·vo·reet

For more sports, see the **dictionary** (p196).

GOING TO A GAME

Would you like to go to a game?	Vous voulez aller voir un match? pol voo voo·lay a·lay vwar um matsh
Who's playing?	Qui joue? kee zhoo
Who's winning?	Qui est en train de gagner? kee ay ton trun der ga·nyay
Q **What was the final score?**	Quel est le score final? kel ay ler skor fee·nal
A **It was a draw.**	Ils ont fait match nul. eel zon fay matsh newl
That was a good/bad game.	C'était vraiment un bon/ mauvais match. say·tay vray·mon um bon/ mo·vay matsh
What's the score?	Quel est le score? kel ay ler skor

PLAYING SPORT

Q **Do you want to play?**	Vous voulez jouer? pol voo voo·lay zhoo·ay
A **Yes, that'd be great.**	Oui, ça serait excellent. wee sa se ray tek·say·lon
A **I have an injury.**	Je suis blessé. zher swee blay·say
Can I join in?	Je peux participer? zher per par·tee·see·pay
Your/My point.	Un point pour vous/moi. pol um pwun poor voo/mwa

LISTEN FOR

match nul	matsh newl	draw/even
égalité	ay·ga·lee·tay	tie
balle de match	bal der matsh	match point
zéro	zay·ro	nil/zero

Kick/Pass it to me!	Passez-le-moi! pol pa·say·ler·mwa
Thanks for the game.	Merci d'avoir joué avec moi. mair·see da·vwar zhoo·ay a·vek mwa
Where's the best place to jog around here?	Où peut-on faire du jogging? oo per·ton fair dew zho·geeng
Where's a nearby gym?	Où y a t-il un gymnase par ici? oo ya teel un zheem·naz par ee·see
Where's a nearby swimming pool?	Où y a t-il une piscine par ici? oo ya teel ewn pee·seen par ee·see
Where's a nearby tennis court?	Où y a t-il un terrain de tennis par ici? oo ya teel un tay·run der tay·nees par ee·see
Can I rent a locker, please?	Puis-je louer un casier, s'il vous plaît? pol pweezh loo·way ung ka·zyay seel voo play
Can I see the gym, please?	Puis-je voir le gymnase, s'il vous plaît? pol pweezh vwar ler zheem·naz seel voo play

What's the charge per ...?	Quel est le prix ...? kel ay ler pree ...	
day	par jour	par zhoor
game	de la séance	der la say·ons
hour	de l'heure	der ler
visit	de la visite	der la vee·zeet

Can I hire a bicycle?	Puis-je louer un vélo? pwee·zher loo·way un vay·lo
Can I hire a tennis court?	Puis-je louer un terrain de tennis? pwee·zher loo·way un tay·run der tay·nees
Can I hire a racquet?	Puis-je louer une raquette? pwee·zher loo·way ewn ra·ket
Where are the changing rooms?	Où sont les vestiaires? oo son lay vays·tyair

CYCLING

Where does the race finish?	Où finit la course? oo fee·nee la koors
Where does it pass through?	Ça passe par où? sa pas par oo
Who's winning?	Qui est en train de gagner? kee ay ton trun der ga·nyay
Is today's leg very hard?	Est-ce que l'étape d'aujourd'hui est très difficile? es ker lay·tap do·zhoor·dwee ay tray dee·fee·seel

cyclist	cycliste m&f see·kleest
hill stage	fortes côtes f fort kot
leg (in race)	étape f ay·tap
time trial	course contre la montre f koors kon·trer la mon·trer
winner	gagnant(e) m/f ga·nyon(t)
the yellow jersey	le maillot jaune m ler ma·yo zhon

For phrases on getting around by bicycle, see **transport** (p38).

FOOTBALL/SOCCER

He's a great (player).	C'est un (joueur) formidable. say tun (zhoo·er) for·mee·da·bler
Which team is at the top of the league?	Quelle équipe est en tête du championnat? kel ay·keep ay ton tet dew shom·pyo·na

LISTEN FOR

corner m	kor·nair	corner
faute f	fot	foul
coup franc m	koo frong	free kick
gardien de but m	gar·dyun der bewt	goalkeeper
hors jeu	or zher	offside
penalty m	pay·nal·tee	penalty

Outdoors

KEY PHRASES

Do we need a guide?	A-t-on besoin d'un guide?	a·tom ber·zwun dung geed
I'm lost.	Je suis perdu(e). m/f	zher swee pair·dew
What's the weather like?	Quel temps fait-il?	kel tom fay·teel

HIKING

Where can I ...?
Où est-ce que je peux ...?
oo es ker zher per ...

buy supplies	acheter des provisions	ash·tay day pro·vee·zyon
find out about hiking trails	me renseigner sur les sentiers à suivre	mer ron·se·nyay sewr lay son·tyay a swee·vrer
find someone who knows this area	trouver quelqu'un qui connaît la région	troo·vay kel·kun kee ko·nay la ray·zhyon
get a map	trouver une carte	troo·vay ewn kart
hire hiking gear	louer du matériel de randonnée	loo·way dew ma·tay·ryel der ron·do·nay

Do I need to take food?
Est-ce qu'il faut apporter des vivres?
es keel fo a·por·tay day vee·vrer

Do I need to take water?	Est-ce qu'il faut apporter de l'eau? es keel fo a·por·tay der lo
How long is the trail?	Le chemin fait combien de kilomètres? ler shmun fay kom·byun der kee·lo·me·trer
Do we need a guide?	A-t-on besoin d'un guide? a·tom ber·zwun dung geed
Are there guided treks?	Est-ce qu'il y a des marches organisées? es keel ya day marsh or·ga·nee·zay
Is it safe?	C'est sans danger? say son don·zhay
Is there a hut there?	Y a-t-il une cabane là-bas? ya·teel ewn ka·ban la·ba
When does it get dark?	À quelle heure fait-il nuit? a kel er fay·teel nwee
Where's the nearest village?	Où est le village le plus proche? oo ay ler vee·lazh ler plew prosh
Which is the easiest route?	Quel est l'itinéraire le plus facile à suivre? kel ay lee·tee·nay·rair ler plew fa·seel a swee·vrer
Which is the most interesting route?	Quel est l'itinéraire le plus intéressant? kel ay lee·tee·nay·rair ler plew zun·tay·ray·son
Where have you come from?	Vous êtes parti d'où? pol voo zet par·tee doo

How long did it take?	Ça a pris combien de temps? sa a pree kom·byun der tom
Does this path go to ...?	Est-ce que ce sentier mène à ...? es ker ser son·tyay men a ...
Can we go through here?	On peut passer par ici? on per pa·say par ee·see
Is the water OK to drink?	Est-ce que l'eau est potable? es ker lo ay po·ta·bler
I'm lost.	Je suis perdu(e). m/f zher swee pair·dew

AT THE BEACH

Where's the nearest beach?	Où est la plage la plus proche? oo ay la plazh la plew prosh
Is it safe to dive/swim here?	On peut plonger/nager sans danger? on per plon·zhay/na·zhay son don·zhay
What time is high/low tide?	À quelle heure est la marée haute/basse? a kel er ay la ma·ray ot/bas
How much for a chair?	Combien coûte une chaise longue? kom·byun koot ewn shez long·ger

LOOK FOR

Baignade Interdite!	be·nyad un·ter·deet	No Swimming!

SOCIAL OUTDOORS

LISTEN FOR

Attention au courant sous-marin.	a·ton·syon o koo·ron soo·ma·run Be careful of the undertow.
C'est dangereux.	say don·zhrer It's dangerous.

How much for a hut?	Combien coûte une cabine de bain? kom·byun koot ewn ka·been der bun
How much for an umbrella?	Combien coûte un parasol? kom·byun koot um pa·ra·sol

WEATHER

Q **What's the weather like?**	Quel temps fait-il? kel tom fay·teel
A **(Today) It's cold.**	(Aujourd'hui) Il fait froid. (o·zhoor·dwee) eel fay frwa
A **It's (very) hot.**	Il fait (très) chaud. eel fay (tray) sho
A **It's windy.**	Il fait du vent. eel fay dew von
A **It's raining.**	Il pleut. eel pler
A **It's snowing.**	Il neige. eel nezh
A **It's cloudy.**	Le temps est couvert. ler tom ay koo·vair
What's the weather forecast?	Quelles sont les prévisions météo? kel son lay pray·vee·zyon may·tay·yo

SAFE TRAVEL

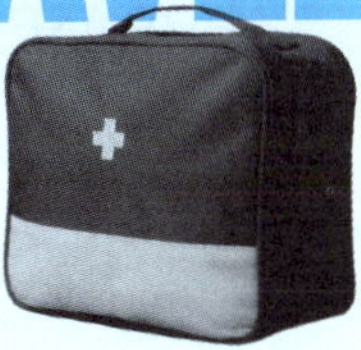

Emergencies

KEY PHRASES

Help!	Au secours!	o skoor
There's been an accident.	Il y a eu un accident.	eel ya ew un ak·see·don
It's an emergency!	C'est urgent!	say tewr·zhon

Help!	Au secours! o skoor
Stop!	Arrêtez! pol a·ray·tay
Go away!	Allez-vous-en! pol a·lay·voo·zon
Thief!	Au voleur! o vo·ler
Fire!	Au feu! o fer
Watch out!	Faites attention! pol fet a·ton·syon
Call the police!	Appelez la police! pol a·play la po·lees
It's an emergency!	C'est urgent! say tewr·zhon
There's been an accident.	Il y a eu un accident. eel ya ew un ak·see·don
Do you have a first-aid kit?	Avez-vous une trousse de première urgence? pol a·vay·voo ewn troos der prer·myair ewr·zhons

Can you help me, please?	Est-ce que vous pourriez m'aider, s'il vous plaît? pol es ker voo poo·ryay may·day seel voo play
Can I use the telephone?	Est-ce que je pourrais utiliser le téléphone? es ker zher poo·ray ew·tee·lee·zay ler tay·lay·fon
I'm lost.	Je suis perdu(e). m/f zher swee pair·dew
Where are the toilets?	Où sont les toilettes? oo son lay twa·let

LANGUAGE TIP: MISUNDERSTANDINGS

As in any language, French words can have a number of meanings that can lead to some funny, or possibly strange, sentences. How about this for an account of a (sure, unlikely) run-in with the law:

Madame Aubergine a posé un papillon sur ma Renault, et les poulets m'ont ramené dans un panier à salade.

ma·dam o·bair·zheen a po·say un pa·pee·yon sewr ma re·no ay lay poo·lay mon ra·me·nay dons un pan·yay a sa·lad

(Lit: Mrs Eggplant/Aubergine put a butterfly on my Renault, and the chickens came and took me away in a salad basket.) A more useful translation of this might be: 'A parking inspector stuck a ticket on my car, then the cops came and took me away in a police car.'

Police

KEY PHRASES

Where's the police station?	Où est le commissariat de police?	oo ay ler ko·mee·sar·ya der po·lees
I want to contact my embassy/ consulate.	Je veux contacter mon ambassade/ consulat.	zher ver kon·tak·tay mon om·ba·sad/ kon·sew·la
My bag was stolen.	On m'a volé mon sac.	on ma vo·lay mon sak

Where's the police station?	Où est le commissariat de police? oo ay ler ko·mee·sar·ya der po·lees
I want to report an offence.	Je veux signaler un délit. zher ver see·nya·lay un day·lee
I've been raped.	J'ai été violé(e). m/f zhay ay·tay vyo·lay
I've been assaulted.	J'ai été violenté(e). m/f zhay ay·tay vyo·lon·tay
He/She has been raped.	Il/Elle a été violé(e). m/f eel/el a ay·tay vyo·lay
I've been robbed.	On m'a volé. on ma vo·lay
He/She has been robbed.	Il/Elle s'est fait voler. eel/el say fay vo·lay
It was him/her.	C'est lui/elle. say lwee/el

I've lost my ...	J'ai perdu ... zhay pair·dew ...
My ... was/were stolen.	On m'a volé ... on ma vo·lay ...

backpack	mon sac à dos	mon sak a do
bags	mes valises	may va·leez
money	mon argent	mon ar·zhon
passport	mon passeport	mom pas·por
wallet	mon portefeuille	mom por·ter·fer·yer

What am I accused of?	Je suis accusé(e) de quoi? m/f zher swee a·kew·zay der kwa
I didn't realise I was doing anything wrong.	Je ne croyais pas que je faisais quelque chose de mal. zher ner krwa·yay pa ker zher fer·zay kel·ker shoz der mal
I'm innocent.	Je suis innocent(e). m/f zher swee zee·no·son(t)
I want to contact my embassy/consulate.	Je veux contacter mon ambassade/consulat. zher ver kon·tak·tay mon om·ba·sad/kon·sew·la
Can I make a phone call?	Je peux téléphoner? zher per tay·lay·fo·nay
Can I have a lawyer (who speaks English)?	Je peux avoir un avocat (qui parle anglais)? zher per a·vwar un a·vo·ka (koo parl ong·glay)
Can I have a copy, please?	Puis-je en avoir un exemplaire? pwee·zhon a·vwar un eg·zom·plair
I have a prescription for this drug/medication.	On m'a prescrit cette drogue/ médicaments. om ma pray·skree set drog/ may·dee·ka·mon

Health

KEY PHRASES

Where's a nearby hospital?	Où y a t-il un hôpital par ici?	oo ee a teel un o·pee·tal par ee·see
I'm sick.	Je suis malade.	zher swee ma·lad
I need a doctor.	J'ai besoin d'un médecin.	zhay ber·zwun dun mayd·sun
I'm on medication for ...	Je prends des médicaments pour ...	zher pron day may·dee·ka·mon poor ...
I'm allergic to ...	Je suis allergique à ...	zher swee za·lair·zheek a ...

Where's a nearby ...? Où y a t-il un/une ... par ici? m/f
oo ee a teel un/ewn ... par ee·see

(night) chemist/ pharmacy	pharmacie (de nuit) f	far·ma·see (der nwee)
dentist	dentiste m	don·teest
doctor	médecin m	mayd·sun
hospital	hôpital m	o·pee·tal

I need a doctor (who speaks English). J'ai besoin d'un médecin (qui parle anglais).
zhay ber·zwun dun mayd·sun (kee parl ong·glay)

Could I see a female doctor?	Est-ce que je peux voir une femme médecin? es ker zher per vwar ewn fam mayd·sun
Can the doctor come here?	Est-ce que le médecin peut venir ici? es ker ler mayd·sun per ver·neer ee·see
I've run out of my medication.	Je n'ai plus de médicaments. zher nay plew der may·dee·ka·mon
I don't want a blood transfusion.	Je ne veux pas de transfusion sanguine. zher ner ver pa der trons·few·zyon song·geen
Please use a new syringe.	Je vous prie d'utiliser une seringue neuve. pol zher voo pree dew·tee·lee·zay ewn ser·rung nerv
He/She has been vaccinated for ...	Il/Elle s'est fait vacciner contre ... eel/el say fay vak·see·nay kon·trer ...

LANGUAGE TIP: FRENCH IDIOMS

Here are a couple of colourful expressions referring to body parts:

J'ai l'estomac dans les talons.	zhay les·to·ma don lay ta·lon I'm starving. (lit: I have my stomach in my heels)
Je n'ai plus de jambes.	zher nay plew der zhomb I'm exhausted. (lit: I don't have any more legs)

I've been vaccinated for hepatitis.	Je me suis fait(e) vacciner contre l'hépatite. m/f zher mer swee fay/fet vak·see·nay kon·trer lay·pa·teet
I've been vaccinated for tetanus.	Je me suis fait(e) vacciner contre le tétanos. m/f zher mer swee fay/fet vak·see·nay kon·trer ler tay·ta·nos
I've been vaccinated for typhoid.	Je me suis fait(e) vacciner contre la typhoïde. m/f zher mer swee fay/fet vak·see·nay kon·trer la tee·fo·eed

SYMPTOMS & CONDITIONS

I'm sick.	Je suis malade. zher swee ma·lad
My friend is sick.	Mon ami(e) est malade. m/f mon a·mee ay ma·lad
It hurts here.	J'ai une douleur ici. zhay ewn doo·ler ee·see
I've been injured.	J'ai été blessé(e). m/f zhay ay·tay blay·say
I've been vomiting.	J'ai vomi. zhay vo·mee
I can't sleep.	Je n'arrive pas à dormir. zher na·reev pa a dor·meer
I have an infection.	J'ai une infection. zhay ewn un·fek·syon
I have a rash.	J'ai des démangeaisons. zhay day day·mon·zhe·zon

LISTEN FOR

Je voudrais prendre votre température.	zher voo·dray pron·drer vo·trer tom·pay·ra·tewr	I'd like to take your temperature.
Depuis quand êtes-vous dans cet état?	der·pwee kon et·voo don sayt ay·ta	How long have you been like this?
Cela vous est déjà arrivé?	ser·la voo zay day·zha a·ree·vay	Have you had this before?
Est-ce que vous buvez?	es·ker voo bew·vay	Do you drink?
Est-ce que vous fumez?	es·ker voo few·may	Do you smoke?
Est-ce que vous vous droguez?	es·ker voo voo dro·gay	Do you take drugs?
Êtes-vous allergique à quelque chose?	et·voo za·lair·zheek a kel·ker shoz	Are you allergic to anything?
Êtes-vous enceinte?	et·voo zon·sunt	Are you pregnant?
Vous avez une vie sexuelle?	voo za·vay ewn vee sek·swel	Are you sexually active?
Vous avez eu des rapports non protégés?	voo za·vay ew day ra·por non pro·tay·zhay	Have you had unprotected sex?
Est-ce que vous prenez des médicaments?	es·ker voo prer·nay day may·dee·ka·mon	Are you on any medication?
Il faut vous faire hospitaliser.	eel fo voo fair os·pee·ta·lee·zay	You need to be admitted to hospital.

I feel ...	Je me sens ...	zher mer son ...
anxious	inquiet/inquiète m/f	un·kyay/un·kyet
better	mieux	myer
weak	faible	fay·bler
worse	pire	peer

I feel ...	J'ai ...	zhay ...
dizzy	des vertiges	day ver·teezh
hot and cold	chaud et froid	sho ay frwa
nauseous	des nausées	day no·zay
shivery	des frissons	day free·son

I have diarrhoea.	J'ai la diarrhée. zhay la dya·ray
I have a headache.	J'ai mal à la tête. zhay mal a la tet
I have a sore throat.	J'ai mal à la gorge. zhay mal a la gorzh
I've recently had ...	J'ai eu récemment ... zhay ew ray·sa·mon ...
I'm on medication for ...	Je prends des médicaments pour ... zher pron day may·dee·ka·mon poor ...
He/She is on medication for ...	Il/Elle prend des médicaments pour ... eel/el pron day may·dee·ka·mon poor ...

For more symptoms and conditions, see the **dictionary** (p196).

ALLERGIES

I'm allergic to ...	Je suis allergique ... zher swee za·lair·zheek ...
He/She's allergic to ...	Il/Elle est allergique ... eel/el ay ta·lair·zheek ...

antibiotics	aux antibiotiques	o zon·tee·byo·teek
anti-inflammatories	aux anti-inflammatoires	o zun·tee·un·fla·ma·twar
aspirin	à l'aspirine	a las·pee·reen
bees	aux abeilles	o za·bay·yer
codeine	à la codéine	a la ko·day·een
sulphur-based drugs	aux sulfamides	o sewl·fa·meed

I have a skin allergy.	J'ai une allergie de peau. zhay ewn a·lair·zhee der po

For food-related allergies, see **vegetarian & special meals** (p174).

WOMEN'S HEALTH

I need a pregnancy test.	J'ai besoin d'un test de grossesse. zhay ber·zwun dun test der gro·ses
I'm on the Pill.	Je prends la pilule. zher pron la pee·lewl
I haven't had my period for ... weeks.	Je n'ai pas eu mes règles depuis ... semaines. zher nay pa ew may re·gler der·pwee ... ser·men
I've noticed a lump here.	J'ai remarqué une grosseur ici. zhay rer·mar·kay ewn gro·ser ee·see

I need contraception.	J'ai besoin d'un contraceptif. zhay ber·zwun dun kon·trer·sep·teef
I need the morning-after pill.	J'ai besoin de la pilule du lendemain. zhay ber·zwun de la pee·lewl dew lon·der·mun

PARTS OF THE BODY

My ... hurts.	Mon/Ma/Mes ... me fait mal. m/f/pl mon/ma/may ... mer fay mal

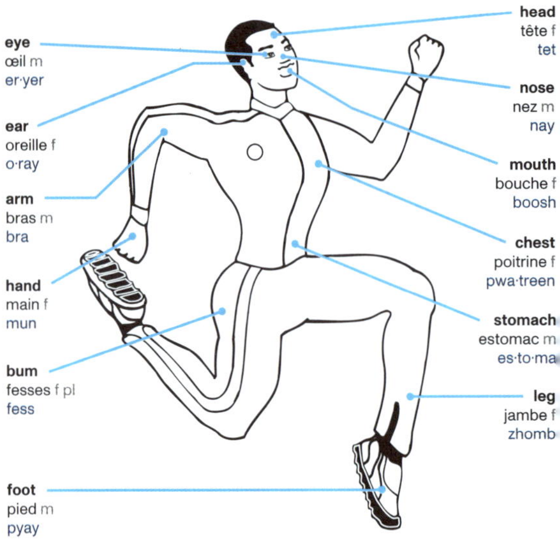

I can't move my ...	Je n'arrive pas à bouger mon/ma ... m/f zher na·reev pa a boo·zhay mon/ma ...
I have a cramp in my ...	J'ai une crampe au/à la ... m/f zhay ewn kromp o/a la ...
My ... is swollen.	Mon/Ma ... est enflé(e). m/f mon/ma ... ay ton·flay

DENTIST

I have a broken tooth.	J'ai une dent cassée. zhay ewn don ka·say
I have a toothache.	J'ai mal aux dents. zhay mal o don
I've lost a filling.	J'ai perdu un plombage. zhay pair·dew un plom·bazh
I don't want it extracted.	Je ne veux pas que vous l'arrachiez. zher ner ver pa ker voo la·rash·yay
My dentures are broken.	Mon dentier est cassé. mon don·tyay ay ka·say
Ouch!	Aïe! a·ee

LISTEN FOR

Ouvrez tout grand.	oo·vray too gron	Open wide.
Rinsez.	run·say	Rinse!
Ça ne fera pas de mal.	sa ne fer·ra pa der mal	This won't hurt a bit.
Ça pourrait faire un peu mal.	sa poo·ray fair un per mal	This might hurt a little.

LISTEN FOR

Avez-vous déjà pris ceci?	a·vay·voo day·zha pree ser·see Have you taken this before?
Deux fois par jour (avec nourriture).	der fwa par zhoor (a·vek noo·ree·tewr) Twice a day (with food).
Cela sera prêt dans (vingt minutes).	ser·la ser·ra pray don (vung mee·newt) It'll be ready to pick up in (20 minutes).
Traitement à suivre jusqu'au bout.	tret·mon a swee·vrer zhews·ko boo You must complete the course.

CHEMIST/PHARMACIST

I need something for ...	J'ai besoin d'un médicament pour ... zhay ber·zwun dun may·dee·ka·mom poor ...
Do I need a prescription for ...?	J'ai besoin d'une ordonnance pour ...? zhay ber·zwun dewn or·do·nons poor ...
How many times a day?	Combien de fois par jour? kom·byun der fwa par zhoor
Will it make me drowsy?	Est-ce que ça peut provoquer des somnolences? es ker sa per pro·vo·kay day som·no·lons

For pharmaceutical items, see the **dictionary** (p196).

FOOD

Eating Out

KEY PHRASES

Can you recommend a restaurant?	Est-ce que vous pouvez me conseiller un restaurant? pol	es ker voo poo·vay mer kon·say·yay un res·to·ron
A table for two people, please.	Une table pour deux personnes, s'il vous plaît. pol	ewn ta·bler poor der pair·son seel voo play
Can I see the menu, please?	Est-ce que je peux voir la carte, s'il vous plaît? pol	es ker zher per vwar la kart seel voo play
I'd like a beer, please.	Je voudrais une bière, s'il vous plaît. pol	zher voo·dray ewn byair seel voo play
Please bring the bill.	Apportez-moi l'addition, s'il vous plaît. pol	a·por·tay·mwa la·dee·syon seel voo play

Petit déjeuner per·tee day·zher·nay (breakfast) typically consists of bread and jam and a coffee or hot chocolate – pastries, yoghurt and cereals might also be eaten. *Déjeuner* day·zher·nay (lunch) is the main meal of the day and may involve a number of courses. *Dîner* dee·nay (dinner) is eaten around 8pm, and is a light version of lunch. Bread and wine feature at both lunch and dinner.

BASICS

breakfast	petit déjeuner m per·tee day·zher·nay
lunch	déjeuner m day·zher·nay

dinner	dîner m dee·nay
snack	casse-croûte m kas·kroot
eat	manger mon·zhay
drink	boire bwar
daily special	suggestion du jour f sew·zhes·tyon dew zhoor
set menu	menu m mer·new
I'd like ...	Je voudrais ... zher voo·dray ...
I'm starving!	Je meurs de faim! zher mer der fum
Enjoy your meal!	Bon appétit! bon a·pay·tee

FINDING A PLACE TO EAT

Can you recommend a cafe?	Est-ce que vous pouvez me conseiller un café? pol es ker voo poo·vay mer kon·say·yay ung ka·fay
Can you recommend a restaurant?	Est-ce que vous pouvez me conseiller un restaurant? pol es ker voo poo·vay mer kon·say·yay un res·to·ron
Where would you go for a cheap meal?	Où est-ce qu'on trouve les restaurants bon marché? oo es kon troov lay res·to·ron bom mar·shay

Where would you go for local specialities?	Où est-ce qu'on trouve les spécialités locales? oo es kon troov lay spay·sya·lee·tay lo·kal
Are you still serving food?	On peut toujours passer des commandes? om per too·zhoor pa·say day ko·mond
How long is the wait?	Il faut attendre combien de temps? eel fo a·ton·drer kom·byun der tom

AT THE RESTAURANT

I'd like to reserve a table for (eight) o'clock.	Je voudrais réserver une table pour (vingt) heures. zher voo·dray ray·zair·vay ewn ta·bler poor (vungt) er
I'd like to reserve a table for (two) people.	Je voudrais réserver une table pour (deux) personnes. zher voo·dray ray·zair·vay ewn ta·bler poor (der) pair·son
I'd like a table in the (non) smoking area, please.	Je voudrais une table dans un endroit pour (non-) fumeurs, s'il vous plaît. pol zher voo·dray ewn ta·bler don zun on·drwa poor (non·)few·mer seel voo play
I'd like a table for (five), please.	Je voudrais une table pour (cinq) personnes, s'il vous plaît. pol zher voo·dray ewn ta·bler poor (sungk) pair·son seel voo play

For five, please.	Pour cinq, s'il vous plaît. pol	poor sungk, seel voo play

Eating Out

CAN I SEE THE MENU, PLEASE?
Est-ce que je peux voir la carte, s'il vous plaît? pol
es ker zher per vwar la kart seel voo play

WHAT WOULD YOU RECOMMEND FOR ...?
Que recommandez vous comme ...? pol
ker rer·ko·mon·day voo kom ...

THE MAIN MEAL
plat principal
pla prun·see·pal

DESSERT
dessert
day·sair

DRINKS
boisson
bwa·son

CAN YOU BRING ME SOME ..., PLEASE?
Apportez-moi ..., s'il vous plaît. pol
a·por·tay·mwa ... seel voo play

I'D LIKE THE BILL, PLEASE.
Je voudrais l'addition, s'il vous plaît. pol
zher voo·dray la·dee·syon seel voo play

LISTEN FOR

Nous sommes complets.	noo som kom·play We're fully booked.
Nous n'avons plus de tables.	noo na·von plew der ta·bler We have no tables.
Où voulez-vous vous asseoir?	oo voo·lay·voo voo zas·war Where would you like to sit?
C'est fermé.	say fair·may We're closed.

I'd like the wine list, please.	Je voudrais la carte des vins, s'il vous plaît. pol zher voo·dray la kart day vun seel voo play
Can I see the menu, please?	Est-ce que je peux voir la carte, s'il vous plaît? pol es ker zher per vwar la kart seel voo play

Menu, please.	La carte, s'il vous plaît. pol	la kart seel voo play

What would you recommend?	Qu'est-ce que vous conseillez? kes ker voo kon·say·yay
Can you tell me which traditional foods I should try?	Pouvez-vous me dire quelle nourriture traditionnelle je dois goûter? poo·vay·voo me deer kel noo·ree·tewr tra·dee·syon·nel zhe dwa goo·tay
I'll have what they're having.	Je prendrai la même chose qu'eux. zher pron·dray la mem shoz ker

What's in that dish?	Quels sont les ingrédients? kel son lay zun·gray·dyon
What's that called?	Ça s'appelle comment? sa sa·pel ko·mon
Do you have children's meals?	Est-ce que vous avez des repas enfants? pol es ker voo za·vay day rer·pa on·fon
Do you have a menu in English?	Est-ce que vous avez une carte en anglais? pol es ker voo za·vay ewn kart on ong·glay
Does it take long to prepare?	Est-ce que la préparation va prendre beaucoup de temps? es ker la pray·pa·ra·syon va pron·drer bo·koo der tom
Is service included in the bill?	Le service est compris? ler sair·vees ay kom·pree
Are these complimentary?	C'est gratuit ça? say gra·twee sa
Is it self-serve?	C'est self-service? say self·sair·vees
We're just having drinks.	C'est juste pour des boissons. say zhewst poor day bwa·son

Just drinks.	Juste des boissons.	zhewst day bwa·son

I'd like a local speciality.	Je voudrais une spécialité locale. zher voo·dray ewn spay·sya·lee·tay lo·kal
I'd like a meal fit for a king.	Je voudrais un repas digne d'un roi. zher voo·dray un rer·pa dee·nyer dun rwa

LISTEN FOR

Vous désirez?	voo day·zee·ray What can I get for you?
Quelle cuisson?	kel kwee·son How would you like it cooked?
Je vous conseille ...	zher voo kon·say ... I suggest ...
Voilà!	vwa·la Here you go!

REQUESTS

I'd like it ...	J'aime ça ... zhem sa ...
I don't want it ...	Je ne veux pas ça ... zher ner ver pa sa ...

boiled	bouilli	boo·yee
fried	frit	free
grilled	grillé	gree·yay
medium	à point	a pwun
rare	saignant	say·nyon
reheated	réchauffé	ray·sho·fay
steamed	à la vapeur	a la va·per
well done	bien cuit	byun kwee
with the dressing on the side	avec la sauce à côté	a·vek la sos a ko·tay
without dressing/sauce	sans sauce	son sos

For phrases to make other specific meal requests, see **vegetarian & special meals** (p174).

I'd like one slice (of pizza), please.	Je voudrais un morceau (de pizza), s'il vous plaît. pol zher voo·dray um mor·so (der peed·za) seel voo play
I'd like a sandwich, please.	Je voudrais un sandwich, s'il vous plaît. pol zher voo·dray un sond·weetsh seel voo play
I'd like that one, please.	Je voudrais ça, s'il vous plaît. pol zher voo·dray sa seel voo play
Please bring a (wine) glass.	Apportez-moi un verre (à vin), s'il vous plaît. pol a·por·tay·mwa un vair (a vun) seel voo play

For typical dishes, see the **menu decoder** (p178). For other food items see the **dictionary** (p196).

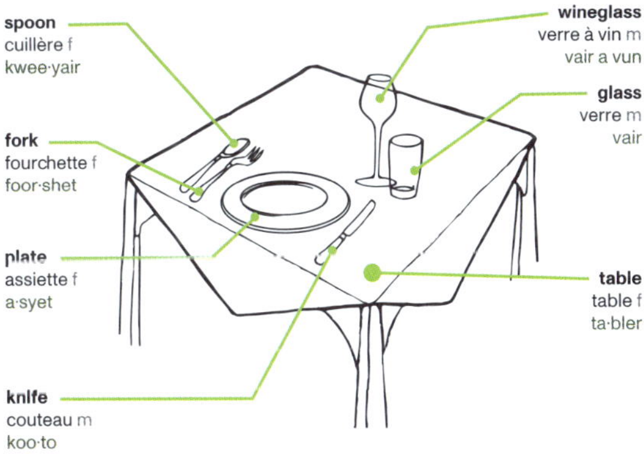

LOOK FOR

Amuse-Gueule	a·mewz·gerl	Appetizers
Soupes	soop	Soups
Entrées	on·tray	Starters
Salades	sa·lad	Salads
Plat Principal	pla prun·see·pal	Main Course
Desserts	day·sair	Desserts
Apéritifs	a·pay·ree·teef	Aperitifs
Spiritueux	spee·ree·twer	Spirits
Bières	byair	Beers
Vins Mousseux	vum moo·ser	Sparkling Wines
Vins Blancs	vum blong	White Wines
Vins Rouges	vun roozh	Red Wines
Vins de Dessert	vun der day·sair	Dessert Wines

COMPLIMENTS & COMPLAINTS

I didn't order this.	Ce n'est pas ce que j'ai commandé. ser nay pa ser ker zhay ko·mon·day
We love the local cuisine.	Nous adorons la cuisine locale. noo za·do·ron la kwee·zeen lo·kal
That was delicious!	C'était délicieux! say·tay day·lee·syer
My compliments to the chef.	Mes compliments au chef. may kom·plee·mon o shef
I'm full.	Je n'ai plus faim. zher nay plew fum
This is burnt.	C'est brûlé. say brew·lay

This is (too) cold.	C'est (trop) froid. say (tro) frwa
This is superb.	C'est superbe. say sew·pairb

PAYING THE BILL

Please bring the bill.	Apportez-moi l'addition, s'il vous plaît. pol a·por·tay·mwa la·dee·syon seel voo play

Bill, please.	L'addition, s'il vous plaît. pol	la·dee·syon seel voo play

There's a mistake in the bill.	Il y a une erreur dans la note. eel ya ewn ay·rer don la not

NONALCOHOLIC DRINKS

sparkling/still mineral water	eau minérale gazeuse/ non-gazeuse o mee·nay·ral ga·zerz/ nong·ga·zerz
orange juice	jus d'orange m zhew do·ronzh
soft drink	boisson non-alcoolisée f bwa·son non·al·ko·lee·zay
(hot) water	eau (chaude) f o (shod)
tea with milk	(un) thé au lait (un) tay o lay
coffee without/with sugar	(un) café sans/avec sucre (ung) ka·fay son/a·vek sew·krer

ALCOHOLIC DRINKS

beer	bière f byair
brandy	cognac m ko·nyak
Champagne	champagne m shom·pan·yer
cocktail	cocktail m kok·tel
a shot of (gin)	un petit verre de (gin) um per·tee vair der (zheen)
a bottle of ... wine	une bouteille de vin ... ewn boo·tay der vun ...
a glass of ... wine	un verre de vin ... un vair der vun ...

dessert	de dessert	der day·sair
red	rouge	roozh
rose	rosé	ro·zay
sparkling	mousseux	moo·ser
table	de table	der ta·bler
white	blanc	blong

a glass of beer	un verre de bière un vair der byair
a pint of beer	un demi de bière un der·mee der byair
a bottle of beer	une bouteille de bière ewn boo·tay der byair

IN THE BAR

Excuse me.	Excusez-moi. pol ek·skew·zay·mwa
I'm next.	C'est mon tour. say mon toor
Q **What would you like?**	Qu'est-ce que vous voulez? kes ker voo voo·lay
A **I'll have (a gin).**	Je prends (un gin). zher pron (un zheen)
Same again, please.	La même chose, s'il vous plaît. pol la mem shoz seel voo play
No ice, thanks.	Pas de glaçons, merci. pa der gla·son mair·see
I'll buy you a drink.	Je vous offre un verre. pol zher voo zo·frer un vair
It's my round.	C'est ma tournée. say ma toor·nay
Do you serve meals here?	Faites-vous les repas ici? pol fet·voo lay rer·pa ee·see

DRINKING UP

Thanks, but I don't feel like it.	Je n'en ai pas envie, merci. zher non ay pa on·vee mair·see

LISTEN FOR

Qu'est-ce que vous desirez prendre?	kes ker voo der·zee·ray pron·drer	What'll it be?
Je pense que ça suffit.	zher pons ker sa sew·fee	I think you've had enough.

LISTEN FOR

Santé!	son·tay	Cheers!
Au chef!	o shef	To the chef!
À tout le monde!	a too ler mond	Here's to everyone!
À la France!	a la frons	Here's to France!
Encore un coup!	ong·kor ung koo	Have another!

No thanks, I'm driving.	Non merci, je conduis. non mair·see zher kon·dwee
This is hitting the spot.	C'est justement ce qu'il me faut. say zhewst·mon ser keel mer fo
I'm tired, I'd better go home.	Je suis fatigué, je dois rentrer. zher swee fa·tee·gay zher dwa ron·tray
I'm feeling drunk.	Je suis ivre. zher swee zee·vrer
I feel fantastic!	Je me sens vachement bien! zher mer son vash·mon byun
I really, really love you.	Je t'aime vraiment beaucoup. zher tem vray·mon bo·koo
Can you call a taxi for me?	Pouvez-vous appeler un taxi pour moi? pol poo·vay·voo a·play un tak·see poor mwa
I don't think you should drive.	Je ne pense pas que vous êtes en état de conduire. pol zher ner pons pa ker voo zet on ay·ta der kon·dweer
I feel ill.	Je me sens malade. zher mer son ma·lad

Self-Catering

KEY PHRASES

What's the local speciality?	Quelle est la spécialité locale?	kel ay la spay·sya·lee·tay lo·kal
Where can I find the ... section?	Où est-ce qu'on trouve le rayon ...?	oo es kon troov ler ray·yon ...
I'd like some ...	Je voudrais quelques ...	zher voo·dray kel·ker ...

BUYING FOOD

How much is ...?	C'est combien ...? say kom·byun ...
What's the local speciality?	Quelle est la spécialité locale? kel ay la spay·sya·lee·tay lo·kal
Do you sell locally produced food?	Est-ce que vous vendez de la nourriture produite localement? pol es ke voo von·day de la noo·ree·tewr pro·dweet lo·kal·mon
What's that?	Qu'est-ce que c'est, ça? kes ker say sa
Can I taste it?	Je peux goûter? zher per goo·tay
Do you have other kinds?	Est-ce que vous avez autre chose? pol es ker voo za·vay o·trer shoz

☑ CULTURE TIP: CHEESE

There are around 400 kinds of cheese in France, from subtle cream cheeses to pungent, whiplash-inducing mould cheeses. Like wines, some cheeses are particular to certain regions and have been awarded an *appellation d'origine* a·pe·la·syon do·ree·zheen, which guarantees the cheese's origin. Cheeses can be broadly grouped into the following styles:

goat's milk cheese	fromage de chèvre fro·mazh der she·vrer
hard cheese	fromage à pâte dure fro·mazh a pat dewr
sheep's milk cheese	fromage de brebis fro·mazh der brer·bee
soft cheese	fromage à pâte molle fro·mazh a pat mol

Can I have a bag, please?	Puis-je avoir un sac, s'il vous plaît? pol pweezh a·vwar un sak seel voo play
I'd like ...	Je voudrais ... zher voo·dray ...

(200) grams	(deux cents) grammes	(der son) gram
(two) kilos	(deux) kilos	(der) kee·lo
(three) pieces	(trois) morceaux	(trwa) mor·so
(six) slices	(six) tranches	(see) tronsh
some of that/ those	de ça	der sa

Do you have anything cheaper?	Est-ce que vous avez quelque chose de moins cher? pol es ker voo za·vay kel·ker shoz der mwun shair
Where can I find the frozen goods section?	Où est-ce qu'on trouve le rayon des surgelés? oo es kon troov ler ray·yon day sewr·zher·lay
Where can I find the fruit and vegetable section?	Où est-ce qu'on trouve le rayon des fruits et legumes? oo es kon troov ler ray·yon day frwee ay lay·gewm
Where can I find the meat section?	Où est-ce qu'on trouve le rayon viande? oo es kon troov ler ray·yon vyond

Je peux goûter?
zher per goo·tay
Can I taste it?

LISTEN FOR

Que puis-je faire pour vous?	ker pwee·zher fair poor voo	Can I help you?
Vous désirez?	voo day·zee·ray	What would you like?
Je n'en ai plus.	zher non ay plew	I don't have any.
Il n'en reste plus.	eel non rest plew	There's none left.
Encore quelque chose?	ong·kor kel·ker shoz	Would you like anything else?
Ça, c'est (un camembert).	sa say (tung ka·mom·bair)	That's (a Camembert).
Ça fait (cinq euros).	sa fay (sungk er·ro)	That's (five euros).

Where is the health-food store?	Où se trouve la boutique bio? oo ser troov la boo·teek bee·yo
Do you sell organic produce?	Est-ce que vous vendez des produits biologiques? pol es ke voo von·day day pro·dwee byo·lo·zheek

For food items, see the **menu decoder** (p178) and the **dictionary** (p196).

COOKING

cooked	cuit(e) m/f kwee(t)
dried	sec/sèche m/f sek/sesh
fresh	frais/fraîche m/f fray/fresh

frozen	surgelé(e) m/f sewr·zher·lay
raw	cru(e) m/f krew
smoked	fumé(e) m/f few·may
stale	rassis(e) m/f ra·see(z)
bottle opener	ouvre-bouteilles m oo·vrer·boo·tay
can opener	ouvre-boîtes m oo·vrer·bwat
chopping board	planche à découper f plonsh a day·koo·pay
corkscrew	tire-bouchon m teer·boo·shon
frying pan	poêle à frire f pwal a freer
saucepan	casserole f kas·rol
toaster	grille-pain m gree·pun

For more cooking implements, see the **dictionary** (p196).

Vegetarian & Special Meals

KEY PHRASES

Do you have vegetarian food?	Vous faites les repas végétariens? pol	voo fet lay rer·pa vay·zhay·ta·ryen
Could you prepare a meal without ...?	Pouvez-vous pré-parer un repas sans ...? pol	poo·vay·voo pray·pa·ray un rer·pa son ...
I'm allergic to ...	Je suis allergique à ...	zher swee za·lair·zheek a ...

SPECIAL DIETS & ALLERGIES

Is there a vegetarian restaurant near here?	Y a-t-il un restaurant végétarien par ici? ya·teel un res·to·ron vay·zhay·ta·ryen par ee·see
Do you have halal food?	Vous faites les repas halal? pol voo fet lay rer·pa a·lal
Do you have kosher food?	Vous faites les repas casher? pol voo fet lay rer·pa ka·shair
I'm a vegan.	Je suis végétalien(ne). m/f zher swee vay·zhay·ta·lyun/ vay·zhay·ta·lyen
I'm a vegetarian.	Je suis végétarien(ne). m/f zher swee vay·zhay·ta·ryun/ vay·zhay·ta·ryen

I'm on a special diet.	Je suis au régime. zher swee zo ray·zheem
I don't eat/drink ...	Je ne mange/bois pas ... zher ner monzh/bwa pa ...
I can't eat it for health reasons.	Je ne mange pas ça pour des raisons de santé. zher ner monzh pa sa poor day ray·zon der son·tay
I can't eat it for religious reasons.	Je ne mange pas ça à cause de ma religion. zher ner monzh pa sa a koz der ma rer·lee·zhyon
I can't eat it for philosophical reasons.	Je ne mange pas ça pour des raisons philosophiques. zher ner monzh pa sa poor day ray·zon fee·lo·zo·feek
I'm allergic to ...	Je suis allergique ... zher swee za·lair·zheek ...

caffeine	à la caféine	a la ka·fay·een
dairy produce	aux produits laitiers	o pro·dwee lay·tyay
eggs	aux œufs	o zer
fish	au poisson	o pwa·son
gelatine/gelatin	à la gélatine	a la zhay·la·teen
honey	au miel	o myel
MSG	au glutamate de sodium	o glew·ta·mat der so·dyom
pork	au porc	o por
poultry	à la volaille	a la vo·lai
red meat	à la viande rouge	a la vyond roozh
seafood	aux fruits de mer	o frwee der mair
shellfish	aux crustacés	o krew·sta·say
wheat flour	à la farine de blé	a la fa·reen der blay

LISTEN FOR

Vous pouvez manger ...?	voo poo·vay mon·zhay ...	Can you eat ...?
C'est cuisiné avec de la viande.	say kee·zee·nay avek der la vyond	It has meat in it.
Je vais demander au cuisinier/chef.	zher vay der·mon·day o kwee·zee·nyay/shef	I'll check with the cook/chef.

ORDERING FOOD

Is this ...?

C'est un produit ...?
say tun pro·dwee ...

free of animal produce	qui n'est pas d'origine animale	kee nay pa do·ree·zheen a·nee·mal
free-range	de ferme	der fairm
genetically modified	qui contient des organismes génétiquement modifiés	kee kon·tyun day zor·ga·nees·mer zhay·nay·teek·mom mo·dee·fyay
gluten-free	sans gluten	son glew·ten
low in sugar	à faible teneur en sucre	a fe·bler ter·ner on sew·krer
low-fat	allégé	a·lay·zhay
organic	biologique	byo·lo·zheek
salt-free	sans sel	son sel

Can I order this without ... in it?

Je peux commander ça sans ...?
zher per ko·mon·day sa son ...

LANGUAGE TIP: TRANSLATING 'NUTS'

There is no single word to translate 'nuts'. You have to say which kind of nut you mean, for example *noix* nwa, 'walnut'; *cacahuète* ka·ka·wet, 'peanut'; or *noisette* nwa·zet, 'hazelnut'.

Could you prepare a meal without butter?	Pouvez-vous préparer un repas sans beurre? poo·vay·voo pray·pa·ray un rer·pa son ber
Could you prepare a meal without eggs?	Pouvez-vous préparer un repas sans œufs? poo·vay·voo pray·pa·ray un rer·pa son zer
Could you prepare a meal without meat stock?	Pouvez-vous préparer un repas sans bouillon de viande? poo·vay·voo pray·pa·ray un rer·pa son boo·yon der vyond

MENU Decoder

LE GLOSSAIRE GASTRONOMIQUE

This miniguide to French cuisine is designed to help you navigate menus. French nouns and adjectives affected by gender have their gender indicated by ⓜ or ⓕ. If it's a plural noun, you'll also see pl. For some dishes, we've added the region thay're from.

A

à la a la served with • in the style of
abats ⓜ a·ba giblets
— de boucherie der boo·shree offal
abricot ⓜ ab·ree·ko apricot
addition ⓕ a·dee·syon bill • check
agneau ⓜ a·nyo lamb
— de lait ⓜ der lay baby lamb • spring lamb
aiguillette ⓕ ay·gwee·yet long & thin slice of meat, usually poultry breast, especially duck
ail ⓜ ai garlic
aile ⓕ el wing (bird or poultry)
aïoli ⓜ ay·o·lee garlic-flavoured mayonnaise sauce, served cold
alcool ⓜ al·kol alcohol
aligot ⓜ a·lee·go mashed potatoes, garlic & melted cheese (Auvergne)
alouette ⓕ al·wet lark
alsacienne (à la —) al·zas·yen (a la —) 'Alsatian style' – dish usually garnished with sauerkraut, pork, sausages or simmered with wine & mushrooms
amande ⓕ a·mond almond
— de mer der mair queen or bay scallop
américaine (à la —) a·may·ree·ken (a la —) 'American style' – generally a dish of fish or shellfish, particularly lobster, flamed in brandy & simmered in white wine & tomatoes
amuse-gueule ⓜ a·mewz·gerl cocktail snack or appetiser
ananas ⓜ a·na·nas pineapple
anchoïade ⓕ on·sho·yad dip of puréed anchovies mixed with garlic & olive oil (Provence)
anchois ⓜ on·shwa anchovy
àncienne ⓕ on·syen 'old style' – depending on the meat used, can be served in a cream sauce with mushrooms, vegetables, onions or shallots, and/or with wine & herbs
andouille ⓕ on·doo·yer smoked sausage made of pork tripe usually eaten cold
andouillette ⓕ on·doo·yet smaller version of *andouille*
aneth ⓜ a·net dill
anglaise (à la —) ong·glayz (a la —) 'English style' – usually boiled meat or vegetables • breaded & fried vegetables, meat, fish or poultry
anguille ⓕ ong·gee·yer eel
anis ⓜ a·nees anis • aniseed

appellation d'origine contrôlée (AOC) ⓕ a·pe·la·syon do·ree·zheen kon·tro·lay (a o say) refers to officially recognised produce with a guarantee of origin
artichaut ⓜ ar·tee·sho artichoke
asperge ⓕ a·spairzh asparagus
assiette ⓕ a·syet plate
— anglaise ong·glayz assorted cold meats & gherkins
— de charcuterie der shar·kew·tree assorted pork & other meat products, including sausages, hams, pates & *rillettes*
— variée va·ree·ay assorted vegetables and/or meat or fish products
assorti(e) ⓜ/ⓕ a·sor·tee assorted
au o served as in • in the style of
aubergine ⓕ o·bair·zheen aubergine/eggplant
avocat ⓜ a·vo·ka avocado

B

baba au rhum ⓜ ba·ba o rom small sponge cake, often with raisins, soaked in a rum-flavoured syrup after baking
bacon ⓜ bay·kon bacon
— fumé few·may smoked bacon
— maigre may·grer lean bacon
baguette ⓕ ba·get long & crispy loaf of bread • chopstick
ballottine ⓕ ba·lo·teen boned meat, stuffed & poached
— de volaille der vo·lai poultry *ballottine* stuffed with forcemeat
banane ⓕ ba·nan banana
barbue ⓕ bar·bew brill or barbel, a carp-like fish
barquette ⓕ bar·ket small boat-shaped shell made of shortcrust pastry (sometimes puff pastry) with sweet or savoury fillings
basilic ⓜ ba·zee·leek basil
basquaise (à la —) bas·kayz (a la —) 'Basque style' – usually prepared with tomatoes & sweet or red peppers
bavarois ⓜ ba·va·rwa Bavarian – a cold mousse-like dessert of cream and/or fruit purée
bavaroise ⓕ ba·va·rwaz syrupy tea that can be set into ice cream
bavette ⓕ ba·vet 'bib apron' – flank steak
béarnaise ⓕ bay·ar·nayz white sauce made of wine or vinegar beaten with egg yolks & flavoured with herbs
bécasse ⓕ bay·kas woodcock, a game bird
Béchamel ⓕ bay·sha·mel milk-based sauce
belon ⓜ ber·lon round pinkish oyster
Bercy bair·see 'Bercy style' – butter, white wine & shallot sauce
betterave ⓕ be·trav beetroot/beet
beurre ⓜ bur butter
— blanc blong white sauce made of a vinegar & white wine reduction blended with softened butter & shallots
— noir nwar 'black butter' – butter browned until nearly burned, sometimes flavoured with capers & parsley
— ravigote ra·vee·got butter with herbs
bien cuit(e) ⓜ/ⓕ byun kwee(t) well-done
bière ⓕ bee·yair beer
— blonde blond light-coloured or pale beer • lager
— en bouteille on boo·tay bottled beer
— brune brewn dark beer or stout
— lager la·ger lager
— pression pre·syon draught • draft beer • beer on tap
bifteck ⓜ beef·tek steak
bio(logique) byo(·lo·zheek) organic
biscuit ⓜ bees·kwee biscuit • cookie
bisque ⓕ beesk spicy shellfish soup or chowder, with cream & Cognac

blanc de blanc blong der blong white wine made of white grapes with white juice
blanc de volaille ⓜ blong der vo·lai boned breast of fowl, cooked without browning
blanquette de veau ⓕ blong·ket der vo veal stew in white sauce enriched with cream
blé ⓜ blay wheat
bleu ⓜ bler blue-veined cheese, often used to flavour dishes or sauces • nearly raw beef • fish boiled in vinegar bouillon
bœuf ⓜ berf beef
— à la mode a la mod larded chunks of beef, braised in wine, either served hot with carrots & onions, or cold in aspic
— bourguignon boor·geen·yon chunks of beef marinated in red wine, spices & herbs, stewed with mushrooms, onions & bacon
— en daube on dob chunks of beef & chopped ham flamed in Armagnac brandy & stewed with red wine, onions, garlic, vegetables & herbs
— miroton mee·ro·ton pre-cooked boiled beef slices, usually left over from *pot-au-feu*, gently stewed with onions
boisson ⓕ bwa·son drink • beverage
— non alcoolisée non al·ko·lee·zay soft drink
bombe glacée ⓕ bom·ber gla·say ice cream dessert – two different ice creams moulded together in a cone shape, decorated with candied (glazed) fruits, candied chestnuts & *Chantilly* cream
bonbon ⓜ bom·bon sweet • candy
bordelaise bor·der·layz red wine sauce with shallots, beef juices, thyme & sometimes boletus mushrooms
bouchée ⓕ boo·shay various types of cocktail snacks or small puffs with a variety of fillings, served hot or cold
boucherie ⓕ boo·shree butcher's shop
boudin ⓜ boo·dun smooth sausage, may be grilled or pan-fried
— blanc blong white veal, pork or chicken sausage
— noir nwar black pork blood sausage (see also *sanguette*)
bouillabaisse ⓕ bwee·ya·bes soup traditionally made of assorted fish stewed in a broth with garlic, orange peel, fennel, tomatoes & saffron. Modern versions include lobster & prawns/shrimps. The broth & the fish may be served separately, with croutons & *rouille*. (Marseilles)
bouillon ⓜ boo·yon broth • stock
boulangerie ⓕ boo·lon·zhree bakery
boulette ⓕ boo·let small meatball or croquette (often leftovers) sautéed, browned or poached in a broth
boulghour ⓜ bool·goor bulgur wheat
bouquet garni ⓜ boo·kay gar·nee mix of herbs tied together – usually parsley, bay leaf & thyme
bourguignonne (à la —) boor·gee·nyon (a la —) 'Burgundy style' – dishes may include button mushrooms, bacon & pearl onions or shallots, braised in red wine
bourride ⓕ boo·reed fish soup or stew using firm whitefish like monkfish
bouteille ⓕ boo·tay bottle
brandade de morue ⓕ bron·dad der mo·rew salt cod puréed with milk, olive oil, garlic & sometimes mashed potatoes
brebis ⓕ brer·bee ewe (female sheep)
brème ⓕ brem bream
brioche ⓕ bree·yosh small roll or cake made of yeast, flour, eggs & butter, sometimes flavoured with nuts, currants or candied fruits

broche ⓕ brosh spit roast
brochet ⓜ bro·shay pike
brochette ⓕ bro·shet grilled skewer of meat, fish or vegetables
brocoli ⓜ bro·ko·lee broccoli
brouillé(e) ⓜ/ⓕ broo·yay scrambled
brûlot ⓜ brew·lo sugar flamed in brandy & added to coffee
brut ⓜ brewt extra dry (Champagne)
bûche de Noël ⓕ bewsh der no·el traditionally served for Christmas – a rolled sponge cake filled & covered with butter-cream (usually chocolate, vanilla or coffee flavoured) or ice cream

C

cabillaud ⓜ ka·bee·yo cod
cacahuète ⓜ ka·ka·wet peanut
cacao ⓜ ka·ka·o cocoa
café ⓜ ka·fay cafe • coffee
caille ⓕ kay·yer quail
caillette ⓕ kay·yet rissole • meatball
calmar ⓜ kal·mar squid
canard ⓜ ka·nar duck
— à la rouennaise a la roo·en·nayz stuffed duck in a red-wine sauce
— à l'orange a lo·ronzh duck braised with Cognac & Cointreau, served with oranges & an orange-based sauce
cannelé ⓜ ka·ner·lay brioche-like pastry made with cornflour, often spelled *canallé* (Bordeaux)
cannelle ⓕ ka·nel cinnamon
câpre ⓕ kap·rer caper
carbonnade ⓕ kar·bo·nad selection of chargrilled meats (often pork)
— de bœuf der berf stew of beef slices, onions & herbs, simmered in beer (Northern France)
carotte ⓕ ka·rot carrot
carpe ⓕ karp carp
carré ⓜ ka·ray loin • rib
— d'agneau da·nyo rack of lamb
— de porc (au chou) der por (o shoo) loin of pork (with cabbage)
carte ⓕ kart menu
— des vins day vun wine list
cassate ⓕ ka·sat ice cream combining different flavours, often studded with candied fruits
casse-croûte ⓜ kas·kroot snack
cassis ⓜ ka·sees blackcurrant (liqueur)
cassoulet ⓜ ka·soo·lay casserole or stew with beans & meat (Southwest France)
céleri ⓜ sayl·ree celery
cendre son·drer baked in the embers
cépage ⓜ say·pazh grape or vine variety
cèpe ⓕ sep wild mushroom of the boletus family known for its full flavour & meaty texture
céréale ⓕ say·ray·al cereal • grain
cerf ⓜ ser venison • stag deer
cerise ⓕ ser·reez cherry
cervelas ⓜ sair·ver·la fat pork sausage cured with garlic & eaten hot
cervelle ⓕ sair·vel brain
champignon ⓜ shom·pee·nyon mushroom
— de Paris der pa·ree button mushroom
chanterelle ⓕ shon·trel boletus mushroom – same as *girolle*
Chantilly ⓕ shon·tee·yee sweetened whipped cream flavoured with vanilla
chapon ⓜ sha·pon capon • castrated cock
charbonnade ⓕ shar·bo·nad chargrilled meat
charcuterie ⓕ shar·kew·tree variety of pork products that are cured, smoked or processed, including sausages, hams, *pâtés* & *rillettes* • the shop where these products are sold

charlotte ⓕ shar·lot dessert of bread slices or sponge fingers, lining a deep, round mould, filled with fruits, whipped cream or a fruit mousse
chasselas ⓜ sha·sla type of white grape
chasseur sha·ser 'hunter' – sauce of white wine with mushrooms, shallots & bacon cubes
châtaigne ⓕ sha·tayn·yer chestnut
chateaubriand ⓜ sha·to·bree·yon thick fillet or rump steak
chaud(e) ⓜ/ⓕ sho(d) hot • warm
chaud-froid ⓜ sho·frwa 'hot-cold' – a piece of poached or roasted meat, poultry or fish that, while cooling, is coated with a white creamy sauce that solidifies
chaudrée ⓕ sho·dray Atlantic fish stew
chef de cuisine ⓜ shef der kwee·zeen chef
cheval ⓜ sher·val horse • horse meat
chèvre ⓕ she·vrer goat • goat's milk cheese
chevreuil ⓜ sher·vrer·yer venison
chicorée ⓕ shee·ko·ray chicory • endive
chipolata ⓕ shee·po·la·ta chipolata • a small sausage
chocolat ⓜ sho·ko·la chocolate
— chaud sho hot chocolate
chou ⓜ shoo cabbage
— de Bruxelles der brew·sel Brussels sprout
— rouge roozh red cabbage
choucroute ⓕ shoo·kroot sauerkraut
chou-fleur ⓜ shoo·fler cauliflower
ciboule ⓕ see·bool spring onion • shallot
cidre ⓜ see·drer cider
citron ⓜ see·tron lemon
— pressé ⓜ see·tron pray·say freshly squeezed lemon juice
citronnade ⓕ see·tro·nad lemon squash • lemonade
citrouille ⓕ see·troo·yer pumpkin
civelle ⓕ see·vel small eel or alevin, generally served fried
civet ⓜ see·vay stew usually containing game marinated in red wine
clam ⓜ klam clam
cochon ⓜ ko·shon pig
— de lait der lay suckling pig
cocktail ⓜ kok·tel cold starter of shellfish & raw vegetables or fruits
cœur ⓜ ker heart
— de filet der fee·lay tenderloin steak
coing ⓜ kwung quince
commande ⓕ ko·mond order
compote ⓕ kom·pot stewed fruit
compris(e) ⓜ/ⓕ kom·pree(z) included
concombre ⓜ kong·kom·brer cucumber
confiserie ⓕ kon·feez·ree confectionery (sweets in general) • sweet shop or candy store
confit ⓜ kon·fee preserved meat, usually duck, goose or pork. The meat is cooked in fat until it is tender, then potted & covered with the fat to preserve it.
confiture ⓕ kon·fee·tewr jam
congolais ⓜ kong·go·lay small coconut meringue cake
consommation ⓕ kon·so·ma·syon consumption • the general term for food & drink ordered in a cafe
consommé ⓜ kon·so·may clarified meat, poultry or fish-based broth used as a base for sauces & soups
— à la printanière a la prun·tan·yair *consommé* with spring vegetables
contre-filet ⓜ kon·trer·fee·lay beef sirloin roast
coq ⓜ kok cockerel • rooster
— de bruyère der brwew·yair grouse
coque ⓕ kok cockle
coquelet ⓜ ko·klay young cockerel
coquillage ⓜ ko·kee·yazh shellfish

coquille Saint-Jacques ⓕ ko·kee·yer sun·zhak scallop
corbeille de fruits ⓕ kor·bay·yer der frwee basket of assorted fruits
cornichon ⓜ kor·nee·shon gherkin/pickle
côte ⓕ kot chop containing eye fillet
côtelette ⓕ kot·let cutlet • chop
coulis ⓜ koo·lee fruit or vegetable purée, usually used as a sauce
courge ⓕ koorzh gourd • marrow
courgette ⓕ koor·zhet courgette/zucchini • baby marrow
couvert ⓜ koo·vair number of people in a group at a restaurant • cover charge
— gratuit gra·twee no cover charge
— vin et service compris vun ay sair·vees kom·pree price includes wine, service & cover charges
crabe ⓜ krab crab
crème ⓜ krem cream • a dessert with cream • a cream-based soup
— anglaise ong·glayz custard
— crue krew raw or unpasteurised cream
— fouettée fwe·tay whipped cream
— fraîche fresh naturally thickened cream, has a slightly sour tang
— glacée gla·say ice cream
crêpe ⓕ krep large, paper-thin pancake served with various fillings
— flambée flom·bay pancake flamed with brandy or other liqueur
— Suzette sew·zet pancake with tangerine or orange sauce & brandy
cresson ⓜ kray·son watercress
crevette grise/rose ⓕ krer·vet greez/roz small prawn/shrimp
croissant ⓜ krwa·son flaky crescent-shaped roll, usually served for breakfast
croquant ⓜ kro·kon butter cookie or biscuit
croque-madame ⓜ krok·ma·dam grilled or pan-fried ham & cheese sandwich, topped with a fried egg
croquembouche ⓜ kro·kom·boosh grand dessert of cream puffs dipped in caramel & assembled into a large pyramid shape
croque-monsieur ⓜ krok·mers·yer grilled or pan-fried ham & cheese sandwich
croustade ⓕ kroo·stad puff pastry shell filled with stewed fish, seafood, meat, poultry, mushrooms or vegetables
croûte ⓕ kroot crust • a puff pastry case filled with various savoury foods
croûte (en —) kroot (on —) 'in crust' – food cooked enclosed in pastry
croûton ⓜ kroo·ton small piece of bread toasted or fried until crisp, used to garnish salads or soups
cru ⓜ krew growth • referring to a particular vineyard & its wine
cru(e) ⓜ/ⓕ krew raw
crudités ⓕ pl krew·dee·tay selection of raw vegetables served sliced, grated or diced with dressing as a starter
crustacé ⓜ krew·sta·say shellfish
cuire kweer to cook
cuisine ⓕ kwee·zeen cooking • kitchen
— bourgeoise boor·zhwaz French home cooking of the highest quality
— campagnarde kom·pan·yard country or provincial cooking, using the finest ingredients & most refined techniques to prepare traditional rural dishes
cuisse ⓕ kwees thigh • leg
cuisses de grenouille kwees der grer·noo·yer frogs' legs
cuit(e) ⓜ/ⓕ kwee(t) cooked
— au four o foor baked
cul de veau ⓜ kew der vo veal fillet or rump steak
cuvée ⓕ kew·vay blend of wine from various vineyards when making Champagne • vintage

D

darne ⓜ darn slice of a large raw fish, such as hake, salmon or tuna
datte ⓕ dat date
daube ⓕ dob beef, poultry or game stewed in a rich wine-laden broth
déjeuner ⓜ day·zher·nay lunch
demi der·mee half • beer glass size, about a pint
— -glace ⓕ ·glas rich brown stock & gravy
— -sec ⓜ ·sek slightly sweet (of wine)
— -sel ⓜ ·sel slightly salty
dieppoise (à la —) dyep·waz (a la —) 'Dieppe style' – soup generally consisting of fish, shrimp, mussels, mushrooms, vegetables, herbs & cream, cooked in cider
digestif ⓜ dee·zhe·steef digestive • drink served after a meal
dijonnaise (à la —) dee·zho·nez (a la —) 'Dijon style' – dishes containing mustard or served with a mustard-based sauce (Burgundy)
dinde/dindon ⓜ/ⓕ dund/dun·don turkey
diplomate ⓜ dee·plo·mat trifle – sponge fingers steeped in milk or liqueur, put into a mould & filled with custard & candied fruits
dodine de canard ⓕ do·deen der ka·nar boned duck stuffed with forcemeat, rolled, cooked & served with a spicy sauce
domaine ⓜ do·mayn vineyard • used on a wine label, it indicates a wine of exceptional quality
dos ⓜ do back • meatiest portion of fish
doux/douce ⓜ/ⓕ doo(s) mild • sweet • soft • without salt (butter)
duxelles ⓕ dewk·sel finely chopped mushrooms sautéed in butter with shallots or onions, used as a seasoning or a sauce

E

eau ⓕ o water
— de source der soors spring water
— du robinet dew ro·bee·nay tap water
— minérale mee·nay·ral mineral water
eau-de-vie ⓕ o·der·vee 'water of life' – clear fruit or nut brandy
écrevisse ⓕ ay·krer·vees crayfish
— à la nage a la nazh crayfish simmered in white wine, usually served with bread & butter as a starter
émincé ⓜ ay·mun·say thinly sliced meat
endive ⓕ on·deev chicory • endive
— à la bruxelloise a la brew·sel·waz chicory/endive leaves rolled in a slice of ham & covered with cheese sauce
entrecôte ⓕ on·trer·kot rib steak
— chasseur sha·ser pan-broiled steak with a brown sauce made of white wine, mushrooms & tomatoes
— marchand de vin mar·shon der vun steak poached in red wine, shallots & onions
entrée ⓕ on·tray the starter or first course
entremets ⓜ on·trer·may cream-based sweet or dessert
épaule ⓕ ay·pol shoulder
épinard ⓜ ay·pee·nar spinach
escabèche ⓕ es·ka·besh highly seasoned marinade used to flavour & preserve small fish
escalope ⓕ es·ka·lop thin boneless slice of meat, usually from the top round
— viennoise vyen·waz breaded veal *escalope* or cutlet
escargot ⓜ es·kar·go snail
espadon ⓜ es·pa·don swordfish
espagnole (à la —) es·pan·yol (a la —) 'Spanish style' – generally including tomatoes, pimentos, peppers/capsicum, onion, garlic & rice

estomac ⓜ es·to·ma stomach
estouffade ⓕ es·too·fad meat, usually beef or pork, stewed in wine with carrots & herbs (Southern France)
estragon ⓜ es·tra·gon tarragon
étouffé(e) ⓜ/ⓕ ay·too·fay food steamed or braised in a tightly sealed vessel with minimal liquid
extra-sec ⓜ ek·stra·sek very dry (of wine)

F

faisan ⓜ fer·zon pheasant
fait(e) maison ⓜ/ⓕ fe(t) may·zon homemade, of the house
farce ⓕ fars forcemeat • stuffing
farci(e) ⓜ/ⓕ far·see stuffed
faux-filet ⓜ fo·fee·lay beef sirloin
fenouil ⓜ fer·noo·yer fennel
feuilletage ⓜ fer·yer·tazh puff pastry
feuilleté ⓜ fer·yer·tay puff pastry usually filled with fruit, cheese, mushrooms, meat, seafood or poultry
fève ⓕ fev broad or lima bean
ficelle ⓕ fee·sel long thin *baguette* • a tender cut of meat, often beef or duck poached in rich broth
figue ⓕ feeg fig
filet ⓜ fee·lay fillet of meat or fish
financière fee·non·syair food served with a rich dressing of pike dumplings, truffles, mushrooms & Madeira wine
financier ⓜ fee·non·syay mall cake made of almond meal and egg white
fines herbes ⓕ pl feen zairb mixture of chopped fresh herbs consisting of tarragon, parsley, chervil & chives
flageolet ⓜ fla·zho·lay kidney bean
flamande (à la —) fla·mond (a la —) 'Flemish style' – usually food with braised carrots, cabbage, turnips & sometimes bacon, potatoes or sausage, occasionally simmered in beer
flambé(e) ⓜ/ⓕ flom·bay dish with liqueur spooned or poured over it & ignited
flamiche ⓕ fla·meesh tart filled with leeks, eggs & cream, & sometimes pumpkin & Maroilles cheese (Picardy)
flan ⓜ flon open-top tart with various fillings • dessert made of baked custard flavoured with caramel
— parisien pa·ree·zyun tart filled with a vanilla cream
florentine (à la —) flo·ron·teen (a la —) 'Florence style' – commonly dishes containing spinach & sometimes a cream sauce
flûte ⓕ flewt long bread roll, similar to baguette
foie ⓜ fwa liver
— gras gra fatted goose or duck liver. The birds are force-fed to speed the fattening process.
fondue ⓕ fon·dew usually a pot of melted cheeses, or hot oil or broth, that diners dip meat or bread in
— bourguignonne boor·geen·yon bite-size pieces of beef cooked in boiling oil & dipped in a variety of sauces
— chocolat sho·ko·la fruits & pieces of cake dipped in hot melted chocolate
— savoyarde sa·vwa·yard bread dipped in hot melted cheeses flavoured with white wine, garlic & cherry brandy (Savoy)
forestière fo·re·styair generally food sautéed with mushrooms & bacon, or with a Cognac-based sauce
four ⓜ foor oven
fourchette ⓕ foor·shet fork
frais/fraîche ⓜ/ⓕ fray/fresh fresh
fraise ⓕ frez strawberry
framboise ⓕ from·bwaz raspberry • raspberry liqueur
frappé ⓜ fra·pay syrup/liquid poured over crushed ice

frappé(e) ⓜ/ⓕ fra·pay chilled • iced
friand ⓜ free·yon pastry stuffed with minced sausage meat, ham & cheese, or almond cream
friandise ⓕ free·on·deez titbit • delicacy • sweets or candy
fricadelle ⓕ free·ka·del small fried mincemeat patty or meatball
fricandeau ⓜ free·kon·do veal fillet simmered in white wine, vegetables herbs & spices • a pork pate
fricassée ⓕ free·ka·say lamb, veal or poultry served in a thick creamy sauce, often with mushrooms & onions • quickly pan-fried foods, sometimes with wild mushrooms
frit(e) ⓜ/ⓕ free(t) fried
frites ⓕ pl freet chips • French fries
friture ⓕ free·tewr deep-fried food, often fish like whitebait
froid(e) ⓜ/ⓕ frwa(d) cold
fromage ⓜ fro·mazh cheese
— blanc blong cream cheese
— de tête der tet brawn • head cheese (usually pork)
— frais fray fermented dairy product similar to curds or cottage cheese
fromagerie ⓕ fro·ma·zhree cheese shop
fruit ⓜ frwee fruit
— confit kon·fee candied or glazed fruit
— de mer der mair seafood
— glacé gla·say candied or glazed fruit
fumé(e) ⓜ/ⓕ few·may smoked
fumet ⓜ few·may aromatic broth used in soups & sauces

G

galantine ⓕ ga·lon·teen pressed cold meat, usually poultry, stuffed with forcemeat, served cold as a starter
galette ⓕ ga·let crêpe made with buckwheat flour • flat plain cake of *brioche*-type dough or puff pastry, with a variety of fillings • small short butter cookies
— sarrasin sa·ra·zun buckwheat flour *crêpe*
gamba ⓕ gom·ba king prawn
garbure ⓕ gar·bewr thick cabbage soup with salted pork, potatoes, vegetables, spices, herbs & sometimes *confit d'oie*. May be covered with bread slices & cheese, then browned in the oven.
garni(e) ⓜ/ⓕ gar·nee garnished
gâteau ⓜ ga·to cake
gaufre ⓕ go·frer waffle
gelée ⓕ zher·lay aspic or fruit jelly
genièvre ⓕ zher·nye·vrer juniper
génoise ⓕ zhay·nwaz very rich sponge cake, eaten as is or used as the foundation for other cake preparations
gésier ⓜ zhay·zyay poultry entrails
gibelotte de lapin ⓕ zhee·blot der la·pun rabbit stewed in wine sauce with bacon, potatoes, mushrooms, garlic, onion & herbs
gibier ⓜ zheeb·yay game
— en saison on say·zon game in season
gigot ⓜ zhee·go leg, generally of lamb or mutton
gigue ⓕ zheeg haunch
gingembre ⓜ zhun·zhom·brer ginger
girolle ⓕ zhee·rol boletus mushroom – same as chanterelle
glace ⓕ glas ice • ice cream
glacé(e) ⓜ/ⓕ gla·say glazed • iced
glaçon ⓜ gla·son ice cube
graisse ⓕ gres grease • fat • suet
grand cru ⓜ gron krew wine of exceptional quality
grand vin ⓜ gron vun wine of exceptional quality
grand(e) ⓜ/ⓕ gron(d) large • big

granité ⓜ gra·nee·tay granular-textured fruit-flavoured water-ice or sorbet
gras-double ⓜ gra·doo·bler tripe – may be cooked in water, moulded in a rectangular block, or cut in strips & braised with tomatoes or onions
grecque (à la —) grek (a la —) 'Greek style' – foods prepared with olive oil, onions, lemon, & sometimes with tomato, peppers or fennel added
grenadin ⓜ grer·na·dun veal (or sometimes poultry) fillet, wrapped in a thin slice of bacon
grenouille ⓕ grer·noo·yer frog
grillade ⓕ gree·yad mixed grill
grillé(e) ⓜ/ⓕ gree·yay grilled
grillons ⓜ gree·yon chunks of fatty pork or duck cooked until crisp
griotte ⓕ gree·yot morello cherry
grive ⓕ greev thrush
groseille ⓕ gro·zay·yer (red) currant
— à maquereau a ma·kro gooseberry

H

haché(e) ⓜ/ⓕ a·shay minced • chopped
hareng ⓜ a·rung herring
— fumé few·may smoked herring • kipper
haricot ⓜ a·ree·ko bean
— blanc blong white haricot or kidney bean
— rouge roozh red kidney bean
— vert vair green bean • French or string bean
haute cuisine ⓕ ot kwee·zeen 'high cuisine' – classic French style of cooking originating in the spectacular feasts of French kings. It's typified by super-rich, elaborately prepared & beautifully presented multicourse meals.
herbe ⓕ airb herb
hollandaise o·lon·dez emulsified oil & egg-yolk sauce, flavoured with fresh lemon juice
homard ⓜ o·mar Atlantic lobster
— à l'armoricaine/à l'américaine a lar·mo·ree·ken/a la·may·ree·ken lobster simmered in white wine, tomatoes, shallots, garlic, pepper, flamed in Cognac or whisky & served with a lobster coral (roe) sauce
— Newburg nyoo·boorg lobster cut into sections, cooked in Madeira wine & served with creamy sauce
— Thermidor ter·mee·dor sautéed lobster, served in its shell with a white wine & *Béchamel* sauce flavoured with shallots, herbs & mustard, sprinkled with cheese & browned
hors-d'œuvre ⓜ or·der·vrer appetiser
huile ⓕ weel oil
huître ⓕ wee·trer oyster

I

île flottante ⓕ eel flo·tont dessert of egg whites floating on a custard surface, coated with caramel sauce
indienne (à la —) un·dyen (a la —) 'Indian style' – generally a dish flavoured with curry
infusion ⓕ un·few·zyon herbal tea

J

jalousie ⓕ zha·loo·zee latticed flaky pastry filled with almond paste & jam
jambon ⓜ zhom·bon ham
— chaud sho baked ham
— cru krew raw ham
— de Bayonne der bay·yon fine raw, slightly salty ham (Basque)
— de canard der ka·nar cured or smoked duck breast
jardinière (à la —) zhar·dee·nyair (a la —) 'gardener's style' – dish of cooked vegetables

jarret ⓜ zha·ray knuckle or shank
joue ⓕ zhoo cheek
julienne ⓕ zhew·lyen usually vegetables, sometimes ham or chicken breast, cut in long, fine strips, cooked in butter or served raw
jus ⓜ zhew juice • gravy

K

kascher ka·shair kosher
kir ⓜ keer white wine sweetened with *cassis*
— royal rwa·yal Champagne with *cassis*
kirsch ⓜ keersh cherry *eau-de-vie* or brandy
kriek ⓕ kreek Belgian beer flavoured with cherries
kugelhopf ⓜ kew·gerl·hopf chocolate, almond & sultana cake (Alsace)

L

lait ⓜ lay milk
— cru krew raw or unpasteurised milk used to make certain cheeses
— écrémé ay·kray·may skimmed milk
laitance ⓕ lay·tons soft roe
laitue ⓕ lay·tew lettuce
langouste ⓕ long·goost spiny lobster • rock lobster (Mediterranean)
langoustine ⓕ long·goo·steen scampi • Dublin Bay prawn • langoustine
langue ⓕ long tongue
lapin ⓜ la·pun rabbit
— de garenne der ga·ren wild rabbit
lard ⓜ lar bacon
— fumé few·may smoked bacon
— maigre may·grer lean bacon
lardon ⓜ lar·don bacon cube
légume ⓜ lay·gewm vegetable
légumes jardinière ⓜ pl lay·gewm zhar·dee·nyair diced fresh vegetables (usually carrots, turnips, beans & cauliflower) with butter, chervil & cream
lentille ⓕ lon·tee·yer lentil
lièvre ⓜ lye·vrer hare
— en civet on see·vay jugged hare (hare stew)
limande ⓕ lee·mond lemon sole • dab
limonade ⓕ lee·mo·nad lemonade
longe ⓕ lonzh loin
— de veau farcie der vo far·see stuffed loin of veal
lorraine (à la —) lo·ren (a la —) 'Lorraine style' – generally a dish garnished with red cabbage & potato croquettes, or bacon slices & Gruyère cheese
lyonnaise (à la —) lee·o·nez (a la —) 'Lyon style' – dish generally including onions cooked golden brown, seasoned with wine, garlic & parsley

M

madeleine ⓕ mad·len small shell-shaped cake, generally flavoured with lemon but also almonds or cinnamon.
madère (à la —) ma·dair (a la —) 'Madeira style' – dishes served with a sauce flavoured with sweet Madeira (Portuguese fortified wine)
magret ⓜ ma·gray breast meat from a fattened mallard or Barbary duck specially raised for *foie gras* (see *jambon de canard*)
maigre may·grer lean, or without meat
maïs ⓜ ma·ees corn/maize
maison (de la —) may·zon (der la —) speciality of the restaurant
mange-tout ⓜ monzh·too snow pea
maquereau ⓜ ma·kro mackerel
marc ⓜ mar drink made from distilled grape skins & pulp left over after being pressed for wine

marcassin ⓜ mar·ka·sun young boar
marchand de vin mar·shon der vun wine merchant • 'wine merchant style' – dish cooked with (red) wine
marengo ⓜ ma·rung·go stewed chicken or veal that is served over toast & garnished with crayfish or prawns/shrimps
marinade ⓕ ma·ree·nad marinade – a highly flavoured liquid; may include wine or vinegar, oil, aromatic vegetables & herbs, that meat, fish or vegetables are steeped in to be flavoured & tenderised
mariné(e) ⓜ/ⓕ ma·ree·nay marinated
marinière (à la —) ma·ree·nyair (a la —) 'mariner's style' – usually mussels or other seafood, simmered in white wine with onions, parsley, thyme & bay leaves
marmelade ⓕ mar·mer·lad thick purée of fresh fruits stewed in sugar or *compote*
marron ⓜ ma·ron chestnut (see also *châtaigne*)
massepain ⓜ mas·pun marzipan – almond paste
matelote ⓕ mat·lot fish stew (often eel) with wine, onions, shallots, garlic & sometimes mushrooms
mayonnaise ⓕ ma·yo·nez mayonnaise
melon ⓜ mer·lon melon
menthe ⓕ mont mint
menu ⓜ mer·new generally means a set meal at a fixed price (*menu à prix fixe*)
— de dégustation der day·gew·sta·syon tasting menu – special menu giving a small sample of several dishes
merguez ⓕ mair·gez spicy red sausage made from beef or mutton, originally from North Africa
merveille ⓕ mair·vay·yer fried pastry shapes, sprinkled with sugar
meunière mer·nyair lightly sautéed in butter, usually with lemon juice & chopped parsley
meurette ⓕ mer·ret red wine sauce
michette ⓕ mee·shet savoury bread stuffed with cheese, olives, onions & anchovies (Nice)
miel ⓜ myel honey
mignon ⓜ meen·yon small piece of tenderloin of beef, pork or veal
mijoté(e) ⓜ/ⓕ mee·zho·tay simmered
millas ⓜ mee·las cornflour & goose fat cake eaten with a meat course
— de Bordeaux der bor·do custard & cherry tart
mille-feuille ⓜ meel·fer·yer '1000 leaves' – flaky pastry layered with custard or thick cream filling
mirabelle ⓕ mee·ra·bel small yellow plum, used in tarts as well as liqueurs & plum brandy (Alsace, Lorraine)
miroton ⓜ mee·ro·ton slices of pre-cooked beef, usually leftovers, simmered with onions, often served as stew
mode (à la —) mod (a la —) 'of the fashion' – often means made according to a local recipe (see also *bœuf à la mode*)
moelle ⓕ mwal bone marrow
mont-blanc ⓜ mon blong canned chestnut purée with or without a meringue base, topped with *crème Chantilly*
morceau ⓜ mor·so morsel or piece
morille ⓕ mo·ree·yer morel mushroom, a wild mushroom, with a honeycomb cap & hollow stem
Mornay (sauce —) ⓕ mor·nay (sos –) Béchamel sauce with Gruyère cheese, sometimes enriched with egg yolks
morue ⓕ mo·rew cod
moule ⓕ mool mussel

mousseline ⓕ moos·leen fine purée or forcemeat lightened with whipped cream • a variation of hollandaise sauce made with whipped cream
mousseron ⓜ moos·ron blewit – fleshy wild mushroom
mousseux ⓜ moo·ser sparkling • sparkling wine
moutarde ⓕ moo·tard mustard
mouton ⓜ moo·ton mutton
mulet ⓜ mu·lay mullet
mûre ⓕ mewr blackberry
muscat ⓜ mew·ska type of grape • a sweet dessert wine
museau ⓜ mew·zo muzzle or snout • pork brawn or head cheese
myrtille ⓕ meer·tee·yer bilberry or European blueberry

N

nature na·tewr plain
navarin ⓜ na·va·run mutton or lamb stew with vegetables & herbs
navet ⓜ na·vay turnip
neige ⓕ nezh 'snow' – stiff beaten egg white
noir(e) ⓜ/ⓕ nwar black
noisette ⓕ nwa·zet hazelnut • a round, boneless cut of lamb or venison
noix ⓕ nwa nut • walnut
— de coco der ko·ko coconut
— du Brésil bray·zeel brazil nut
normande (à la —) nor·mond (a la —) 'Norman style' – usually a dish of meat, shellfish or vegetables, served with cream
note ⓕ not bill or check (restaurant)
nouilles ⓕ noo·yer noodles
nouvelle cuisine ⓕ noo·vel kwee·zeen food prepared & presented to emphasise the inherent textures & colours of the ingredients – features rather small portions served with light sauces

O

œuf ⓜ erf egg
— à la coque a la kok soft-boiled egg
— brouillé broo·yay scrambled egg
— dur dewr hard-boiled egg
— frit free fried egg
oie ⓕ wa goose
oignon ⓜ on·yon onion
olive ⓕ o·leev olive
omelette ⓕ om·let omelette
onglet ⓜ ong·glay prime cut of beef
orange ⓕ o·ronzh orange
— pressée ⓕ pray·say freshly squeezed orange juice
oreille ⓕ o·ray·yer ear
orge ⓕ orzh barley
os ⓜ os bone
— à moelle a mwal marrow-bone

P

pain ⓜ pun bread
palmier ⓜ pal·myay sweet pastry shaped like a heart or a palm leaf
palourde ⓕ pa·loord medium-sized clam
pamplemousse ⓜ pom·pler·moos grapefruit
panaché ⓜ pa·na·shay shandy (beer & lemonade)
panais ⓜ pa·nay parsnip
pan-bagnat ⓜ pun ban·ya small round bread loaves, split or hollowed out, soaked with olive oil & filled with onions, vegetables, anchovies & black olives (Nice)
pané(e) ⓜ/ⓕ pa·nay coated in breadcrumbs • breaded
panisse ⓜ pa·nees pancake or patty of chickpea flour, fried & served with certain meat dishes (Provence)
papillote ⓕ pa·pee·yot dish cooked encased in greaseproof paper or foil
parfait ⓜ par·fay ice cream dessert, often served in a tall glass, sometimes with custard, fruit, nuts & liqueur

Paris-Brest ⓜ pa·ree·brest ring-shaped cake of choux pastry, filled with butter-cream, decorated with flaked almonds & icing sugar
Parmentier ⓜ par·mon·tyay any dish containing potatoes
pastèque ⓕ pas·tek watermelon
pastis ⓜ pa·stees an aniseed-flavoured drink, drunk as an aperitif & always mixed with water
patate douce ⓕ pa·tat doos sweet potato
pâté ⓜ pa·tay pate – thick paste, often pork. Sometimes called terrine.
— de foie gras der fwa gra goose or duck liver paste
— maison may·zon pate made with the restaurant's own recipe
pâtes ⓕ pl pat pasta • noodles
pâtisserie ⓕ pa·tees·ree pastries, cakes & other sweetmeats • the place where they are sold
pavé ⓜ pa·vay thickly-cut steak
paysanne (à la —) pay·zan (a la —) 'peasant style' – dish containing various vegetables & wine, or assorted chopped vegetables, usually used to garnish a soup or an omelette
pêche ⓕ pesh peach
perche ⓕ persh perch
perdrix ⓕ per·dree partridge
périgourdine (à la —) pay·ree·goor·deen (a la —) 'Périgourd style' – dish containing truffles & sometimes *foie gras*
persil ⓜ pair·seel parsley
persillade ⓕ pair·see·yad mixture of chopped parsley & garlic, added to recipes at the end of cooking
pet-de-nonne ⓜ pay·der·non 'nun's fart' – small deep-fried fritter or choux pastry, served hot with sugar or with fruit coulis
pied ⓜ pyay foot • trotter
pigeon ⓜ pee·zhon pigeon
pignon ⓜ pee·nyon pine nut/kernel
piment ⓜ pee·mon pimento, small red pepper • allspice
pintade ⓕ pun·tad guinea fowl
pistache ⓕ pees·tash pistachio nut
pistache (en —) pee·stash (on —) dish prepared with garlic
pistou ⓜ pee·stoo pesto – basil & garlic paste
plat ⓜ pla plate • dish
— du jour dew zhoor speciality of the day
— principal prun·see·pal main course or dish
plateau de fromage ⓜ pla·to der fro·mazh cheese board or platter
pleurote ⓜ pler·rot pleurotus – mild white mushroom with tender flesh
pluvier ⓜ plew·vyay plover (small game bird)
poché(e) ⓜ/ⓕ po·shay poached
poêlé(e) ⓜ/ⓕ pwa·lay pan-fried
point (à —) pwun (a —) medium meat, usually still pink
poire ⓕ pwar pear
poiré ⓜ pwa·ray perry (pear cider)
poireau ⓜ pwa·ro leek
pois ⓜ pwa pea
— cassé ka·say split pea
— chiche sheesh chickpea
poisson ⓜ pwa·son fish
— de mer der mair saltwater fish
— d'eau douce do doos freshwater fish
poissonnerie ⓕ pwa·son·ree fish shop
poitrine ⓕ pwa·treen chest (meat from the chest area)
poivre ⓜ pwa·vrer pepper
poivron ⓜ pwa·vron pepper (bell)/capsicum
pomme ⓕ pom apple
pomme chips pom sheeps crisps or potato chips
pomme de terre ⓕ pom der tair potato

pomme duchesse pom dew·shes deep-fried fritter of mashed potato, butter & egg yolk
porc ⓜ por pig • pork
porto ⓜ por·to port
potage ⓜ po·tazh usually a thickened soup of puréed vegetable base
pot-au-feu ⓜ po·to·fer beef, root vegetable & herb stockpot. Traditionally, the stock is served as a starter & the meat & vegetables are served as a main course.
potée ⓕ po·tay meat (usually pork) & vegetables cooked in an earthenware pot
potimarron ⓜ po·tee·ma·ron gourd – variety of squash
potiron ⓜ po·tee·ron pumpkin
pouding ⓜ poo·deeng pudding
poularde ⓕ poo·lard pullet or fattened chicken
poulet ⓜ poo·lay chicken
— au pot o po whole chicken filled with giblets, ham & bread, stewed with vegetables
— chasseur sha·ser chicken sautéed in white wine with mushrooms, shallots & bacon
poulpe ⓕ poolp octopus
poussin ⓜ poo·sun very young chicken
praire ⓕ prair clam
praline ⓕ pra·leen almonds, sometimes flavoured with coffee or chocolate & a sugar coating
premier cru prer·myay krew high-quality wines from specific vineyards
pré-salé ⓜ pray·sa·lay lamb pastured in the salty meadows of the Atlantic or the English Channel
primeur ⓜ pree·mer spring or early vegetable or fruit
printanière prun·ta·nyair dish often prepared or served with fresh spring vegetables
produits de la mer ⓜ pl pro·dwee der la mair seafood
profiterole ⓜ pro·fee·trol small ball of choux pastry with savoury or sweet fillings
provençale (à la —) pro·von·sal (a la —) 'Provence style' – dish usually cooked with olive oil, tomatoes, garlic, onions, olives, peppers & various herbs
prune ⓕ prewn plum
pruneau ⓜ prew·no prune
puits d'amour ⓜ pwee da·moor small puff pastry shell filled with custard or jam & sprinkled with sugar

Q

quenelle ⓕ ker·nel oval-shaped dumpling of fish or meat, forcemeat, egg & flour, often served poached
— de brochet der bro·shay pike dumpling
queue ⓕ ker tail
quiche ⓕ keesh open-top tart with meat, fish or vegetable filling, baked with beaten eggs & cream

R

raclette ⓕ ra·klet hot melted cheese scraped from a block of cheese placed in front of a grill, served with potatoes & gherkins/pickles (Savoy)
radis ⓜ ra·dee radish
ragoût ⓜ ra·goo stew of meat, poultry or fish and/or vegetables
raie ⓕ ray skate • ray
raisin ⓜ ray·zun grape
rascasse ⓕ ras·kas scorpion fish – grotesque but delicious fish essential in *bouillabaisse* (Mediterranean)
ratatouille ⓕ ra·ta·too·ee vegetable 'stew' – tomatoes, courgette/zucchini, aubergine/eggplant, peppers & onions, flavoured with garlic, herbs & olive oil, served with lemon juice

reine (à la —) ren (a la —) 'queen's style' – a dish with poultry
religieuse ⓕ rer·lee·zhyerz double-decker choux pastry puff, filled with coffee or chocolate-flavoured custard & coated with icing
rémoulade ⓕ re·moo·lad classic sauce made by combining mayonnaise with mustard, capers, chopped gherkins/pickles, herbs & anchovies, served chilled with grated celery, or as an accompaniment to cold meat or seafood
rillettes ⓕ pl ree·yet coarsely shredded, potted meat (usually pork), eaten as a spread on toast or bread
rillons ⓜ ree·yon chunks of fatty pork or duck cooked until crisp
ris de veau ⓜ ree der vo sweetbreads
rissole ⓕ ree·sol fried or baked pastry turnover, filled with a savoury filling of meat, poultry or vegetables
riz ⓜ ree rice
rognon ⓜ ron·yon kidney
romarin ⓜ ro·ma·run rosemary
rosbif ⓜ ros·beef roast beef
rosette de Lyon ⓕ ro·zet der lee·on large pork sausage (like salami)
rôti ⓜ ro·tee roast
rouget ⓜ roo·zhay mullet
rouille ⓕ roo·ee thick *aïoli* sauce
roulade ⓕ roo·lad slice of meat or fish rolled around stuffing • a rolled-up vegetable souffle
roulé(e) ⓜ/ⓕ roo·lay rolled

S

sabayon ⓜ sa·ba·yon creamy dessert of beaten eggs, sugar & wine or liqueur, flavoured with lemon juice
sablé ⓜ sa·blay rich shortbread biscuit
safran ⓜ sa·fron saffron
saignant(e) ⓜ/ⓕ sen·yon(t) rare (meat)
saisi(e) ⓜ/ⓕ say·zee seared
salade ⓕ sa·lad salad • lettuce
— composée kom·po·zay mixed salad
— verte vairt green salad
salé(e) ⓜ/ⓕ sa·lay salted
salmis ⓜ sal·mee game or poultry partially roasted, then simmered in wine
sang ⓜ song blood
sanglier (sauvage) ⓜ song·glee·yay (so·vazh) (wild) boar
sanguette ⓕ song·get *boudin* sausage (often flat) made from rabbit, duck or goose blood (Périgord)
sauce ⓕ sos sauce • gravy
saucisse ⓕ so·sees sausage
— de Francfort der frongk·for frankfurt
— de Strasbourg der straz·boor knackwurst
— de Toulouse der too·looz mild pork sausage
saucisson ⓜ so·see·son large sausage usually air-dried & eaten cold
— à l'ail a lai garlic sausage
— de Lyon der lee·on long air-dried pork sausage, flavoured with garlic & pepper, or a boiling sausage similar to *saucisson à l'ail*
— sec sek air-dried sausage (like salami)
saumon ⓜ so·mon salmon
sauté(e) ⓜ/ⓕ so·tay sautéed
sauvage so·vazh wild
savarin ⓜ sa·va·run ring shaped sponge cake soaked with a rum syrup & filled with custard or whipped cream & fresh or poached fruits
savoie ⓕ sav·wa light, airy cake made with beaten egg whites
sec/sèche ⓜ/ⓕ sek/sesh dry
séché(e) ⓜ/ⓕ say·shay dried
seiche ⓕ sesh cuttlefish
sel ⓜ sel salt
semoule ⓕ ser·mool semolina

service ⓜ sair·vees service (charge)
— compris kom·pree service included (often abbreviated as 's.c.' at the bottom of the bill) – service charge is built into the price of each dish
— en sus on sews service charge is calculated after the food & drink ordered is added up
serviette ⓕ sair·vyet serviette • napkin
sésame ⓜ say·zam sesame
sirop ⓜ see·ro fruit syrup or cordial served mixed with water, soda or with carbonated mineral water
soja ⓜ so·zha soya bean
solette ⓕ so·let baby sole
sorbet ⓜ sor·bay sorbet
soubise ⓕ soo·beez dish served with creamed onion purée & rice
soufflé ⓜ soof·lay soufflé
soupe ⓕ soop soup
spéciale ⓕ spay·syal top-quality oyster
spécialité (de la maison) ⓕ spay·sya·lee·tay (der la may·zon) speciality of the house
steak ⓜ stek steak
— tartare tar·tar steak tartare – raw minced beef served with raw onion, egg yolk, capers & parsley
sucre ⓜ soo·krer sugar
sucré(e) ⓜ/ⓕ soo·kray sweetened
suprême de volaille ⓕ sew·prem der vo·lai boned chicken breast with creamy sauce
sur commande sewr ko·mond to your special order

T

table d'hôte ⓕ ta·bler dot meal at a set price & hour
taboulé ⓜ ta·boo·lay tabouli – common salad of couscous with parsley & mint, tomatoes & onions, seasoned with olive oil & lemon juice
tapenade ⓕ ta·per·nad savoury spread or dip of puréed olives, anchovies, capers, olive oil & lemon, eaten with bread or hard-boiled eggs
tarte ⓕ tart flan • tart
— aux fraises o frez strawberry tart
— Tatin ta·tun type of tart with pastry baked on top of fruit (usually apples)
tartiflette ⓕ tar·tee·flet dish of potatoes, Reblochon cheese & sometimes bacon (Savoy)
tartine ⓕ tar·teen slice of bread with any topping or garnish, such as butter, jam, honey, cream cheese
tendron ⓜ ton·dron cut of meat from the end of ribs to the breastbone
terrine ⓕ tay·reen preparation of meat, poultry, fish or game, baked in a ceramic dish called a *terrine*, & served cold
tête ⓕ tet head
thé ⓜ tay tea
— au citron o see·tron tea with lemon
— au lait o lay tea with milk
— nature na·tewr plain tea (no milk)
thon ⓜ ton tuna
timbale ⓕ tum·bal meat, fish, or seafood stew cooked in a pastry case • rice or pasta with vegetables, cooked in a round or cup-shaped mould, served with sauce
tisane ⓕ tee·zan herbal tea
— de camomille der ka·mo·mee·yer chamomile tea
— de menthe der mont mint tea
— de tilleul der tee·yerl tea made with dried linden blossoms
tomate ⓕ to·mat tomato
topinambour ⓕ to·pee·nom·boor Jerusalem artichoke
tournedos ⓜ toor·ner·do thick round slice of beef fillet
— Rossini ro·see·nee *tournedos* garnished with *foie gras* & truffles, served with Madeira wine sauce

tourte ⓕ toort sweet or savoury pie
tourteau ⓜ toor·to large crab
tourtière ⓕ toor·tyair sweet or savoury pie
tout compris too kom·pree all-inclusive (price)
traiteur ⓜ tray·ter caterer or delicatessen selling prepared dishes
tranche ⓕ tronsh slice
tranché ⓜ tron·shay sliced
tripes ⓕ pl treep tripe
— à la mode de Caen a la mod der kon tripe simmered with cider, leeks & carrots
troquet ⓜ tro·kay bistro • tavern • cafe • small restaurant
truffe ⓕ trewf truffle
— en chocolat on sho·ko·la melted chocolate enriched with butter, cream & egg yolks, rolled into small balls & covered with cocoa
truite ⓕ trweet trout
— au bleu o bler trout poached in a *court-bouillon* broth of vinegar, white wine, vegetables & herbs
tuile ⓕ tweel 'tile' – fragile, wing-like almond biscuit

V

vache ⓕ vash cow
vanille ⓕ va·nee·yer vanilla
vapeur ⓕ va·per steam
vapeur (à la —) va·per (a la —) steamed
varié(e) ⓜ/ⓕ var·yay assorted
veau ⓜ vo veal
velouté ⓜ ver·loo·tay rich, creamy soup, usually prepared with vegetables, shellfish or fish purée
venaison ⓕ ver·nay·zon venison
verdure ⓕ vair·dewr green vegetables
viande ⓕ vyond meat
— froide frwad cold meat
— hachée ha·shay minced meat
— séchée say·shay dried beef served in paper-thin slices as *hors d'œuvre*
viennoiserie ⓕ vyen·wa·zree baked goods like *croissants* & *brioches*
vin ⓜ vun wine
— blanc blong white wine
— de pays der pay·yee reasonable quality & generally drinkable wine
— de table der ta·bler table wine – very cheap lower-quality wine
— doux doo sweet, dessert wine
— mousseux moo·ser sparkling wine
— ordinaire or·dee·nair table wine
— rouge roozh red wine
— sec sek dry wine
vinaigre ⓜ vee·nay·grer vinegar
volaille ⓕ vo·lai poultry • fowl
vol-au-vent ⓜ vo·lo·von round puff-pastry cases filled with a mixture of sauce & meat, poultry, seafood or vegetables

W

waterzoï ⓜ wa·ter·zoy chicken, or sometimes fish, poached with shredded vegetables (especially leeks) & served with a sauce of broth, cream & egg yolks (Northern France)

Y

yaourt ⓜ ya·oort yoghurt
— à boire a bwar yoghurt drink
— brassé bra·say thick creamy yoghurt
— maigre may·grer low-fat yoghurt

DICTIONARY
English to French
ANGLAIS–FRANÇAIS

Nouns have their gender indicated by ⓜ or ⓕ. You'll also see sg and pl for singular and plural nouns. Where a word that could be either a noun or a verb has no gender indicated, it's a verb.

A

a/an un(e) ⓜ/ⓕ un/ewn
a little un peu ⓜ um per
a lot (of) beaucoup (de) bo·koo (der)
aboard à bord a bor
abortion avortement ⓜ a·vor·ter·mon
about environ on·vee·ron
above au-dessus o·der·sew
abroad à l'étranger a lay·tron·zhay
accept accepter ak·sep·tay
accident accident ⓜ ak·see·don
accommodation logement ⓜ lozh·mon
account compte ⓜ kont
ache douleur ⓕ doo·ler
achievement réussite ⓕ ray·ew·seet
acid (drug) acide ⓜ a·seed
across de l'autre côté de der lo·trer ko·tay der
act jouer zhoo·ay
activist militant/militante ⓜ/ⓕ mee·lee·ton(t)
actor acteur/actrice ⓜ/ⓕ ak·ter/ak·trees
acupuncture acupuncture ⓕ a·kew·pongk·tewr
adaptor adaptateur ⓜ a·dap·ta·ter
addicted (to drugs) drogué dro·gay
addiction dépendance ⓕ day·pon·dons
additional supplémentaire sew·play·mon·tair
address adresse ⓕ a·dres
administration administration ⓕ ad·mee·nee·stra·syon
admire admirer ad·mee·ray
admission (price) prix d'entrée ⓜ pree don·tray
admit admettre ad·me·trer
adult adulte ⓜ&ⓕ a·dewlt
advertisement publicité ⓕ pewb·lee·see·tay
advice conseil ⓜ kon·say
aerobics aérobic ⓜ a·ay·ro·beek
aeroplane avion ⓜ a·vyon
affair liaison ⓕ lyay·zon
Africa Afrique ⓕ a·freek
after après a·pray
afternoon après-midi ⓜ a·pray·mee·dee
aftershave après-rasage ⓜ a·pray·ra·zazh
again encore ong·kor
against contre kon·trer
age âge ⓜ azh

aggressive agressif/agressive ⓜ/ⓕ a·gray·seef/a·gray·seev
agree être d'accord e·trer da·kor
agriculture agriculture ⓕ a·gree·kewl·tewr
ahead en avant on a·von
AIDS SIDA ⓜ see·da
air air ⓜ air
air-conditioned climatisé kee·ma·tee·zay
airline ligne aérienne ⓕ lee·nyer a·ay·ryen
airmail par avion par a·vyon
airplane avion ⓜ a·vyon
airport aéroport ⓜ a·ay·ro·por
airport tax taxe d'aéroport ⓕ taks da·ay·ro·por
aisle (on plane) couloir ⓜ koo·lwar
alarm clock réveil ⓜ ray·vay
alcohol alcool ⓜ al·kol
alive vivant(e) ⓜ/ⓕ vee·von(t)
all tout too
allergy allergie ⓕ a·lair·zhee
allow permettre pair·me·trer
almost presque pres·ker
alone tout(e) seul(e) ⓜ/ⓕ too(t) serl
already déjà day·zha
also aussi o·see
altar autel ⓜ o·tel
alternative alternative ⓕ al·tair·na·teev
altitude altitude ⓕ al·tee·tewd
always toujours too·zhoor
amateur amateur ⓜ a·ma·ter
amazing stupéfiant(e) ⓜ/ⓕ stew·pay·fyon(t)
ambassador ambassadeur/ ambassadrice ⓜ/ⓕ om·ba·sa·der/ om·ba·sa·drees
ambulance ambulance ⓕ om·bew·lons
among parmi par·mee
amount (money) somme ⓕ som
ancient antique on·teek
and et ay
angry fâché(e) ⓜ/ⓕ fa·shay
animal animal ⓜ a·nee·mal
ankle cheville ⓕ sher·vee·yer
annual annuel(le) ⓜ/ⓕ a·nwel
another un/une autre ⓜ/ⓕ un/ewn o·trer
answer réponse ⓕ ray·pons
answer répondre ray·pon·drer
ant fourmi ⓕ foor·mee
antibiotics antibiotiques ⓜ on·tee·byo·teek
antinuclear anti-nucléaire on·tee·new·klay·air
antique antiquité ⓕ on·tee·kee·tay
antiseptic antiseptique ⓜ on·tee·sep·teek
any n'importe quel/quelle ⓜ/ⓕ num·port kel
anyone n'importe qui num·port kee
anything n'importe quoi num·port kwa
anywhere n'importe où num·port oo
apartment appartement ⓜ a·par·ter·mon
appendix appendice a·pun·dees
appointment rendez-vous ⓜ ron·day·voo
approximately à peu près a per pray
April avril ⓜ a·vreel
archaeology archéologie ⓕ ar·kay·o·lo·zhee
architect architecte(e) ⓜ/ⓕ ar·shee·tekt
architecture architecture ar·shee·tek·tewr
argue se disputer ser dees·pew·tay
argument débat ⓜ day·ba
arm bras ⓜ bra
armchair fauteuil ⓜ fo·ter·yee
aromatherapy aromathérapie ⓕ a·ro·ma·tay·ra·pee
around autour o·toor
arrest arrêter a·ray·tay
arrivals arrivées ⓕ a·ree·vay
arrive arriver a·ree·vay
art art ⓜ ar
art gallery galerie ⓕ gal·ree
artist artiste ⓜ/ⓕ ar·teest
as comme kom

ashtray cendrier ⓜ son·dree·yay
Asia Asie ⓕ a·zee
ask (a question) poser po·zay
ask for (something) demander der·mon·day
aspirin aspirine ⓕ as·pee·reen
ass (bum) cul ⓜ kew
asthma asthme ⓜ as·mer
at à a
athletics athlétisme ⓜ at·lay·tees·mer
atmosphere atmosphère ⓕ at·mos·fair
attached attaché(e) ⓜ/ⓕ a·ta·shay
auction vente aux enchères ⓕ vont o zon·shair
August août ⓜ oot
aunt tante ⓕ tont
Australia Australie ⓕ o·stra·lee
Austria Autriche ⓕ o·treesh
automatic automatique o·to·ma·teek
automatic teller machine (ATM) guichet ⓜ automatique de banque (GAB) gee·shay o·to·ma·teek der bonk
autumn automne ⓜ o·ton
avenue avenue ⓕ av·new
awful affreux/affreuse ⓜ/ⓕ a·frer/a·frerz

B

B&W (film) noir et blanc nwar ay blong
baby bébé ⓜ bay·bay
baby food bouillie ⓕ boo·yee
baby powder talc ⓜ talk
back (body) dos ⓜ do
backpack sac à dos ⓜ sak a do
bad mauvais(e) ⓜ/ⓕ mo·vay(z)
bag sac ⓜ sak
baggage bagages ⓜ ba·gazh
baggage allowance franchise ⓕ fron·sheez
baggage claim retrait des bagages ⓜ rer·tray day ba·gazh
bakery boulangerie ⓕ boo·lon·zhree
balance (account) solde ⓜ sold
balcony balcon ⓜ bal·kon
ball (tennis/football) balle/ballon ⓕ/ⓜ bal/ba·lon
ballet ballet ⓜ ba·lay
band (music) bande ⓕ bond
bandage pansement ⓜ pons·mon
Band-Aid sparadrap ⓜ spa·ra·dra
bank banque ⓕ bonk
bank account compte bancaire ⓜ kont bong·kair
bank draft traite bancaire ⓕ tret bong·kair
banknote billet de banque ⓜ bee·yay der bonk
baptism baptême ⓜ ba·tem
bar bar ⓜ bar
bar work travail dans un bar ⓜ tra·vai don zun bar
baseball baseball ⓜ bez·bol
basic fondamental fon·da·mon·tal
basket panier ⓜ pan·yay
basketball basket(ball) ⓜ bas·ket(·bol)
bastard salaud ⓜ sa·lo
bath baignoire ⓕ bey·nwar
bath (have a) (prendre un) bain (pron·drer un) bun
bathing suit maillot de bain ⓜ may·yo der bun
bathroom salle de bain ⓕ sal der bun
battery pile ⓕ peel
battery (car) batterie ⓕ bat·ree
be être e·trer
beach plage ⓕ plazh
beautiful beau/belle ⓜ/ⓕ bo/bel
beauty salon salon de beauté ⓜ sa·lon der bo·tay
because parce que pars ker
become devenir derv·neer
bed lit ⓜ lee
bed linen draps ⓜ dra
bedding literie ⓕ leet·ree
bedroom chambre à coucher ⓕ shom·brer a koo·shay
bee abeille ⓕ a·bay
beer bière ⓕ byair
before avant a·von
begin commencer ko·mon·say

behind derrière dair·yair
Belgium Belgique ⓕ bel·zheek
belief croyance ⓕ krwa·yons
believe croire krwar
below sous soo
beside à côté de a ko·tay der
best le/la meilleur(e) ⓜ/ⓕ ler/la may·yer
bet pari ⓜ pa·ree
bet parier par·yay
better meilleur(e) ⓜ/ⓕ may·yer
between entre on·trer
bib bavoir ⓜ ba·vwar
bible bible ⓕ bee·bler
bicycle vélo ⓜ vay·lo
big grand(e) ⓜ/ⓕ gron(d)
bigger plus grand(e) ⓜ/ⓕ plew gron(d)
biggest le/la plus grand(e) ⓜ/ⓕ ler/la plew gron(d)
bike vélo ⓜ vay·lo
bike chain chaîne de bicyclette ⓕ shen der bee·see·klet
bike path piste cyclable ⓕ peest see·kla·bler
bill (restaurant) addition ⓕ a·dee·syon
bird oiseau ⓜ wa·zo
birth certificate acte de naissance ⓜ akt der nay·sons
birthday anniversaire ⓜ a·nee·vair·sair
bitch salope ⓕ sa·lop
bite mordre mor·drer
bite (dog) morsure ⓕ mor·sewr
bite (insect) piqûre ⓕ pee·kewr
bitter amer/amère ⓜ/ⓕ a·mair
black noir(e) ⓜ/ⓕ nwar
blanket couverture ⓕ koo·vair·tewr
blessing grâce ⓕ gras
blind aveugle a·ver·gler
blister ampoule ⓕ om·pool
blocked bloqué(e) ⓜ/ⓕ blo·kay
blood sang ⓜ son
blood group groupe sanguin ⓜ groop song·gun
blood pressure tension artérielle ⓕ ton·syon ar·tay·ryel
blood test analyse de sang ⓕ a·na·leez der son
blue bleu(e) ⓜ/ⓕ bler
board (a plane, ship) monter à bord de mon·tay a bor der
boarding house pension ⓕ pon·syon
boarding pass carte d'embarquement ⓕ kart dom·bar·ker·mon
boat bateau ⓜ ba·to
body corps ⓜ kor
bone os ⓜ os
book livre ⓜ leev·rer
book (make a booking) réserver ray·zair·vay
booked up complet/complète ⓜ/ⓕ kom·play/kom·plet
bookshop librairie ⓕ lee·bray·ree
boot (footwear) botte ⓕ bot
border frontière ⓕ fron·tyair
bored (be) s'ennuyer son·nwee·yay
boring ennuyeux/ennuyeuse ⓜ/ⓕ on·nwee·yer/on·nwee·yerz
born né(e) ⓜ/ⓕ nay
borrow emprunter om·prun·tay
botanic garden jardin botanique ⓜ zhar·dun bo·ta·neek
both tous les deux too lay der
bottle bouteille ⓕ boo·tay
bottle opener ouvre-bouteille ⓜ oo·vrer·boo·tay
boulevard boulevard ⓜ bool·var
bowl bol ⓜ bol
box boîte ⓕ bwat
boxer shorts boxer-short ⓜ bok·sair·short
boxing boxe ⓕ boks
boy garçon ⓜ gar·son
boyfriend petit ami ⓜ per·tee ta·mee
bra soutien-gorge ⓜ soo·tyung gorzh
Braille braille ⓜ bra·yer
brakes freins ⓜ frun
brave courageux/courageuse ⓜ/ⓕ koo·ra·zher/koo·ra·zherz
bread pain ⓜ pun
break casser ka·say

break down tomber en panne tom·bay on pan
breakfast petit déjeuner ⓜ per·tee day·zher·nay
breast sein ⓜ sun
breathe respirer res·pee·ray
brewery brasserie ⓕ bra·ser·ree
bribe pot-de-vin ⓜ po·der·vun
bribe suborner sew·bor·nay
bridge pont ⓜ pon
briefcase serviette ⓕ sair·vyet
brilliant génial(e) ⓜ/ⓕ zhay·nyal
bring (a person) amener am·nay
bring (a thing) apporter a·por·tay
brochure brochure ⓕ bro·shewr
broken cassé(e) ⓜ/ⓕ ka·say
broken down (tombé) en panne (tom·bay) on pan
bronchitis bronchite ⓕ bron·sheet
brother frère ⓜ frair
brown brun/brune ⓜ/ⓕ brun/brewn
bruise bleu ⓜ bler
brush brosse ⓕ bros
bucket seau ⓜ so
Buddhist bouddhiste boo·deest
budget budget ⓜ bew·dzay
buffet buffet ⓜ bew·fay
bug (insect) insecte ⓜ un·sekt
build construire kon·strweer
building bâtiment ⓜ ba·tee·mon
burn brûlure ⓕ brew·lewr
burn brûler brew·lay
bus (city) (auto)bus ⓜ (o·to)bews
bus (intercity) (auto)car ⓜ (o·to)kar
bus station gare routière ⓕ gar roo·tyair
bus stop arrêt d'autobus ⓜ a·ray do·to·bews
business affaires ⓕ a·fair
business class classe affaires ⓕ klas a·fair
business man/woman homme/ femme d'affaires ⓜ/ⓕ om/fum da·fair
business trip voyage d'affaires ⓜ vwa·yazh da·fair
busker musicien(ne) des rues ⓜ/ⓕ mew·zee·syun/mew·zee·syen day rew
busy occupé(e) ⓜ/ⓕ o·kew·pay
but mais may
butcher's shop boucherie ⓕ boosh·ree
butterfly papillon ⓜ pa·pee·yon
button bouton ⓜ boo·ton
buy acheter ash·tay
by par par

C

cable câble ⓜ ka·bler
cable car téléphérique ⓜ tay·lay·fay·reek
cafe café ⓜ ka·fay
cake shop pâtisserie ⓕ pa·tees·ree
calculator calculatrice ⓕ kal·kew·la·trees
calendar calendrier ⓜ ka·lon·dree·yay
call appeler a·play
camera appareil photo ⓜ a·pa·ray fo·to
camp camp ⓜ kon
camping ground camping ⓜ kom·peeng
camping store magasin pour équi-pement de camping ⓜ ma·ga·zun poor ay·keep·mon der kom·peeng
campsite terrain de camping ⓜ tay·run der kom·peeng
can (be able) pouvoir poo·vwar
can (have permission) pouvoir poo·vwar
can (tin) boîte ⓕ bwat
can opener ouvre-boîte ⓜ oo·vrer·bwat
Canada Canada ⓜ ka·na·da
cancel annuler a·new·lay
cancer cancer ⓜ kon·sair
candle bougie ⓕ boo·zhee
capitalism capitalisme ⓜ ka·pee·ta·lees·mer
car voiture ⓕ vwa·tewr
car hire location de voitures ⓕ lo·ka·syon der vwa·tewr
car owner's title carte grise ⓕ kart greez

car registration immatriculation ee·ma·tree·kew·la·syon
caravan caravane ⓕ ka·ra·van
care for (someone) soigner swa·nyay
career carrière ⓕ kar·ryair
careful soigneux/soigneuse ⓜ/ⓕ swa·nyer/swa·nyerz
caring aimant(e) ⓜ/ⓕ ay·mon(t)
carpark parking ⓜ par·keeng
carpenter menuisier ⓜ mer·nwee·zyay
carry porter por·tay
carton (for ice cream) boîte ⓕ bwat
carton (for yoghurt) pot ⓜ po
cartoon dessin animé ⓜ day·sun a·nee·may
cash argent ⓜ ar·zhon
cash (a cheque) encaisser ong·kay·say
cash register caisse (enregistreuse) ⓕ kes (on·rer·zhee·strerz)
cashier caissier/caissière ⓜ/ⓕ kay·syay/kay·syair
castle château ⓜ sha·to
casual work travail intermittent ⓜ tra·vai un·tair·mee·ton
cat chat ⓜ sha
catch attraper a·tra·pay
cathedral cathédrale ⓕ ka·tay·dral
Catholic catholique ka·to·leek
cause cause ⓕ koz
caution prudence ⓕ prew·dons
cave grotte ⓕ grot
CD CD ⓜ say·day
celebration fête ⓕ fet
cemetery cimetière ⓜ seem·tyair
cent cent ⓜ sent
centimetre centimètre ⓜ son·tee·me·trer
centre centre ⓜ son·trer
ceramic céramique ⓕ say·ra·meek
certain certain(e) ⓜ/ⓕ sair·tun/·ten
certificate certificat ⓜ sair·tee·fee·ka
chain chaîne ⓕ shen
chair chaise ⓕ shez
chairlift (skiing) télésiège ⓜ tay·lay·syezh
Champagne champagne ⓜ shom·pa·nyer
championship championnat ⓜ shom·pyo·na
chance hasard ⓜ a·zar
change changer shon·zhay
change (coins) monnaie ⓕ mo·nay
change (money) échanger ay·shon·zhay
changing room (in shop) cabine d'essayage ⓕ ka·been day·say·yazh
channel chaîne ⓕ shen
charming charmant(e) ⓜ/ⓕ shar·mon(t)
chat bavarder ba·var·day
chat up draguer dra·gay
cheap bon marché ⓜ bon mar·shay
cheat tricheur/tricheuse ⓜ/ⓕ tree·sher/tree·sherz
check vérifier vay·ree·fyay
check (banking) chèque ⓜ shek
check (bill) addition ⓕ la·dee·syon
check-in (desk) enregistrement on·rer·zhee·strer·mon
checkpoint contrôle ⓜ kon·trol
cheese fromage fro·mazh
chef chef de cuisine ⓜ shef der kwee·zeen
chemist pharmacie ⓕ far·ma·see
chemist (person) pharmacien(ne) ⓜ/ⓕ far·ma·syun/far·ma·syen
cheque (banking) chèque ⓜ shek
chess échecs ⓜ ay·shek
chess board échiquier ⓜ ay·shee·kyay
chest poitrine ⓕ pwa·treen
chicken poulet ⓜ poo·lay
child enfant ⓜ&ⓕ on·fon
child seat siège pour enfant ⓜ syezh poor on·ton
childminding garderie ⓕ gard·ree
children enfants ⓜ&ⓕ pl on·fon
chiropractor chiropracteur ⓜ kee·ro·prak·ter
chocolate chocolat ⓜ sho·ko·la
choice choix ⓜ shwa
choose choisir shwa·zeer

Christian chrétien(ne) ⓜ/ⓕ kray·tyun/kray·tyen
Christian name prénom ⓜ pray·non
Christmas Noël ⓜ no·el
Christmas Day jour de Noël ⓜ zhoor der no·el
Christmas Eve veille de Noël ⓕ vay der no·el
church église ⓕ ay·gleez
cigar cigare ⓜ see·gar
cigarette cigarette ⓕ see·ga·ret
cigarette lighter briquet ⓜ bree·kay
cinema cinéma ⓜ see·nay·ma
circle cercle ⓜ sair·kler
circus cirque ⓜ seerk
citizen citoyen(ne) ⓜ/ⓕ see·twa·yun/see·twa·yen
citizenship citoyenneté ⓕ see·twa·yen·tay
city ville ⓕ veel
city centre centre-ville ⓜ son·trer·veel
city hall mairie ⓕ may·ree
civil rights droits civils ⓜ pl drwa see·veel
class classe ⓕ klas
classical classique kla·seek
clean propre pro·prer
clean nettoyer net·wa·yay
cleaning nettoyage ⓜ net·wa·yazh
clear clair(e) ⓜ/ⓕ klair
client client(e) ⓜ/ⓕ klee·on(t)
cliff falaise ⓕ fa·lez
climb monter mon·tay
cloak cape ⓕ kap
cloakroom vestiaire ⓜ vays·tyair
clock pendule ⓕ pon·dewl
close proche prosh
close fermer fair·may
closed fermé(e) ⓜ/ⓕ fair·may
clothes line corde à linge ⓕ kord a lunzh
clothing vêtements ⓜ vet·mon
clothing store magasin de vêtements ⓜ ma·ga·zun der vet·mon
cloud nuage ⓜ nwazh
cloudy nuageux/nuageuse ⓜ/ⓕ nwa·zher/nwa·zherz
clutch embrayage om·bray·yazh
coach entraîneur ⓜ on·tray·ner
coast côte ⓕ kot
coat manteau ⓜ mon·to
cocaine cocaïne ⓕ ko·ka·een
cockroach cafard ⓜ ka·far
cocktail cocktail ⓜ kok·tel
coffee café ⓜ ka·fay
coins pièces ⓕ pyes
cold froid(e) ⓜ/ⓕ frwa(d)
colleague collègue ⓜ/ⓕ ko·leg
collect (stamps etc) collectionner ko·lek·syo·nay
collect call appel en PCV ⓜ a·pel on pay·say·vay
collection accumulation ⓕ a·kew·mew·la·syon
college institut universitaire ⓜ un·stee·tew ew·nee·vair·see·tair
college (vocational) école professionnelle ⓕ ay·kol pro·fay·syo·nel
colour couleur ⓕ koo·ler
comb peigne ⓜ pe·nyer
combination combinaison ⓕ kom·bee·nay·zon
come venir ver·neer
comedy comédie ⓕ ko·may·dee
comfortable confortable kon·for·ta·bler
comic (magazine) bande dessinée ⓕ bond day·see·nay
commission commission ⓕ ko·mee·syon
common commun(e) ⓜ/ⓕ ko·mun/ko·mewn
communism communisme ⓜ ko·mew·nees·mer
communist communiste ko·mew·neest
community communauté ⓕ ko·mew·no·tay
companion compagnon/compagne ⓜ/ⓕ kom·pa·nyon/kom·pa·nyer
company entreprise ⓕ on·trer·preez
compass boussole ⓕ boo·sol
competition compétition ⓕ kom·pay·tees·yon

complain se plaindre ser plun·drer
complaint plainte ⓕ plunt
complimentary (free) gratuit(e) ⓜ/ⓕ gra·twee(t)
computer ordinateur ⓜ or·dee·na·ter
computer game jeu électronique ⓜ zher ay·lek·tro·neek
concert concert ⓜ kon·sair
concussion commotion cérébrale ⓕ ko·mo·syon say·ray·bral
conditioner (hair) après-shampooing ⓜ a·pray·shom·pwung
condom préservatif ⓜ pray·zair·va·teef
conductor (bus) receveur ⓜ rer·ser·ver
conference (big) congrès ⓜ kong·gray
conference (small) colloque ⓜ ko·lok
confession (religious) confession ⓕ kon·fay·syon
confirm (a booking) confirmer kon·feer·may
congratulations félicitations fay·lee·see·ta·syon
connection rapport ⓜ ra·por
conservative conservateur/conservatrice ⓜ/ⓕ kon·sair·va·ter/kon·sair·va·trees
constipation constiptation ⓕ kon·stee·pa·syon
consulate consulat ⓜ kon·su·la
contact lenses verres de contact ⓜ vair der kon·takt
contraceptive contraceptif ⓜ kon·trer·sep·teef
contract contrat ⓜ kon·tra
convenience store supérette de quartier ⓕ sew·pay·ret der kar·tyay
convent couvent ⓜ koo·von
conversation conversation ⓕ kon·vair·sa·syon
cook cuisinier/cuisinière ⓜ/ⓕ kwee·zee·nyay/kwee·zee·nyair
cook cuire kweer
cool frais/fraîche ⓜ/ⓕ fray/fresh
cooperate coopérer ko·o·pay·ray
cop flic ⓜ fleek
corkscrew tire-bouchon ⓜ teer·boo·shon
corner coin ⓜ kwun
correct correct(e) ⓜ/ⓕ ko·rekt
corrupt corrompu(e) ⓜ/ⓕ ko·rom·pew
cost coût ⓜ koo
cotton coton ⓜ ko·ton
cotton balls ouate de coton ⓕ wat der ko·ton
cough toux ⓕ too
cough medicine syrop contre la toux ⓜ see·ro kon·trer la too
count compter kon·tay
counter (at bar) comptoir ⓜ kon·twar
country pays ⓜ pay·ee
countryside campagne ⓕ kom·pa·nyer
coupon coupon ⓜ koo·pon
court (legal) tribunal ⓜ tree·bew·nal
court (tennis) court ⓜ koor
cover charge couvert ⓜ koo·vair
cow vache ⓕ vash
crafts artisanat ⓜ ar·tee·za·na
crash accident ⓜ ak·see·don
crazy fou/folle ⓜ/ⓕ foo/fol
cream crème ⓕ krem
creche crèche ⓕ kresh
credit crédit ⓜ kray·dee
credit card carte de crédit ⓕ kart der kray·dee
creek crique ⓕ kreek
crime délit ⓜ day·lee
crop (gathered) récolte ⓕ ray·kolt
crop (grown) culture ⓕ kewl·tewr
cross traverser tra·vair·say
cross (angry) fâché(e) ⓜ/ⓕ fa·shay
cross (religious) croix ⓕ krwa
crowd foule ⓕ fool
crowded bondé(e) ⓜ/ⓕ bon·day
cry pleurer pler·ray
cup tasse ⓕ tas
cupboard placard ⓜ pla·kar
current actuel(le) ⓜ/ⓕ ak·twel

currency exchange taux de change ⓜ to der shonzh
current (electricity) courant ⓜ koo·ron
current affairs actualité ak·twa·lee·tay
custom coutume ⓕ koo·tewm
customer client(e) ⓜ/ⓕ klee·on(t)
customs douane ⓕ dwan
cut couper koo·pay
cute mignon/mignonne ⓜ/ⓕ mee·nyo/mee·nyon
cutlery couverts ⓜ koo·vair
CV CV ⓜ say·vay
cycle faire du vélo fair dew vay·lo
cycling cyclisme ⓜ see·klee·smer
cyclist cycliste ⓜ/ⓕ see·kleest

D

dad papa ⓜ pa·pa
daily quotidien(ne) ⓜ/ⓕ ko·tee·dyun/ko·tee·dyen
damage dégâts ⓜ day·ga
dance danser don·say
dancing danse ⓕ dons
dangerous dangereux/dangereuse ⓜ/ⓕ don·zhrer/don·zhrerz
dark obscur(e) ⓜ/ⓕ ob·skewr
dark (of colour) foncé(e) ⓜ/ⓕ fon·say
date (appointment) rendez-vous ⓜ ron·day·voo
date (day) date ⓕ dat
date (go out with) sortir avec sor·teer a·vek
date of birth date de naissance ⓕ dat der nay·sons
daughter fille ⓕ fee·yer
dawn aube ob
day jour ⓜ zhoor
day after tomorrow après-demain a·pray·der·mun
day before yesterday avant-hier a·von·tyair
dead mort(e) ⓜ/ⓕ mor(t)
deaf sourd(e) ⓜ/ⓕ soor(d)
deal (cards) donner do·nay
death mort ⓕ mor
December décembre ⓜ day·som·brer
decide se décider ser day·see·day
decision décision ⓕ day·see·zyon
deep profond(e) ⓜ/ⓕ pro·fon(d)
definite bien déterminé byun day·tair·mee·nay
deforestation déboisement ⓜ day·bwaz·mon
degree diplôme ⓜ dee·plom
delay retard ⓜ rer·tard
delicatessen charcuterie ⓕ shar·kew·tree
deliver livrer leev·ray
demand exiger eg·zee·zhay
democracy démocratie ⓕ day·mo·kra·see
demonstration manifestation ⓕ ma·nee·fay·sta·syon
Denmark Danemark ⓜ dan·mark
dental floss fil dentaire ⓜ feel don·tair
dentist dentiste ⓜ don·teest
deny nier nee·ay
deodorant déodorant ⓜ day·o·do·ron
depart (leave) partir par·teer
department store grand magasin ⓜ gron ma·ga·zun
departure départ ⓜ day·par
deposit dépôt ⓜ day·po
descendant descendant(e) ⓜ/ⓕ day·son·don(t)
desert désert ⓜ day·zair
design concevoir kon·ser·vwar
dessert dessert ⓜ day·sair
destination destination ⓕ des·tee·na·syon
destroy détruire day·trweer
detail détail ⓜ day·tai
development développement ⓜ day·vlop·mon
diabetes diabète ⓜ dya·bet
dial tone tonalité ⓕ to·na·lee·tay
diaper couche ⓕ koosh
diaphragm diaphragme ⓜ dya·frag·mer

diarrhoea diarrhée ⓕ dya·ray
diary agenda ⓜ a·zhun·da
dice dés ⓜ day
dictionary dictionnaire ⓜ deek·syo·nair
die mourir moo·reer
diesel gas-oil ⓜ gaz·wal
diet régime ⓜ ray·zheem
different différent(e) ⓜ/ⓕ dee·fay·ron(t)
difficult difficile dee·fee·seel
digital camera appareil photo numérique ⓜ a·pa·ray fo·to new·may·reek
dining car wagon-restaurant ⓜ va·gon·res·to·ron
dinner dîner ⓜ dee·nay
diploma diplôme ⓜ dee·plom
direct direct(e) ⓜ/ⓕ dee·rekt
direct (a film) réaliser ray·a·lee·zay
direction direction ⓕ dee·rek·syon
director (film) réalisateur/réalisatrice ⓜ/ⓕ ray·a·lee·za·ter/ray·a·lee·za·trees
dirty sale sal
disabled handicapé(e) ⓜ/ⓕ on·dee·ka·pay
disappointed déçu(e) ⓜ/ⓕ day·sew
disaster désastre ⓜ day·zas·trer
discount remise ⓕ rer·meez
discover découvrir day·koov·reer
discrimination discrimination ⓕ dee·skree·mee·na·syon
discuss discuter dee·skew·tay
disease maladie ⓕ ma·la·dee
dish plat ⓜ pla
dishonest malhonnête mal·o·net
disinfectant désinfectant ⓜ day·zun·fek·ton
disposable camera appareil photo jetable ⓜ a·pa·ray fo·to zhay·ta·bler
distance distance ⓕ dees·tons
distributor concessionnaire ⓜ kon·say·syo·nair
disturb déranger day·ron·zhay
dive plonger plon·zhay
diving plongée sous-marine ⓕ plon·zhay soo·ma·reen
diving equipment équipement de plongée ⓜ ay·keep·mon der plon·zhay
divorced divorcé(e) ⓜ/ⓕ dee·vor·say
dizzy (be dizzy) avoir la tête qui tourne a·vwar la tet kee toorn
do faire fair
doctor médecin ⓜ mayd·sun
dog ⓜ chien shyun
dole (benefits) allocation de chômage ⓕ a·lo·ka·syon der sho·mazh
doll poupée ⓕ poo·pay
door porte ⓕ port
dope (drugs) drogue ⓕ drog
dose dose ⓕ doz
double double doo·bler
double bed grand lit ⓜ gron lee
double room chambre double ⓕ shom·brer doo·bler
down en bas on ba
dozen douzaine ⓕ doo·zen
drama (theatre) théâtre ⓜ tay·a·trer
draw (picture) dessiner day·see·nay
dream rêver ray·vay
dress robe ⓕ rob
dress (oneself) s'habiller sa·bee·yay
drink boisson ⓕ bwa·son
drink boire bwar
drink (alcoholic) verre ⓜ vair
drive conduire kon·dweer
driver's licence permis de conduire ⓜ pair·mee der kon·dweer
drop laisser tomber lay·say tom·bay
drug drogue ⓕ drog
drug addiction toxicomanie ⓕ tok·see·ko·ma·nee
drug dealer trafiquant de drogue ⓜ tra·fee·kon der drog
drugs drogue ⓕ drog
drum tambour ⓜ tom·boor
drums batterie ⓕ ba·tree
drunk ivre ee·vrer
dry sec/sèche ⓜ/ⓕ sek/sesh
dry (clothes) sécher say·shay
duck canard ⓜ ka·nar
dummy (pacifier) tétine ⓕ tay·teen
during pendant pon·don

dust poussière ⓕ poo·syair
duty devoir ⓜ der·vwar

E

each chaque shak
ear oreille ⓕ o·ray
early tôt to
earn gagner ga·nyay
earrings boucles d'oreille ⓕ boo·kler do·ray
Earth Terre ⓕ tair
earth (ground) terre ⓕ tair
earthquake tremblement de terre ⓜ trom·bler·mon der tair
east est ⓜ est
Easter Pâques pak
easy facile fa·seel
eat manger mon·zhay
economy économie ⓕ ay·ko·no·mee
economy class classe touriste ⓕ klas too·reest
ecstasy (drug) ecstasy ⓜ ek·sta·zee
eczema eczéma ⓜ eg·zay·ma
edge bord ⓜ bor
editor rédacteur/rédactrice ⓜ/ⓕ ray·dak·ter/ray·dak·trees
education éducation ⓕ ay·dew·ka·syon
effect effet ⓜ ay·fay
eight huit weet
elderly âgé(e) ⓜ/ⓕ a·zhay
election élection ⓕ ay·lek·syon
electrical store magasin qui vend des appareils électriques ⓜ ma·ga·zunkee von day za·pa·ray ay·lek·treek
electricity électricité ⓕ ay·lek·tree·see·tay
elevator ascenseur ⓜ a·son·ser
email e-mail ⓜ ee·mel
embarrass gêner zhay·nay
embarrassed gêné(e) ⓜ/ⓕ zhay·nay
embarrassing gênant(e) ⓜ/ⓕ zhay·non(t)
embassy ambassade ⓕ om·ba·sad
embroidery broderie ⓕ bro·dree
emergency cas urgent ⓜ ka ewr·zhon
emotional (person) facilement ému fa·seel·mon ay·mew
employee employé/employée ⓜ/ⓕ om·plwa·yay/om·plwa·yay
employer employeur ⓜ om·plwa·yer
empty vide veed
end bout ⓜ boo
end finir fee·neer
endangered species espèce menacée de disparition ⓕ es·pes mer·na·say der dees·pa·rees·yon
energy énergie ⓕ ay·nair·zhee
engaged fiancé(e) ⓜ/ⓕ fyon·say
engagement fiançailles ⓕ fyon·sai
engine moteur ⓜ mo·ter
engineer ingénieur ⓜ un·zhay·nyer
engineering ingénierie un·zhay·nee·ree
England Angleterre ⓕ ong·gler·tair
English anglais(e) ⓜ/ⓕ ong·glay(z)
enjoy (oneself) s'amuser sa·mew·zay
enough assez a·say
enter entrer on·tray
entertainment guide programme des spectacles ⓜ pro·gram day spek·tak·ler
enthusiastic enthousiaste on·tooz·yast
entry entrée ⓕ on·tray
envelope enveloppe ⓕ on·vlop
environment environnement ⓜ on·vee·ron·mon
epilepsy épilepsie ⓕ ay·pee·lep·see
equal égale ay·gal
equal opportunity égalité des chances ⓕ ay·ga·lee·tay day shons
equality égalité ⓕ ay·ga·lee·tay
equipment équipement ⓜ ay·keep·mon
escalator escalier roulant ⓜ es·ka·lyay roo·lon
escape échapper ay·sha·pay
estate agency agence immobilière ⓕ a·zhons ee·mo·bee·lyair

euro euro ⓜ er·ro
Europe Europe ⓕ er·rop
euthanasia euthanasie ⓕ er·ta·na·zee
evening soir ⓜ swar
event événement ⓜ ay·ven·mon
every chaque shak
every day tous les jours too lay zhoor
everyone tout le monde too ler mond
everything tout too
exactly exactement eg·zak·ter·mon
exam examen ⓜ eg·za·mun
example exemple ⓜ eg·zom·pler
excellent excellent(e) ⓜ/ⓕ ek·say·lon
except sauf sof
excess (baggage) excédent ek·say·don
exchange échange ⓜ ay·shonzh
exchange échanger ay·shon·zhay
exchange rate taux de change ⓜ to der shonzh
excluded pas compris pa kom·pree
exercise exercice ⓜ eg·zair·sees
exhaust (car) pot d'échappement ⓜ po day·shap·mon
exhausted épuisé(e) ⓜ/ⓕ ay·pwee·zay
exhibition exposition ⓕ ek·spo·zee·syon
exit sortie ⓕ sor·tee
expensive cher/chère ⓜ/ⓕ shair
experience expérience ⓕ eks·pair·yons
explain expliquer eks·plee·kay
exploitation exploitation ⓕ eks·plwa·ta·syon
export exporter eks·por·tay
express (mail) exprès eks·pres
express mail (by) par exprès par eks·pres
extension (visa) prolongation ⓕ pro·long·ga·syon
extra supplémentaire soop·lay·mon·tair
extraordinary extraordinaire eks·tra·or·dee·nair
eye œil ⓜ er·yee
eyes yeux ⓜ yer

F

fabric tissu ⓜ tee·sew
face visage ⓜ vee·zazh
face cloth gant de toilette ⓜ gon der twa·let
fact fait ⓜ fet
factory usine ⓕ ew·zeen
factory worker ouvrier/ouvrière d'usine ⓜ/ⓕ oo·vree·yay/oo·vree·yair dew·zeen
failure échec ⓜ ay·shek
faith foi ⓕ fwa
fall tomber tom·bay
fall (autumn) automne ⓜ o·ton
false faux/fausse ⓜ/ⓕ fo/fos
family famille ⓕ fa·mee
family name nom de famille ⓜ non der fa·mee
famous célèbre say·leb·rer
fan (of person) fan ⓜ/ⓕ fan
fan (machine) ventilateur ⓜ von·tee·la·ter
fanbelt courroie de ventilateur ⓕ koor·wa der von·tee·la·ter
far lointain(e) ⓜ/ⓕ lwun·tun/lwun·ten
fare tarif ⓜ ta·reef
farm ferme ⓕ ferm
farmer agriculteur/agricultrice ⓜ/ⓕ a·gree·kewl·ter/a·gree·kewl·trees
fascist fasciste fa·sheest
fashion mode ⓕ mod
fast rapide ra·peed
fat gras/grasse ⓜ/ⓕ gra/gras
fate destin ⓜ des·tun
father père ⓜ pair
father-in-law beau-père ⓜ bo·pair
faucet robinet ⓜ ro·bee·nay
fault (someone's) faute ⓕ fot
faulty défectueux/défectueuse ⓜ/ⓕ day·fek·twer/day·fek·twerz
fear peur ⓕ per
February février ⓜ fayv·ree·yay
feed nourrir noo·reer

feel (touch) toucher too·shay
feeling (emotion) sentiment ⓜ son·tee·mon
feeling (physical) sensation ⓕ son·sa·syon
female femelle fer·mel
fence barrière ⓕ bar·yair
fencing escrime ⓕ es·kreem
ferry bac ⓜ bak
festival fête ⓕ fet
fever fièvre ⓕ fyev·rer
few peu per
fiancé fiancé ⓜ fyon·say
fiancée fiancée ⓕ fyon·say
fiction fiction ⓕ feek·syon
field champ ⓜ shom
fight bagarre ⓕ ba·gar
fill remplir rom·pleer
film (cinema) film ⓜ feelm
film (for camera) pellicule ⓕ pay·lee·kewl
find trouver troo·vay
fine (penalty) amende ⓕ a·mond
finger doigt ⓜ dwa
finish finir fee·neer
fire feu ⓜ fer
firewood bois de chauffage ⓜ bwa der sho·fazh
first premier/première ⓜ/ⓕ prer·myay/prer·myair
first class première classe ⓕ prer·myair klas
first-aid kit trousse à pharmacie ⓕ troos a far·ma·see
fish poisson ⓜ pwa·son
fish shop poissonnerie ⓕ pwa·son·ree
fishing pêche ⓕ pesh
five cinq sungk
flag drapeau ⓜ dra·po
flannel (washing) gant de toilette ⓜ gon der twa·let
flashlight lampe de poche ⓕ lomp der posh
flat plat(e) ⓜ/ⓕ pla(t)
flavour goût ⓜ goo
flea puce ⓕ pews
flea market marché aux puces ⓜ mar·shay o pews
flight vol ⓜ vol
flood inondation ⓕ ee·non·da·syon
flooding inondation ⓕ ee·non·da·syon
floor plancher ⓜ plon·shay
floor (storey) étage ⓜ ay·tazh
florist fleuriste ⓜ&ⓕ fler·reest
flower fleur ⓕ fler
flu grippe ⓕ greep
fly mouche ⓕ moosh
fly voler vo·lay
foggy brumeux/brumeuse ⓜ/ⓕ brew·mer/brew·merz
follow suivre swee·vrer
food nourriture ⓕ noo·ree·tewr
food supplies provisions ⓕ pl pro·vee·zyon
foot pied ⓜ pyay
football (soccer) football ⓜ foot·bol
footpath sentier ⓜ son·tyay
for pour poor
forecast prévision ⓕ pray·vee·zyon
forecast prévoir pray·vwar
foreign étranger/étrangère ⓜ/ⓕ ay·tron·zhay/ay·tron·zhair
forest forêt ⓕ fo·ray
forever pour toujours poor too·zhoor
forget oublier oo·blee·yay
forgive pardonner par·do·nay
fork fourchette ⓕ foor·shet
fortnight quinze jours ⓜ pl kunz zhoor
fortune (money) fortune ⓕ for·tewn
fortune teller diseuse de bonne aventure ⓕ dee·zerz der bon a·von·tewr
foul (football) faute ⓕ fot
four quatre ka·trer
foyer (of cinema) hall ⓜ ol
fragile fragile fra·zheel
France France ⓕ frons
free (at liberty) libre lee·brer
free (available) disponible dees·po·nee·bler
free (gratis) gratuit(e) ⓜ/ⓕ gra·twee(t)

freedom liberté ⓕ lee·bair·tay
freeze geler zher·lay
frequent fréquent(e) ⓜ/ⓕ fray·kon(t)
fresh frais/fraîche ⓜ/ⓕ fray/fresh
Friday vendredi von·drer·dee
fridge réfrigérateur ⓜ ray·free·zhay·ra·ter
friend ami/amie ⓜ/ⓕ a·mee
friendly amical(e) ⓜ/ⓕ a·mee·kal
friendship amitié ⓕ a·mee·tyay
frog grenouille ⓕ grer·noo·yer
from de der
frost gel ⓜ zhel
frozen gelé(e) ⓜ/ⓕ zher·lay
fruit fruit ⓜ frwee
fruit picking cueillette de fruits ⓕ ker·yet der frwee
fry faire frire fair freer
frying pan poêle ⓕ pwal
full plein(e) ⓜ/ⓕ plun/plen
full-time à plein temps a plun ton
fun (have fun) s'amuser sa·mew·zay
funeral enterrement ⓜ on·tair·mon
funny drôle ⓜ&ⓕ drol
furnished meublé(e) ⓜ/ⓕ mer·blay
furniture meubles ⓜ pl mer·bler
future avenir av·neer

G

game jeu ⓜ zher
game (football) match ⓜ matsh
garage garage ⓜ ga·razh
garbage ordures ⓕ pl or·dewr
garbage can poubelle ⓕ poo·bel
garden jardin ⓜ zhar·dun
gardening jardinage ⓜ zhar·dee·nazh
gas (for cooking) gaz ⓜ gaz
gas (petrol) essence ⓕ ay·sons
gas cartridge cartouche de gaz ⓕ kar·toosh der gaz
gastroenteritis gastro-entérite ⓕ gastro·on·tay·reet
gate barrière ⓕ bar·yair
gay homosexuel(le) ⓜ/ⓕ o·mo·sek·swel
general général(e) ⓜ/ⓕ zhay·nay·ral
generous généreux/généreuse ⓜ/ⓕ zhay·nay·rer/zhay·nay·rerz
Germany Allemagne ⓕ al·ma·nyer
get off (a train, etc) descendre day·son·drer
gift cadeau ⓜ ka·do
gig concert ⓜ kon·sair
girl fille ⓕ fee·yer
girlfriend petite amie ⓕ per·teet a·mee
give donner do·nay
glandular fever mononucléose infectieuse ⓕ mo·no·new·klay·oz un·fek·syerz
glass verre ⓜ vair
glasses (spectacles) lunettes ⓕ pl lew·net
gloves gants ⓜ pl gon
glue colle ⓕ kol
go aller a·lay
go down (stairs, etc) descendre day·son·drer
go out sortir sor·teer
go out with sortir avec sor·teer a·vek
go shopping faire les courses fair lay koors
go to bed se coucher ser koo·shay
go window-shopping faire du lèche-vitrines fair dew lesh·vee·treen
goal but ⓜ bewt
goalkeeper gardien ⓜ de but gar·dyun der bewt
goat chèvre ⓕ shev·rer
god dieu ⓜ dyer
goggles (skiing) lunettes ⓕ pl lew·net
gold or ⓜ or
golf course terrain de golf ⓜ tay·run der golf
good bon/bonne ⓜ/ⓕ bon/bon
goodbye au revoir o rer·vwar
government gouvernement ⓜ goo·vair·ner·mon
gram gramme ⓜ gram
grandchild petit-fils/petite-fille ⓜ/ⓕ per·tee fees/per·teet fee·yer

grandfather grand-père ⓜ grom·pair
grandmother grand-mère ⓕ grom·mair
grandparents grands-parents ⓜ pl grom·pa·ron
grass (lawn) gazon ⓜ ga·zon
grass (marijuana) herbe ⓕ airb
grateful reconnaissant(e) ⓜ/ⓕ rer·ko·nay·son(t)
grave tombe ⓕ tomb
gray gris(e) ⓜ/ⓕ gree(z)
great (fantastic) génial(e) ⓜ/ⓕ zhay·nyal
greedy (food) gourmand(e) ⓜ/ⓕ goor·mon(d)
greedy (money) avide a·veed
green vert(e) ⓜ/ⓕ vair(t)
greengrocer marchand de légumes ⓜ mar·shon der lay·gewm
grey gris(e) ⓜ/ⓕ gree(z)
grocery épicerie ⓕ ay·pee·sree
grow pousser poo·say
G-string cache-sexe ⓜ kash·seks
guaranteed garanti(e) ⓜ/ⓕ ga·ron·tee
guess deviner der·vee·nay
guesthouse pension (de famille) ⓕ pon·syon (der fa·mee)
guide (person) guide ⓜ geed
guide dog chien d'aveugle ⓜ shyun da·ver·gler
guidebook guide ⓜ geed
guided tour visite guidée ⓕ vee·zeet gee·day
guilty coupable koo·pa·bler
guitar guitare ⓕ gee·tar
gun pistolet ⓜ pees·to·lay
gym (place) gymnase ⓜ zheem·naz
gymnastics gymnastique ⓕ zheem·na·steek
gynaecologist gynécologue ⓜ/ⓕ zhee·nay·ko·log

H

habit habitude ⓕ a·bee·tewd
hair cheveux ⓜ shver
hairbrush brosse à cheveux ⓕ bros a shver
haircut coupe ⓕ koop
hairdresser coiffeur/coiffeuse ⓜ/ⓕ kwa·fer/kwa·ferz
halal halal a·lal
half moitié ⓕ mwa·tyay
half a litre demi-litre ⓜ der·mee·lee·trer
hallucinate avoir des hallucinations a·vwar day za·lew·see·na·syon
ham jambon ⓜ zhom·bon
hammer marteau ⓜ mar·to
hammock hamac ⓜ a·mak
hand main ⓕ mun
handbag sac à main ⓜ sak a mun
handicrafts objets artisanaux ⓜ pl ob·zhay ar·tee·za·no
handkerchief mouchoir ⓜ moo·shwar
handlebars guidon ⓜ gee·don
handmade fait/faite à la main ⓜ/ⓕ fay/fet a la mun
handsome beau/belle ⓜ/ⓕ bo/bel
happy heureux/heureuse ⓜ/ⓕ er·rer/er·rerz
harassment harcèlement ⓜ ar·sel·mon
harbour port ⓜ por
hard (not easy) difficile dee·fee·seel
hard (not soft) dur(e) ⓜ/ⓕ dewr
hardware store quincaillerie ⓕ kung·kay·ree
hare lièvre ⓜ lyev·rer
hash teush ⓜ tersh
hat chapeau ⓜ sha·po
hate détester day·tes·tay
have avoir a·vwar
have a cold être enrhumé e·trer on·rew·may
have fun s'amuser sa·mew·zay
hay fever rhume des foins ⓜ rewm day fwun
he il eel
head tête ⓕ tet
headache mal à la tête ⓜ mal a la tet
headlights phares ⓜ pl far
health santé ⓕ son·tay

hear entendre on·ton·drer
hearing aid appareil acoustique ⓜ a·pa·ray a·koos·teek
heart cœur ⓜ ker
heart condition maladie de cœur ⓕ ma·la·dee der ker
heat chaleur ⓕ sha·ler
heated chauffé(e) ⓜ/ⓕ sho·fay
heater appareil de chauffage ⓜ a·pa·ray der sho·fazh
heavy lourd(e) ⓜ/ⓕ loor(d)
height hauteur ⓕ o·ter
helmet casque ⓜ kask
help aider ay·day
help aide ⓕ ed
hepatitis hépatite ⓕ ay·pa·teet
her son/sa/ses ⓜ/ⓕ/pl son/sa/say
herbalist herboriste ⓜ/ⓕ air·bo·reest
herbs fines herbes ⓕ feen zairb
here ici ee·see
heroin héroïne ⓕ ay·ro·een
high haut(e) ⓜ/ⓕ o(t)
high school établissement d'enseignement secondaire ⓜ ay·ta·blees·mon don·say·nyer·mon zgon·dair
highway autoroute ⓕ o·to·root
hike faire la randonnée fair la ron·do·nay
hiking randonnée ⓕ ron·do·nay
hiking boots chaussures de marche ⓕ pl sho·sewr der marsh
hiking route itinéraire de randonnée ⓜ ee·tee·nay·rair der ron·do·nay
hill colline ⓕ ko·leen
Hindu hindou(e) ⓜ/ⓕ un·doo
hire louer loo·ay
his son/sa/ses ⓜ/ⓕ/pl son/sa/say
historical historique ees·to·reek
history histoire ⓕ ees·twar
hitchhike faire du stop fair dew stop
HIV VIH (virus immunodéficitaire humain) ⓜ vay·ee·ash (vee·rewsee·mew·no·day·fee·see·tair ew·mun)
HIV positive séropositif/séropositive ⓜ/ⓕ say·ro·po·zee·teef/say·ro·po·zee·teev
hobby passe-temps ⓜ pas·ton
hockey hockey ⓜ o·kay
hole trou ⓜ troo
holidays vacances ⓕ pl va·kons
home à la maison a la may·zon
homeless sans-abri son·za·bree
homemaker femme au foyer ⓕ fum o fwa·yay
homesick nostalgique nos·tal·zheek
homework devoirs ⓜ der·vwar
homosexual homosexuel(le) ⓜ/ⓕ o·mo·sek·swel
honest honnête o·net
honeymoon lune de miel ⓕ lewn der myel
hope espoir ⓜ es·pwar
hope espérer es·pay·ray
horoscope horoscope ⓜ o·ro·skop
horse cheval ⓜ shval
horse riding équitation ⓕ ay·kee·ta·syon
hospital hôpital ⓜ o·pee·tal
hospitality hospitalité ⓕ os·pee·ta·lee·tay
hot chaud(e) ⓜ/ⓕ sho(d)
hotel hôtel ⓜ o·tel
hour heure ⓕ er
house maison ⓕ may·zon
housework ménage ⓜ may·nazh
how comment ko·mon
hug serrer dans ses bras say·ray don say bra
huge énorme ay·norm
human humain ⓜ ew·mun
human rights droits de l'homme ⓜ pl drwa der lom
humanities lettres classiques ⓕ pl le·trer kla·seek
humour humour ⓜ ew·moor
hundred cent son
hungry (to be) avoir faim a·vwar fum
hunting chasse ⓕ shas
hurt blessé(e) ⓜ/ⓕ blay·say
husband mari ⓜ ma·ree

I

I je zher
ice glace ⓕ glas

ice cream glace ⓕ glas
ice hockey hockey sur glace ⓜ o·kay sewr glas
idea idée ⓕ ee·day
identification pièce d'identité ⓕ pyes dee·don·tee·tay
identification card (ID) carte d'identité ⓕ kart dee·don·tee·tay
idiot idiot(e) ⓜ/ⓕ ee·dyo(t)
if si see
ignorant ignorant(e) ⓜ/ⓕ ee·nyo·ron(t)
ill malade ma·lad
illegal illégal(e) ⓜ/ⓕ ee·lay·gal
imagination imagination ⓕ ee·ma·zhee·na·syon
immediately/right now immédiatement ee·may·dyat·mon
immigration immigration ⓕ ee·mee·gra·syon
impolite impoli(e) ⓜ/ⓕ um·po·lee
import importer um·por·tay
important important(e) ⓜ/ⓕ um·por·ton(t)
impossible impossible um·po·see·bler
improve améliorer a·may·lyo·ray
in dans don
in a hurry pressé(e) ⓜ/ⓕ pray·say
in front of devant der·von
included compris(e) ⓜ/ⓕ kom·pree(z)
income revenus ⓜ pl rerv·new
income tax impôt sur le revenu ⓜ um·po sewr ler rerv·new
inconvenient inopportun(e) ⓜ/ⓕ ee·no·por·tun/ee·no·por·tewn
independent indépendant(e) ⓜ/ⓕ un·day·pon·don(t)
India Inde ⓕ und
indicator (on car) clignotant ⓜ klee·nyo·ton
indigestion indigestion ⓕ un·dee·zhes·tyon
individual individu ⓜ un·dee·vee·dew
industrial industriel/industrielle ⓜ/ⓕ un·dews·tree·el
industry industrie ⓕ un·dews·tree
infection infection ⓕ un·fek·syon
inflammation inflammation ⓕ un·fla·ma·syon
influence influence ⓕ un·flew·ons
influenza grippe ⓕ greep
information renseignements ⓜ pl ron·sen·yer·mon
ingredient ingrédient ⓜ ung·gray·dyon
inject injecter un·zhek·tay
injection piqûre ⓕ pee·kewr
injured blessé(e) ⓜ/ⓕ blay·say
injury blessure ⓕ blay·sewr
innocent innocent(e) ⓜ/ⓕ ee·no·son(t)
insect insecte ⓜ un·sekt
inside dedans der·don
insurance assurance ⓕ a·sew·rons
insure assurer a·sew·ray
intelligent intelligent(e) ⓜ/ⓕ un·tay·lee·zhon(t)
interesting intéressant(e) ⓜ/ⓕ un·tay·ray·son(t)
intermission entracte ⓜ on·trakt
international international(e) ⓜ/ⓕ un·tair·na·syo·nal
internet internet ⓜ un·tair·net
interpreter interprète ⓜ/ⓕ un·tair·pret
intersection carrefour ⓜ kar·foor
interview entrevue ⓕ on·trer·vew
intimate intime un·teem
into dans don
introduce (people) présenter pray·zon·tay
invite inviter un·vee·tay
Ireland Irlande ⓕ eer·lond
iron (clothes) repasser rer·pa·say
iron (for clothes) fer à repasser ⓜ fair a rer·pa·say
island île ⓕ eel
IT informatique ⓕ un·for·ma·teek
Italy Italie ⓕ ee·ta·lee
itch démangeaison ⓕ day·mon·zhay·zon
itemised détaillé(e) ⓜ/ⓕ day·ta·yay
itinerary itinéraire ⓜ ee·tee·nay·rair
IUD stérilet ⓜ stay·ree·lay

J

jacket veste ⓕ vest
jail prison ⓕ pree·zon
January janvier ⓜ zhon·vyay
Japan Japon ⓜ zha·pon
jar (jam) pot ⓜ po
jaw mâchoire ⓕ ma·shwar
jealous jaloux/jalouse ⓜ/ⓕ zha·loo/zha·looz
jeans jean ⓜ zheen
jeep jeep ⓕ zheep
jet lag fatigue due au décalage horaire ⓕ fa·teeg dew o day·ka·lazh o·rair
jewellery bijoux ⓜ pl bee·zhoo
Jewish juif/juive ⓜ/ⓕ zhweef/zhweev
job travail ⓜ tra·vai
jockey jockey ⓜ zho·kay
jogging jogging ⓜ zho·geeng
join joindre zhwun·drer
joke plaisanterie ⓕ play·zon·tree
journalist journaliste ⓜ/ⓕ zhoor·na·leest
journey voyage ⓜ vwa·yazh
joy joie ⓕ zhwa
judge juge ⓜ zhewzh
July juillet ⓜ zhwee·yay
jump sauter so·tay
jumper (sweater) pull ⓜ pewl
jumper leads câbles de démarrage ⓜ pl ka·bler der day·ma·razh
June juin ⓜ zhwun
justice justice ⓕ zhew·stees

K

kerb bord du trottoir ⓜ bor dew tro·twar
key clé ⓕ klay
keyboard clavier ⓜ kla·vyay
kick (person) donner un coup de pied à do·nay ung koo der pyay a
kick (football) donner un coup de pied dans do·nay ung koo der pyay don
kid (child) gamin/gamine ⓜ/ⓕ ga·mun/ga·meen
kill tuer tew·way
kilo kilo ⓜ kee·lo
kilogram kilogramme ⓜ kee·lo·gram
kilometre kilomètre ⓜ kee·lo·may·trer
kind (nice) gentil/gentille ⓜ/ⓕ zhon·tee
kind (type) genre ⓜ zhon·rer
kindergarten jardin d'enfants ⓜ zhar·dun don·fon
king roi ⓜ rwa
kingdom royaume ⓜ rwa·yom
kiosk kiosque ⓜ kyosk
kiss baiser ⓜ bay·zay
kiss embrasser om·bra·say
kitchen cuisine ⓕ kwee·zeen
kitten chaton ⓜ sha·ton
knee genou ⓜ zhnoo
kneel se mettre à genoux ser may·trer a zher·noo
knife couteau ⓜ koo·to
knitting tricot ⓜ tree·ko
know savoir sa·vwar
know (be familiar with) connaître ko·nay·trer
kosher casher/kascher ka·shair

L

labourer manoeuvre ⓜ ma·ner·vrer
lace dentelle ⓕ don·tel
lake lac ⓜ lak
lamp lampe ⓕ lomp
land terre ⓕ tair
landlady propriétaire ⓕ prop·ryay·tair
landlord propriétaire ⓜ prop·ryay·tair
lane (city) ruelle ⓕ rwel
lane (country) chemin ⓜ shmun
language langue ⓕ long
laptop ordinateur ⓜ or·dee·na·ter
large grand(e) ⓜ/ⓕ gron(d)
last (previous) dernier/dernière ⓜ/ⓕ dair·nyay/dair·nyair
late en retard on rer·tar
later plus tard plew·tar
laugh rire reer
launderette laverie ⓕ lav·ree

L ENGLISH – FRENCH

laundry (clothes) linge ⓜ lunzh
laundry (place) blanchisserie ⓕ blon·shees·ree
law loi ⓕ lwa
law (study, professsion) droit ⓜ drwa
lawyer avocat(e) ⓜ/ⓕ a·vo·ka(t)
laxative laxatif ⓜ lak·sa·teef
lazy paresseux/paresseuse ⓜ/ⓕ pa·ray·ser/pa·ray·serz
leader chef ⓜ shef
leaf feuille ⓕ fer·yee
learn apprendre a·pron·drer
lease bail ⓜ ba·yer
lease louer à bail loo·way a ba·yer
least moins ⓜ mwun
leather cuir ⓜ kweer
leave partir par·teer
leave (something) laisser lay·say
lecturer professeur (à l'université) ⓜ pro·fay·ser (a lew·nee·vair·see·tay)
ledge rebord ⓜ rer·bor
left (direction) à gauche a gosh
left luggage (office) consigne ⓕ kon·see·nyer
left-wing de gauche der gosh
leg jambe ⓕ zhomb
legal légal(e) ⓜ/ⓕ lay·gal
legislation législation ⓕ lay·zhee·sla·syon
length longueur ⓕ long·ger
lens objectif ⓜ ob·zhek·teef
lesbian lesbienne ⓕ les·byen
less moins mwun
less moins de mwun der
letter lettre ⓕ lay·trer
level niveau ⓜ nee·vo
liar menteur/menteuse ⓜ/ⓕ mon·ter/mon·terz
library bibliothèque ⓕ bee·blee·o·tek
lice poux ⓜ pl poo
licence plate number plaque d'immatriculation ⓕ plak dee·ma·tree·kew·la·syon
lie mensonge ⓜ mon·sonzh
lie (not stand) s'allonger sa·lon·zhay
lie (tell lies) mentir mon·teer
life vie ⓕ vee
life jacket gilet de sauvetage ⓜ zhee·lay der sov·tazh
lift (arm) lever ler·vay
lift (elevator) ascenseur ⓜ a·son·ser
lift (something heavy) soulever sool·vay
light lumière ⓕ lew·myair
light (on vehicle) phare ⓜ far
light (not heavy) léger/légère ⓜ/ⓕ lay·zhay/lay·zhair
light (of colour) clair(e) ⓜ/ⓕ klair
light bulb ampoule ⓕ om·pool
light meter posemètre ⓜ poz·may·trer
lighter briquet ⓜ bree·kay
lights (on car) phares ⓜ pl far
like (as) comme kom
like (love) aimer ay·may
line ligne ⓕ lee·nyer
linen (material) lin ⓜ lun
linen (sheets etc) linge ⓜ lunzh
lingerie lingerie ⓕ lun·zhree
lip lèvre ⓕ lay·vrer
lip balm pommade pour les lèvres ⓕ po·mad poor lay lay·vrer
lipstick rouge à lèvres ⓜ roozh a lay·vrer
liquor store magasin de vins et spiritueux ⓜ ma·ga·zun der vun ay spee·ree·twer
listen (to) écouter ay·koo·tay
little petit(e) ⓜ/ⓕ per·tee(t)
little bit peu ⓜ per
live vivre vee·vrer
live (in a place) habiter a·bee·tay
liver foie ⓜ fwa
lizard lézard ⓜ lay·zar
local local(e) ⓜ/ⓕ lo·kal
lock fermer à clé fair·may a klay
lock serrure ⓕ say·rewr
locked fermé(e) à clé ⓜ/ⓕ fair·may a klay
long long/longue ⓜ/ⓕ long
long-distance (flight) long-courrier long·koo·ryay
look regarder rer·gar·day
look after s'occuper de so·kew·pay der
look at regarder rer·gar·day
look for chercher shair·shay

look out faire attention fair a·ton·syon
loose (clothes) ample om·pler
loose change petite monnaie ⓕ per·teet mo·nay
lorry camion ⓜ ka·myon
lose perdre pair·drer
loser perdant(e) ⓜ/ⓕ pair·don(t)
loss perte ⓕ pairt
lost perdu(e) ⓜ/ⓕ pair·dew
lost property office bureau des objets trouvés ⓜ bew·ro day zob·zhay troo·vay
loud fort(e) ⓜ/ⓕ for(t)
love amour a·moor
love aimer ay·may
lover amant(e) ⓜ/ⓕ a·mon(t)
low bas/basse ⓜ/ⓕ ba(s)
loyal loyal(e) ⓜ/ⓕ lwa·yal
lubricant lubrifiant ⓜ lew·bree·fyon
luck chance ⓕ shons
lucky (to be) avoir de la chance a·vwar der la shons
luggage bagages ⓜ pl ba·gazh
luggage lockers consigne automatique ⓕ kon·see·nyer o·to·ma·teek
luggage tag étiquette ⓕ ay·tee·ket
lump grosseur ⓕ gro·ser
lunch déjeuner ⓜ day·zher·nay
lung poumon ⓜ poo·mon
luxury luxe ⓜ lewks
luxury de luxe der lewks

M

machine machine ⓕ ma·sheen
mad (angry) fâché(e) ⓜ/ⓕ fa·shay
mad (crazy) fou/folle ⓜ/ⓕ foo/fol
made of (cotton, wood etc) en on
magazine magazine ⓜ ma·ga·zeen
magician magicien/magicienne ⓜ/ⓕ ma·zhee·syun/ma·zhees·yen
mail (letters) courrier ⓜ koo·ryay
mail (postal system) poste ⓕ post
mailbox boîte aux lettres ⓕ bwat o ay·trer
main principal(e) ⓜ/ⓕ prun·see·pal
main road grande route ⓕ grond root
main square place centrale ⓕ plas son·tral
majority majorité ⓕ ma·zho·ree·tay
make faire fair
make-up maquillage ⓜ ma·kee·yazh
mammogram mammographie ⓕ ma·mo·gra·fee
man homme ⓜ om
manage (business) diriger dee·ree·zhay
manager directeur/directrice ⓜ/ⓕ dee·rek·ter/dee·rek·trees
manager (restaurant, hotel) gérant(e) ⓜ/ⓕ zhay·ron(t)
manner façon ⓕ fa·son
manual ⓜ/ⓕ manuel ma·nwel
manual worker ouvrier/ouvrière ⓜ/ⓕ oo·vree·yay/oo·vree·yair
many beaucoup de bo·koo der
map (of country) carte ⓕ kart
map (of town) plan ⓜ plon
March mars ⓜ mars
marijuana marihuana ⓕ ma·ree·wa·na
marital status situation familiale ⓕ see·twa·syon fa·mee·lyal
market marché ⓜ mar·shay
marriage mariage ⓜ ma·ryazh
married marié(e) ⓜ/ⓕ ma·ryay
marry épouser ay·poo·zay
martial arts arts martiaux ⓜ pl ar mar·syo
mass (Catholic) messe ⓕ mes
massage massage ⓜ ma·sazh
massage masser ma·say
masseur/masseuse masseur/masseuse ⓜ/ⓕ ma·ser/ma·serz
mat petit tapis ⓜ per·tee ta·pee
match (sports) match ⓜ matsh
matches (for lighting) allumettes ⓕ pl a·lew·met
material matériel ⓜ ma·tay·ryel
mattress matelas ⓜ mat·la
May mai ⓜ may
maybe peut-être per·tay·trer
mayor maire ⓜ mair
me moi mwa
meal repas ⓜ rer·pa

measles rougeole ⓕ roo·zhol
meat viande ⓕ vyond
mechanic mécanicien/ mécanicienne ⓜ/ⓕ may·ka·nee·syun/ may·ka·nee·syen
media médias ⓜ pl may·dya
medicine médecine ⓕ med·seen
medicine (medication) médicament ⓜ may·dee·ka·mon
meditation méditation ⓕ may·dee·ta·syon
meet rencontrer ron·kon·tray
member membre ⓜ mom·brer
memory (ability to remember) mémoire ⓕ may·mwar
memory (recollection) souvenir ⓜ soov·neer
menstruation menstruation ⓕ mon·strew·a·syon
menu carte kart
message message ⓜ may·sazh
messy en désordre on day·zor·drer
metal métal ⓜ may·tal
metre mètre ⓜ may·trer
metro station station de métro ⓕ sta·syon der may·tro
microwave (oven) four à micro-ondes ⓜ foor a mee·kro·ond
midday/noon midi mee·dee
midnight minuit mee·nwee
migraine migraine ⓕ mee·gren
military militaire mee·lee·tair
military service service militaire ⓜ sair·vees mee·lee·tair
milk lait ⓜ lay
millennium millénaire ⓜ mee·lay·nair
millimetre millimètre ⓜ mee·lee·may·trer
million million ⓜ mee·lyon
mind esprit ⓜ ay·spree
mineral water eau minérale ⓕ o mee·nay·ral
minority minorité ⓕ mee·no·ree·tay
minute minute ⓕ mee·newt
mirror miroir ⓜ mee·rwar
miscarriage (to have a) faire une fausse couche fair ewn fos koosh
miss manquer mong·kay
mistake erreur ⓕ ay·rer
mix mélanger may·lon·zhay
mix up (confuse) confondre kon·fon·drer
mobile phone téléphone portable ⓜ tay·lay·fon por·ta·bler
modem modem ⓜ mo·dem
modern moderne mo·dairn
moisturiser crème hydratante ⓕ krem ee·dra·tont
mom/mum maman ⓕ ma·mon
monarchy monarchie ⓕ mo·nar·shee
monastery monastère ⓜ mo·na·stair
Monday lundi ⓜ lun·dee
money argent ⓜ ar·zhon
monkey singe ⓜ sunzh
month mois ⓜ mwa
monument monument ⓜ mo·new·mon
more plus de plews der
more plus plew
morning matin ⓜ ma·tun
morning sickness nausées matinales ⓕ no·zay ma·tee·nal
mosque mosquée ⓕ mo·skay
mosquito moustique ⓜ moo·steek
mosquito coil allume-feu anti-moustiques ⓜ a·lewm·fer on·tee·moo·steek
mosquito net moustiquaire ⓕ moo·stee·kair
most plus ⓜ plews
motel motel ⓜ mo·tel
mother mère ⓕ mair
mother-in-law belle-mère ⓕ bel·mair
motorboat canot automobile ⓜ ka·no o·to·mo·beel
motorcycle moto ⓕ mo·to
motorway (tollway) autoroute ⓕ o·to·root
mountain montagne ⓕ mon·ta·nyer
mountain bike vélo tout terrain (VTT) ⓜ vay·lo too tay·run (vay·tay·tay)
mountain path chemin de montagne ⓜ shmun der mon·ta·nyer

mountain range chaîne de montagnes Ⓕ shen der mon·ta·nyer
mountaineering alpinisme Ⓜ al·pee·nee·smer
mouse souris Ⓕ soo·ree
mouth bouche Ⓕ boosh
move bouger boo·zhay
movie film Ⓜ feelm
Miss Mademoiselle mad·mwa·zel
Mr Monsieur mer·syer
Mrs/Ms Madame ma·dam
mud boue Ⓕ boo
mum maman Ⓕ ma·mon
muscle muscle Ⓜ mews·kler
museum musée Ⓜ mew·zay
music musique Ⓕ mew·zeek
music shop disquaire Ⓜ dee·skair
musician musicien/musicienne Ⓜ/Ⓕ mew·zees·yun/mew·zees·yen
Muslim musulman(e) Ⓜ/Ⓕ mew·zewl·mon/mew·zewl·man
my mon/ma/mes Ⓜ/Ⓕ/pl mon/ma/may

N

nail clippers coupe-ongles Ⓜ koop·ong·gler
name nom Ⓜ nom
napkin serviette Ⓕ sair·vyet
nappy couche Ⓕ koosh
narcotic stupéfiant Ⓜ stew·pay·fyon
national park parc national Ⓜ park na·syo·nal
nationality nationalité Ⓕ na·syo·na·lee·tay
nature nature Ⓕ na·tewr
naturopath naturopathe Ⓜ/Ⓕ na·tew·ro·pat
nausea nausée Ⓕ no·zay
near près de pray der
nearby tout près too pray
nearest le/la plus proche Ⓜ/Ⓕ ler/la plew prosh
necessary nécessaire nay·say·sair
necklace collier Ⓜ ko·lyay
need avoir besoin de a·vwar ber·zwun de
needle aiguille Ⓕ ay·gwee·yer
neither ni nee
net filet Ⓜ fee·lay
Netherlands Pays-Bas Ⓜ pl pay·ee·ba
network réseau Ⓜ ray·zo
never jamais zha·may
new nouveau/nouvelle Ⓜ/Ⓕ noo·vo/noo·vel
New Year's Day jour de l'An Ⓜ zhoor der lon
New Year's Eve Saint-Sylvestre Ⓕ sun·seel·ves·trer
New Zealand Nouvelle-Zélande Ⓕ noo·vel·zay·lond
news les nouvelles lay noo·vel
news (on TV etc) les actualités lay zak·twa·lee·tay
newsagent marchand de journaux Ⓜ mar·shon der zhoor·no
newspaper journal Ⓜ zhoor·nal
next (month) prochain(e) Ⓜ/Ⓕ pro·shun/pro·shen
next to ... à côté de ... a ko·tay der
nice (kind) gentil/gentille Ⓜ/Ⓕ zhon·tee/zhon·tee·yer
nice (pleasant) agréable a·gray·a·bler
nickname surnom Ⓜ sewr·nom
night nuit Ⓕ nwee
night out soirée Ⓕ swa·ray
nightclub boîte Ⓕ bwat
nine neuf nerf
no non non
no vacancy complet kom·play
noisy bruyant(e) Ⓜ/Ⓕ brew·yon(t)
nondirect non-direct non·dee·rekt
none aucun(e) Ⓜ/Ⓕ o·kun/o·kewn
nonsmoking non-fumeur non·few·mer
noon midi mee·dee
north nord Ⓜ nor
northern hemisphere hémisphère nord Ⓜ ay·mees·fair nor
nose nez Ⓜ nay
not bad pas mal pa mal
not yet pas encore pa zong·kor
notebook carnet Ⓜ kar·nay
nothing rien ryun
novel roman Ⓜ ro·mon

now maintenant mun·ter·non
nuclear energy énergie nucléaire ⓕ ay·nair·zhee new·klay·air
nuclear power puissance nucléaire ⓕ pwee·sons new·klay·air
nuclear test essai nucléaire ⓜ ay·say new·klay·air
nuclear waste déchets nucléaires ⓜ day·shay new·klay·air
number numéro ⓜ new·may·ro
nun religieuse ⓕ rer·lee·zhyerz
nurse infirmier/infirmière ⓜ/ⓕ un·feer·myay/un·feer·myair

O

obtain obtenir op·ter·neer
obvious évident(e) ⓜ/ⓕ ay·vee·don(t)
occupation occupation ⓕ o·kew·pa·syon
ocean océan ⓜ o·say·on
off (meat) mauvais(e) ⓜ/ⓕ mo·vay(z)
offence délit ⓜ day·lee
office bureau ⓜ bew·ro
office worker employé(e) de bureau ⓜ/ⓕ om·plwa·yay der bew·ro
officer officier ⓜ o·fees·yay
officer (police) agent de police ⓜ a·zhon der po·lees
offside (sport) hors jeu or·zher
often souvent soo·von
oil huile ⓕ weel
oil (petrol) pétrole ⓜ pay·trol
old vieux/vieille ⓜ/ⓕ vyer/vyay
Olympic Games Les Jeux Olympiques lay zher zo·lum·peek
on sur sewr
on strike en grève ong grev
on the corner au coin o kwun
on time à l'heure a ler
once une fois ewn fwa
one un(e) ⓜ/ⓕ un/ewn
one-way (ticket) (billet) simple (bee·yay) sum·pler
only seul(e) ⓜ/ⓕ serl
open ouvert(e) ⓜ/ⓕ oo·vair(t)
open ouvrir oo·vreer
opening hours heures d'ouverture ⓕ pl lay zer doo·vair·tewr
opera opéra ⓜ o·pay·ra
operation opération ⓕ o·pay·ra·syon
operator opérateur/opératrice ⓜ/ⓕ o·pay·ra·ter/o·pay·ra·trees
opinion avis ⓜ a·vee
opponent adversaire ⓜ/ⓕ ad·vair·sair
opportunity occasion ⓕ o·ka·zyon
opposite en face de on fas der
or ou oo
orange (colour) orange o·ronzh
order ordre ⓜ or·drer
order ordonner or·do·nay
ordinary ordinaire or·dee·nair
organisation organisation ⓕ or·ga·nee·za·syon
organise organiser or·ga·nee·zay
orgasm orgasme ⓜ or·gas·mer
original original(e) ⓜ/ⓕ o·ree·zhee·nal
other autre o·trer
our notre no·trer
out of order hors service or sair·vees
outside dehors der·or
oven four ⓜ foor
over (above) par-dessus par·der·sew
over (finished) fini(e) ⓜ/ⓕ fee·nee
overdose overdose ⓕ o·vair·doz
overnight pendant la nuit pon·don la nwee
overseas outre-mer oo·trer·mair
owe devoir der·vwar
owner propriétaire ⓜ/ⓕ pro·pree·ay·tair
ox bœuf ⓜ berf
oxygen oxygène ⓜ ok·see·zhen
ozone layer couche d'ozone ⓕ koosh do·zon

P

pacemaker pacemaker ⓜ pes·may·ke
pacifier (dummy) tétine ⓕ tay·teen

package paquet ⓜ pa·kay
packet (general) paquet ⓜ pa·kay
padlock cadenas ⓜ kad·na
page page ⓕ pazh
pain douleur ⓕ doo·ler
painful douloureux/douloureuse ⓜ/ⓕ doo·loo·rer/doo·loo·rerz
painkiller analgésique ⓜ a·nal·zhay·zeek
painter peintre ⓜ pun·trer
painting (a work) tableau ⓜ ta·blo
painting (the art) peinture ⓕ pun·tewr
pair (couple) paire ⓕ pair
palace palais ⓜ pa·lay
pan casserole ⓕ kas·rol
panties slip ⓜ sleep
pants (trousers) pantalon ⓜ pon·ta·lon
pants (underpants) slip ⓜ sleep
panty liners protège-slips ⓜ pl pro·tezh·sleep
pantyhose collant ⓜ ko·lon
pap smear frottis ⓜ fro·tee
paper papier ⓜ pa·pyay
paperwork paperasserie ⓕ pa·pras·ree
parade (ceremony) parade ⓕ pa·rad
paraplegic paraplégique pa·ra·play·zheek
parcel colis ⓜ ko·lee
parents parents ⓜ pl pa·ron
park parc ⓜ park
park (a car) garer (une voiture) ga·ray (ewn vwa·tewr)
part partie ⓕ par·tee
participate participer par·tee·see·pay
particular particulier/particulière ⓜ/ⓕ par·tee·kew·lyay/par·tee·kew·lyair
part-time à temps partiel a tom par·syel
party (night out) soirée ⓕ swa·ray
party (politics) parti ⓜ par·tee
pass passer pa·say
pass (football) passe ⓕ pas
passenger voyageur/voyageuse ⓜ/ⓕ vwa·ya·zher/vwa·ya·zherz
passport passeport ⓜ pas·por
passport number numéro de passeport ⓜ new·may·ro der pas·por
past passé ⓜ pa·say
path chemin ⓜ shmun
pay payer pay·yay
payment paiement ⓜ pay·mon
peace paix ⓕ pay
peak cime ⓕ seem
pedal pédale ⓕ pay·dal
pedestrian piéton ⓜ pyay·ton
pen (ballpoint) stylo ⓜ stee·lo
pencil crayon ⓜ kray·yon
penicillin pénicilline ⓕ pay·nee·see·leen
penis pénis ⓜ pay·nees
penknife canif ⓜ ka·neef
pensioner retraité(e) ⓜ/ⓕ rer·tray·tay
people gens ⓜ pl zhon
per (day) par par
percent pour cent poor son
perfect parfait(e) ⓜ/ⓕ par·fay(t)
performance spectacle ⓜ spek·ta·kler
perfume parfum ⓜ par·fum
period pain règles douloureuses ⓕ pl ray·gler doo·loo·rerz
permanent permanent(e) ⓜ/ⓕ pair·ma·non(t)
permission permission ⓕ pair·mee·syon
permit permis ⓜ pair·mee
permit permettre pair·may·trer
person personne ⓕ pair·son
personal personnel(le) ⓜ/ⓕ pair·so·nel
personality personnalité ⓕ pair·so·na·lee·tay
pet animal familier ⓜ a·nee·mal fa·mee·lyay
petition pétition ⓕ pay·tees·yon
petrol essence ⓕ ay·sons
petrol station station-service ⓕ sta·syon·sair·vees
pharmacy pharmacie ⓕ far·ma·see
phone book annuaire ⓜ an·wair

phone box cabine téléphonique ⓕ ka·been tay·lay·fo·neek
phone card télécarte ⓕ tay·lay·kart
photo photo ⓕ fo·to
photographer photographe ⓜ/ⓕ fo·to·graf
photography photographie ⓕ fo·to·gra·fee
phrase expression ⓕ ek·spray·syon
phrasebook recueil d'expressions ⓜ rer·ker·yer dek·spray·syon
physiotherapist kinésithérapeute ⓜ&ⓕ kee·nay·zee·tay·ra·pert
physiotherapy kinésithérapie ⓕ kee·nay·zee·tay·ra·pee
pick (choose) choisir shwa·zeer
pick up (something) ramasser ra·ma·say
picnic pique-nique ⓜ peek·neek
picture image ⓕ ee·mazh
piece morceau ⓜ mor·so
pig cochon ⓜ ko·shon
pill pilule ⓕ pee·lewl
pillow oreiller ⓜ o·ray·yay
pillowcase taie d'oreiller ⓕ tay do·ray·yay
pin épingle ⓕ ay·pung·gler
pink rose roz
pipe pipe ⓕ peep
place lieu ⓜ lyer
place of birth lieu de naissance ⓜ lyer der nay·sons
plane avion ⓜ a·vyon
planet planète ⓕ pla·net
plastic plastique ⓜ plas·teek
plate assiette ⓕ a·syet
platform quai ⓜ kay
play (cards etc) jouer zhoo·ay
play (football etc) jouer au zhoo·ay o
play (guitar etc) jouer de zhoo·ay der
play (theatre) pièce de théâtre ⓕ pyes der tay·a·trer
playground terrain de jeux ⓜ tay·run der zher
plenty abondance ⓕ a·bon·dons
plenty beaucoup de bo·koo der
plug (bath) bonde ⓕ bond
plug (electricity) prise ⓕ preez
pocket poche ⓕ posh
poetry poésie ⓕ po·ay·zee
point pointe ⓕ pwunt
point indiquer un·dee·kay
poisonous venimeux/venimeuse ⓜ/ⓕ ver·nee·mer/ver·nee·merz
police police ⓕ po·lees
police car voiture de police ⓕ vwa·tewr der po·lees
police officer (in city) policier ⓜ po·lee·syay
police officer (in country) gendarme ⓜ zhon·darm
police station commissariat ⓜ ko·mee·sar·ya
policy politique ⓕ po·lee·teek
politician homme/femme politique ⓜ/ⓕ om/fum po·lee·teek
politics politique ⓕ po·lee·teek
pollen pollen ⓜ po·len
pollution pollution ⓕ po·lew·syon
pond étang ⓜ ay·tong
pool (game) billard américain ⓜ bee·yar a·may·ree·kun
pool (swimming) piscine ⓕ pee·seen
poor pauvre po·vrer
popular populaire po·pew·lair
port port ⓜ por
positive positif/positive ⓜ/ⓕ po·zee·teef/po·zee·teev
possible possible po·see·bler
post code code postal ⓜ kod pos·tal
post office bureau de poste ⓜ bew·ro der post
postage tarifs postaux ⓜ pl ta·reef pos·to
postcard carte postale ⓕ kart pos·tal
postman facteur ⓜ fak·ter
pot (ceramics) pot ⓜ po
pottery poterie ⓕ po·tree
pound (money, weight) livre ⓕ leev·re
poverty pauvreté ⓕ po·vrer·tay
power pouvoir ⓜ poo·vwar
practical pratique pra·teek
practise pratiquer pra·tee·kay

prayer prière ⓕ pree·yair
prefer préférer pray·fay·ray
pregnancy test kit test de grossesse ⓜ test der gro·ses
pregnant enceinte on·sunt
premenstrual tension syndrome prémenstruel ⓜ sun·drom pray·mon·strwel
prepare préparer pray·pa·ray
prescription ordonnance ⓕ or·do·nons
present (gift) cadeau ⓜ ka·do
present (time) présent ⓜ pray·zon
president président ⓜ pray·zee·don
pressure pression ⓕ pray·syon
pretend faire semblant fair som·blon
pretty joli(e) ⓜ/ⓕ zho·lee
prevent empêcher om·pay·shay
previous précédent(e) ⓜ/ⓕ pray·say·don(t)
price prix ⓜ pree
priest prêtre ⓜ pray·trer
prime minister premier ministre ⓜ prer·myay mee·nee·strer
printer (computer) imprimante ⓕ um·pree·mont
prison prison ⓕ pree·zon
prisoner prisonnier/prisonnière ⓜ/ⓕ pree·zo·nyay/pree·zo·nyair
private privé(e) ⓜ/ⓕ pree·vay
private hospital clinique privée ⓕ klee·neek pree·vay
probable probable pro·ba·bler
problem problème ⓜ pro·blem
produce produire pro·dweer
professional professionnel(le) ⓜ/ⓕ pro·fay·syo·nel
profit bénéfice ⓜ bay·nay·fees
programme programme ⓜ pro·gram
projector projecteur ⓜ pro·zhek·ter
promise promesse ⓕ pro·mes
promise promettre pro·may·trer
promote promouvoir pro·moo·vwar
prostitute prostituée ⓕ pro·stee·tway
protect protéger pro·tay·zhay
protected (species) protégé(e) ⓜ/ⓕ pro·tay·zhay
protection protection ⓕ pro·tek·syon
protest manif(estation) ⓕ ma·neef(ay·sta·syon)
protest manifester ma·nee·fay·stay
provisions provisions ⓕ pl pro·vee·zyon
psychotherapy psychothérapie ⓕ psee·ko·tay·ra·pee
pub (bar) bar ⓜ bar
public public ⓜ pewb·leek
public telephone téléphone public ⓜ tay·lay·fon pewb·leek
public toilet toilettes ⓕ pl twa·let
pull tirer tee·ray
pump pompe ⓕ pomp
puncture crevaison ⓕ krer·vay·zon
punish punir pew·neer
puppy chiot ⓜ shyo
pure pur(e) ⓜ/ⓕ pewr
purple violet(te) ⓜ/ⓕ vyo·lay(·let)
purpose objet ⓜ ob·zhay
purse porte-monnaie ⓜ port·mo·nay
push pousser poo·say
pushchair poussette ⓕ poo·set
put mettre may·trer

Q

qualification qualification ⓕ ka·lee·fee·ka·syon
quality qualité ⓕ ka·lee·tay
quantity quantité ⓕ kon·tee·tay
quarantine quarantaine ⓕ ka·ron·ten
quarrel dispute ⓕ dees·pewt
quarter quart ⓜ kar
queen reine ⓕ ren
question question ⓕ kay·styon
queue queue ⓕ ker
quick rapide ra·peed
quiet tranquille trong·keel
quit quitter kee·tay

R

rabbit lapin ⓜ la·pun
race race ⓕ ras
race (sport) course ⓕ koors

racetrack champ de courses ⓜ shon der koors
racism racisme ⓜ ra·sees·mer
racquet raquette ⓕ ra·ket
radiator radiateur ⓜ ra·dya·ter
radical radical(e) ⓜ/ⓕ ra·dee·kal
radio radio ⓕ ra·dyo
rail garde-fou ⓜ gard·foo
railway chemin de fer ⓜ shmun der fair
railway station gare ⓕ gar
rain pluie ⓕ plwee
rain pleuvoir pler·vwar
raincoat imperméable um·pair·may·abler
raise (lift) soulever sool·vay
rape violer vyo·lay
rare rare rar
rash rougeur ⓕ roo·zher
rat rat ⓜ ra
rave rave ⓕ raiv
raw cru(e) ⓜ/ⓕ krew
razor rasoir ⓜ ra·zwar
razor blade lame de rasoir ⓕ lam der ra·zwar
reach atteindre a·tun·drer
read lire leer
ready prêt(e) ⓜ/ⓕ pray/pret
real vrai(e) ⓜ/ⓕ vray
real estate agent agent immobilier ⓜ a·zhon ee·mo·bee·lyay
realise se rendre compte de ser ron·drer kont der
realistic réaliste ray·a·leest
reality réalité ⓕ ray·a·lee·tay
really vraiment vray·mon
rear (seat etc) arrière a·ryair
reason raison ⓕ ray·zon
receipt reçu ⓜ rer·sew
receive recevoir rer·ser·vwar
recently récemment ray·sa·mon
recognise reconnaître rer·ko·nay·trer
recommend recommander rer·ko·mon·day
record enregistrer on·rer·zhees·tray
record (music) disque ⓜ deesk
recording enregistrement ⓜ on·rer·zhees·trer·mon
recyclable recyclable rer·see·kla·bler
recycle recycler rer·see·klay
recycling recyclage ⓜ rer·see·klazh
red rouge roozh
reduce réduire ray·dweer
referee arbitre ⓜ ar·bee·trer
reference référence ⓕ ray·fay·rons
reflexology réflexologie ⓕ ray·flek·so·lo·zhee
refrigerator réfrigérateur ⓜ ray·free·zhay·ra·ter
refugee réfugié(e) ⓜ/ⓕ ray·few·zhyay
refund remboursement ⓜ rom·boor·ser·mon
refuse refuser rer·few·zay
region région ⓕ ray·zhyon
registered mail/post (by) en recommandé on rer·ko·mon·day
regular normal(e) ⓜ/ⓕ nor·mal
relationship relation ⓕ rer·la·syon
relax (rest) se reposer ser rer·po·zay
relevant pertinent(e) ⓜ/ⓕ pair·tee·non(t)
religion religion ⓕ rer·lee·zhyon
religious religieux/religieuse ⓜ/ⓕ rer·lee·zhyer/rer·lee·zhyerz
remember se souvenir ser soo·ver·neer
remote éloigné(e) ⓜ/ⓕ ay·lwa·nyay
remote control télécommande ⓕ tay·lay·ko·mond
rent louer loo·ay
repair réparer ray·pa·ray
reply répondre ray·pon·drer
represent représenter rer·pray·zon·tay
republic république ⓕ ray·pewb·leek
research recherches ⓕ pl rer·shairsh
reservation réservation ⓕ ray·zair·va·syon
response réponse ⓕ ray·pons
rest repos ⓜ rer·po
restaurant restaurant ⓜ res·to·ron
resumé CV ⓜ say·vay
retired retraité(e) ⓜ/ⓕ rer·tray·tay

return revenir rerv·neer
return (ticket) aller retour ⓜ a·lay rer·toor
review (article) critique ⓕ kree·teek
revolution révolution ⓕ ray·vo·lew·syon
rhythm rythme ⓜ reet·mer
rice riz ⓜ ree
rich (wealthy) riche reesh
ride promenade ⓕ prom·nad
ride (horse) monter à (cheval) mon·tay a (shval)
right (direction) à droite a drwat
right (entitlement) droite ⓜ drwa
right (to be right) avoir raison a·vwar ray·zon
right-wing de droite der drwat
ring (of phone) sonner so·nay
ring (on finger) bague ⓕ bag
ring (shape) anneau ⓜ a·no
ring road (boulevard) périphérique (BP) ⓜ (bool·var) pay·ree·fay·reek (bay pay)
rip-off arnaque ⓕ ar·nak
risk risque ⓜ reesk
river rivière ⓕ ree·vyair
road route ⓕ root
road map carte routière ⓕ kart roo·tyair
rob (person) voler vo·lay
robbery vol ⓜ vol
rock rocher ⓜ ro·shay
rock climbing varappe ⓕ va·rap
rock group groupe de rock ⓜ groop der rok
rock music rock ⓜ rok
rollerblading roller ⓜ ro·lair
romantic romantique ro·mon·teek
roof toit ⓜ twa
room chambre ⓕ shom·brer
room number numéro de chambre ⓜ new·may·ro der shom·brer
rooster coq ⓜ kok
rope corde ⓕ kord
round rond(e) ⓜ/ⓕ ron(d)
roundabout (traffic) rond-point ⓜ rom·pwun
route itinéraire ⓜ ee·tee·nay·rair
rowing aviron ⓜ a·vee·ron
rubbish ordures ⓕ or·dewr
rubbish bin poubelle ⓕ poo·bel
rubbish dump décharge ⓕ day·sharzh
rude impoli(e) ⓜ/ⓕ um·po·lee
rug tapis ⓜ ta·pee
rugby rugby ⓜ rewg·bee
ruins ruines ⓕ pl rween
rules règles ⓕ ray·gler
run courir koo·reer
run out of manquer de mong·kay der

S

Sabbath sabbat ⓜ sa·ba
sad triste treest
saddle selle ⓕ sel
safe sans danger son don·zhay
safe coffre-fort ⓜ kof·rer·for
safe sex rapports sexuels protégés ⓜ pl ra·por seks·wel pro·tay·zhay
safety sécurité ⓕ say·kew·ree·tay
sail voile ⓕ vwal
sailing voile ⓕ vwal
saint saint(e) ⓜ/ⓕ sun(t)
salary salaire ⓜ sa·lair
sale vente ⓕ vont
sales tax taxe à la vente ⓕ taks a la vont
salt sel ⓜ sel
same même mem
sand sable ⓜ sa·bler
sandals sandales ⓕ son·dal
sanitary napkin serviette hygiénique ⓕ sair·vyet ee·zhyay·neek
satisfied satisfait(e) ⓜ/ⓕ sa·tees·fay/ sa·tees·fet
Saturday samedi ⓜ sam·dee
sauna sauna ⓜ so·na
save sauver so·vay
say dire deer
scared effrayé(e) ⓜ/ⓕ ay·fray·yay
scarf écharpe ⓕ ay·sharp
scenery paysage ⓜ pay·yee·zazh
school école ⓕ ay·kol
science science ⓕ syons

science fiction science-fiction ⓕ syons·feek·syon
scientist scientifique ⓜ/ⓕ syon·tee·feek
scissors ciseaux ⓜ pl see·zo
score score ⓜ skor
scoreboard tableau d'affichage ⓜ ta·blo da·fee·shazh
Scotland Ecosse ⓕ ay·kos
screen écran ⓜ ay·kron
script scénario ⓜ say·na·ryo
sculpture sculpture ⓕ skewl·tewr
sea mer ⓕ mair
seashell coquillage ⓜ ko·kee·yazh
seasick (to be) avoir le mal de mer a·vwar ler mal der mair
seaside bord de la mer ⓜ bor der la mair
season saison ⓕ say·zon
seat (place) place ⓕ plas
seatbelt ceinture de sécurité ⓕ sun·tewr der say·kew·ree·tay
second second(e) ⓜ/ⓕ skon/skond
second class de seconde classe der skond klas
second (clock) seconde ⓕ skond
secondhand d'occasion do·ka·zyon
secret secret ⓜ ser·kray
secretary secrétaire ⓜ/ⓕ ser·kray·tair
security sécurité ⓕ say·kew·ree·tay
see voir vwar
self service libre-service ⓜ lee·brer·sair·vees
self-employed indépendant(e) ⓜ/ⓕ un·day·pon·don(t)
selfish égoïste ay·go·eest
sell vendre von·drer
seminar séminaire ⓜ say·mee·nair
send envoyer on·vwa·yay
sensible raisonnable ray·zo·na·bler
sensual sensuel(le) ⓜ/ⓕ son·swel
separate séparé(e) ⓜ/ⓕ say·pa·ray
September septembre ⓜ sep·tom·brer
series série ⓕ say·ree
serious sérieux/sérieuse ⓜ/ⓕ say·ree·yer/say·ree·yerz
service service ⓜ sair·vees
service charge service ⓜ sair·vees
service station station-service ⓕ sta·syon·sair·vees
seven sept set
several plusieurs plew·zyer
sew coudre koo·drer
sex sexe ⓜ seks
sexism sexisme ⓜ sek·see·smer
sexist sexiste sek·seest
sexy sexy sek·see
shade ombre ⓕ om·brer
shadow ombre ⓕ om·brer
shake (something) agiter a·zhee·tay
shallow peu profond ⓜ per pro·fon(d)
shampoo shampooing ⓜ shom·pwung
shape forme ⓕ form
shape façonner fa·so·nay
share (a dorm etc) partager par·ta·zhay
share (with) partager (avec) par·ta·zhay (a·vek)
sharp (blade etc) tranchant(e) ⓜ/ⓕ tron·shon(t)
shave se raser ser ra·zay
shaving cream mousse à raser ⓕ moos a ra·zay
she elle el
sheep mouton ⓜ moo·ton
sheet (bed) drap ⓜ dra
sheet (of paper) feuille ⓕ fer·yee
shelf étagère ⓕ ay·ta·zhair
shelter abri ⓜ a·bree
ship navire ⓜ na·veer
shirt chemise ⓕ sher·meez
shoe chaussure ⓕ sho·sewr
shoe shop magasin de chaussures ⓜ ma·ga·zun der sho·sewr
shoot tirer tee·ray
shop magasin ⓜ ma·ga·zun
shop faire des courses fair day koors
shopping centre centre commercial ⓜ son·trer ko·mair·syal
short (height) court(e) ⓜ/ⓕ koor(t)

shortage manque ⓜ mongk
shorts short ⓜ short
shoulder épaule ⓕ ay·pol
shout crier kree·yay
show montrer mon·tray
show spectacle ⓜ spek·ta·kler
shower douche ⓕ doosh
shrine lieu saint ⓜ lyer sun
shut fermé(e) ⓜ/ⓕ fair·may
shy timide tee·meed
sick malade ma·lad
sickness maladie ⓕ ma·la·dee
side côté ⓜ ko·tay
sign signe ⓜ see·nyer
signature signature ⓕ see·nya·tewr
silk soie ⓕ swa
silver argent ⓜ ar·zhon
similar semblable som·bla·bler
simple simple sum·pler
since (May etc) depuis der·pwee
sing chanter shon·tay
Singapore Singapour sung·ga·poor
singer chanteur/chanteuse ⓜ/ⓕ shon·ter/shon·terz
single (person) célibataire say·lee·ba·tair
single room chambre pour une personne ⓕ shom·brer poor ewn pair·son
singlet maillot de corps ⓜ ma·yo der kor
sister sœur ⓕ ser
sit s'asseoir sa·swar
situation situation ⓕ see·twa·syon
six six sees
size (general) taille ⓕ tai
skateboarding skateboard ⓜ sket·bord
ski skier skee·yay
skiing ski ⓜ skee
skill compétence ⓕ kom·pay·tons
skin peau ⓕ po
skirt jupe ⓕ zhewp
skis skis ⓜ skee
sky ciel ⓜ syel
sleep sommeil ⓜ so·may
sleep dormir dor·meer
sleeping bag sac de couchage ⓜ sak der koo·shazh
sleeping car wagon-lit ⓜ va·gon·lee
sleeping pill somnifère ⓜ som·nee·fair
sleepy (to be sleepy) avoir sommeil a·vwar so·may
slice tranche ⓕ tronsh
slow lent(e) ⓜ/ⓕ lon(t)
slowly lentement lon·ter·mon
small petit(e) ⓜ/ⓕ per·tee/per·teet
smaller plus petit(e) ⓜ/ⓕ plew per·tee/·teet
smallest le plus petit/la plus petite ⓜ/ⓕ ler plew per·tee/la plew per·teet
smell odeur ⓕ o·der
smell sentir son·teer
smile sourire ⓜ soo·reer
smile sourire soo·reer
smoke fumée ⓕ few·may
smoke fumer few·may
snack casse-croûte ⓜ kas·kroot
snail escargot ⓜ es·kar·go
snake serpent ⓜ sair·pon
snorkel nager avec un tuba na·zhay a·vek un tew·ba
snow neige ⓕ nezh
snow neiger nay·zhay
snowboarding surf (des neiges) ⓜ serf (day nezh)
soap savon ⓜ sa·von
soccer foot(ball) ⓜ foot(bol)
social welfare sécurité sociale ⓕ say·kew·ree·tay so·syal
socialism socialisme ⓜ so·sya·lees·mer
socialist socialiste so·sya·leest
society societé ⓕ so·syay·tay
socks chaussettes ⓕ sho·set
soft doux/douce ⓜ/ⓕ doo/doos
software logiciel ⓜ lo·zhee·syel
soldier soldat ⓜ sol·da
solid solide so·leed
some quelques kel·ker
some du/de la/des ⓜ/ⓕ/pl dew/der la/day

someone quelqu'un kel·kun
something quelque chose kel·ker shoz
sometimes quelquefois kel·ker·fwa
son fils ⓜ fees
song chanson ⓕ shon·son
soon bientôt byun·to
sore douloureux/douloureuse ⓜ/ⓕ doo·loo·rer/doo·loo·rerz
south sud ⓜ sewd
southern hemisphere hémisphère sud ⓜ ay·mees·fair sewd
souvenir souvenir ⓜ soov·neer
souvenir shop magasin de souvenirs ⓜ ma·ga·zun der soov·neer
space espace ⓜ es·pas
Spain Espagne ⓕ es·pa·nyer
speak parler par·lay
special spécial(e) ⓜ/ⓕ spay·syal
specialist spécialiste ⓜ/ⓕ spay·sya·leest
speech discours ⓜ dees·koor
speed vitesse ⓕ vee·tes
speed limit limitation de vitesse ⓕ lee·mee·ta·syon der vee·tes
speedometer compteur (de vitesse) ⓜ kon·ter (der vee·tes)
spend (money) dépenser day·pon·say
spend (time) passer pa·say
spicy épicé(e) ⓜ/ⓕ ay·pee·say
spider araignée ⓕ a·ray·nyay
spine colonne vertébrale ⓕ ko·lon vair·tay·bral
spirit esprit ⓜ es·pree
spoon cuillère ⓕ kwee·yair
sport sport ⓜ spor
sports ground terrain de sport ⓜ tay·run der spor
sports store/shop magasin de sports ⓜ ma·ga·zun der spor
sportsperson sportif/sportive ⓜ/ⓕ spor·teef/spor·teev
sprain entorse ⓕ on·tors
spring (coil) ressort ⓜ rer·sor
spring (season) printemps ⓜ prun·tom
square (town) place ⓕ plas
stadium stade ⓜ stad
stage scène ⓕ sen
stairway escalier ⓜ es·ka·lyay
stale pas frais/fraîche ⓜ/ⓕ pa fray/fresh
stale (bread) rassis(e) ⓜ/ⓕ ra·see(z)
stamp timbre ⓜ tum·brer
stand-by ticket billet stand-by ⓜ bee·yay stond·bai
stars étoiles ⓕ ay·twal
start commencement ⓜ ko·mons·mon
start commencer ko·mon·say
station gare ⓕ gar
stationer's (shop) papeterie ⓕ pa·pet·ree
stay rester res·tay
steal voler vo·lay
steep raide red
step marche ⓕ marsh
stereo (system) chaîne hi-fi ⓕ shen ee·fee
stockings bas ⓜ ba
stolen volé(e) ⓜ/ⓕ vo·lay
stomach estomac ⓜ es·to·ma
stomachache (to have a) avoir mal au ventre a·vwar mal o von·trer
stone pierre ⓕ pyair
stop arrêt ⓜ a·ray
stop (doing) s'arrêter sa·ray·tay
stop (something, someone) arrêter a·ray·tay
storm orage ⓜ o·razh
story histoire ⓕ ees·twar
stove réchaud ⓜ ray·sho
straight droit(e) ⓜ/ⓕ drwa(t)
straight ahead tout droit too drwa
strange étrange ay·tronzh
stranger étranger/étrangère ⓜ/ⓕ ay·tron·zhay/ay·tron·zhair
stream ruisseau ⓜ rwee·so
street rue ⓕ rew
street market braderie ⓕ bra·dree
strike (go on strike) se mettre en grève ser may·trer ong grev
string ficelle ⓕ fee·sel
stroller poussette ⓕ poo·set

strong fort(e) ⓜ/ⓕ for(t)
student étudiant(e) ⓜ/ⓕ ay·tew·dyon(t)
studio atelier ⓜ a·ter·lyay
study étudier ay·tew·dyay
stupid stupide stew·peed
style style ⓜ steel
subtitles sous-titres ⓜ soo·tee·trer
suburb banlieue ⓕ bon·lyer
subway métro ⓜ may·tro
suffer souffrir soo·freer
suitcase valise ⓕ va·leez
summer été ⓜ ay·tay
sun soleil ⓜ so·lay
sunblock écran solaire total ⓜ ay·kron so·lair to·tal
sunburn coup de soleil ⓜ koo der so·lay
Sunday dimanche ⓜ dee·monsh
sunglasses lunettes de soleil ⓕ lew·net der so·lay
sunny ensoleillé(e) ⓜ/ⓕ on·so·lay·yay
sunrise lever du soleil ⓜ ler·vay dew so·lay
sunscreen écran solaire ⓜ ay·kron so·lair
sunset coucher du soleil ⓜ koo·shay dew so·lay
supermarket supermarché ⓜ sew·pair·mar·shay
superstition superstition ⓕ sew·pair·stee·syon
support supporter sew·por·tay
sure sûr(e) ⓜ/ⓕ sewr
surf surfer ser·fay
surface mail (land) voie de terre vwa der tair
surface mail (sea) voie maritime vwa ma·ree·teem
surfboard planche de surf ⓕ plonsh der serf
surname nom de famille ⓜ nom der fa·mee
surprise surprise ⓕ sewr·preez
survive survivre sewr·vee·vrer
sweater pull ⓜ pewl
Sweden Suède ⓕ swayd
sweet sucré(e) ⓜ/ⓕ sew·kray
swim nager na·zhay
swimming pool piscine ⓕ pee·seen
swimsuit maillot de bain ⓜ ma·yo der bun
Switzerland Suisse ⓕ swees
synagogue synagogue ⓕ see·na·gog
synthetic synthétique sun·tay·teek
syringe seringue ⓕ ser·rung

T

table table ⓕ ta·bler
table tennis tennis de table ⓜ tay·nees der ta·bler
tablecloth nappe ⓕ nap
tail queue ⓕ ker
tailor tailleur ⓜ ta·yer
take prendre pron·drer
take a photo prendre en photo pron·drer on fo·to
talk parler par·lay
talk conversation ⓕ kon·vair·sa·syon
talk (lecture) exposé ⓜ eks·po·zay
tall grand(e) ⓜ/ⓕ gron(d)
tampon tampon hygiénique ⓜ tom·pon ee·zhyay·neek
tanning lotion crème de bronzage ⓕ krem der bron·zazh
tap robinet ⓜ ro·bee·nay
tasty délicieux/délicieuse ⓜ/ⓕ day·lees·yer/day·lees·yerz
tax taxe ⓕ taks
taxi taxi ⓜ tak·see
taxi stand station de taxi ⓕ sta·syon der tak·see
teacher professeur ⓜ pro·fay·ser
team équipe ⓕ ay·keep
teaspoon petite cuillère ⓕ per·teet kwee·yair
technique technique ⓕ tek·neek
teeth dents ⓕ don
telegram télégramme ⓜ tay·lay·gram
telephone téléphone ⓜ tay·lay·fon
telephone téléphoner tay·lay·fo·nay
telephone box cabine téléphonique ⓕ ka·been tay·lay·fo·neek

telescope télescope ⓜ tay·lay·skop
television télé(vision) ⓕ tay·lay(vee·zyon)
tell dire deer
tell (a story) raconter ra·kon·tay
teller caissier/caissière ⓜ/ⓕ kay·syay/kay·syair
temperature (fever) température ⓕ tom·pay·ra·tewr
temperature (weather) température ⓕ tom·pay·ra·tewr
temple temple ⓜ tom·pler
ten dix dee(s)
tenant locataire ⓜ/ⓕ lo·ka·tair
tennis tennis ⓜ tay·nees
tennis court court de tennis ⓜ koor der tay·nees
tent tente ⓕ tont
tent pegs piquets de tente ⓜ pee·kay der tont
terrible affreux/affreuse ⓜ/ⓕ a·frer/a·frerz
terrorism terrorisme ⓜ tay·ro·rees·mer
test essai ⓜ ay·say
thank remercier rer·mair·syay
that ce/cette ⓜ/ⓕ ser/set
that (one) cela ser·la
theatre théâtre ⓜ tay·a·trer
their leur/leurs sg/pl ler
then (at the time) alors a·lor
then (next) puis pwee
there là la
therefore donc dongk
they ils/elles ⓜ/ⓕ eel/el
thick épais/épaisse ⓜ/ⓕ ay·pay/ay·pes
thief voleur/voleuse ⓜ/ⓕ vo·ler/vo·lerz
thin maigre may·grer
thing chose ⓕ shoz
think penser pon·say
third troisième trwa·zyem
thirsty (to be) avoir soif a·vwar swaf
this ce/cette ⓜ/ⓕ ser/set
this (one) ceci ser·see
three trois trwa
throat gorge ⓕ gorzh
throw jeter zher·tay
thrush (illness) muguet ⓜ mew·gay
Thursday jeudi ⓜ zher·dee
ticket billet ⓜ bee·yay
ticket collector contrôleur ⓜ kon·tro·ler
ticket machine distributeur de tickets ⓜ dee·stree·bew·ter der tee·kay
ticket office guichet ⓜ gee·shay
tide marée ⓕ ma·ray
tie (draw) match nul ⓜ matsh newl
tight étroit(e) ⓜ/ⓕ ay·trwa(t)
time heure ⓕ er
time difference décalage horaire ⓜ day·ka·lazh o·rair
time (general) temps ⓜ tom
timetable horaire ⓜ o·rair
tin (can) boîte ⓕ bwat
tin opener ouvre-boîte ⓜ oo·vrer·bwat
tiny minuscule mee·new·skewl
tip (gratuity) pourboire ⓜ poor·bwar
tire pneu ⓜ pner
tired fatigué(e) ⓜ/ⓕ fa·tee·gay
tissues mouchoirs en papier ⓜ pl moo·shwar om pa·pyay
to à a
toast pain grillé ⓜ pung gree·yay
toaster grille-pain ⓜ greey·pun
tobacco tabac ⓜ ta·ba
tobacconist bureau de tabac ⓜ bew·ro der ta·ba
today aujourd'hui o·zhoor·dwee
toe orteil ⓜ or·tay
together ensemble on·som·bler
toilet toilettes ⓕ pl twa·let
toilet paper papier hygiénique ⓜ pa·pyay ee·zhyay·neek
tomorrow demain der·mun
tomorrow afternoon demain après-midi der·mun a·pray·mee·dee
tomorrow evening demain soir der·mun swar
tomorrow morning demain matin der·mum ma·tun
tonight ce soir ser swar
too (expensive etc) trop tro
too much/many trop tro

too much (rain etc)/too many (people etc) trop de tro der
tooth dent ⓕ don
toothache mal de dents ⓜ a·vwar mal o don
toothbrush brosse à dents ⓕ bros a don
toothpaste dentifrice ⓜ don·tee·frees
toothpick cure-dent ⓜ kewr·don
torch (flashlight) lampe de poche ⓕ lomp der posh
touch toucher too·shay
touch (sense) toucher ⓜ too·shay
tour voyage ⓜ vwa·yazh
tourist touriste ⓜ/ⓕ too·reest
tourist office office de tourisme ⓜ o·fees·der too·rees·mer
tournament tournoi ⓜ toor·nwa
tow truck dépanneuse ⓕ day·pa·nerz
toward (direction) vers vair
toward (feelings) envers on·vair
towel serviette ⓕ sair·vyet
tower tour ⓕ toor
town ville ⓕ veel
toxic waste déchets toxiques ⓜ pl day·shay tok·seek
toy jouet ⓜ zhway
track (path) chemin (de randonnée) ⓜ sher·mun (der ron·do·nay)
track (sports) piste ⓕ peest
trade commerce ⓜ ko·mairs
traffic circulation ⓕ seer·kew·la·syon
traffic jam bouchon ⓜ boo·shon
traffic lights feux ⓜ fer
trail piste ⓕ peest
train train ⓜ trun
train station gare ⓕ gar
transfer transfert ⓜ trons·fair
transit lounge salle de transit ⓕ sal der tron·zeet
translate traduire tra·dweer
transport transport ⓜ trons·por
travel voyager vwa·ya·zhay
travel agency agence de voyage ⓕ a·zhons der vwa·yazh
travel sickness mal des transports ⓜ mal day trons·por
travellers cheque chèque de voyage ⓜ shek der vwa·yazh
treatment traitement ⓜ tret·mon
tree arbre ⓜ ar·brer
trek randonnée ⓜ ran·do·nay
trick ruse ⓕ rewz
trick tromper trom·pay
trip voyage ⓜ vwa·yazh
trolley chariot ⓜ shar·yo
trouble peine ⓕ pen
trousers pantalon ⓜ pon·ta·lon
truck camion ⓜ ka·myon
true vrai(e) ⓜ/ⓕ vray
trust faire confiance à fair kon·fyons a
trust confiance ⓕ kon·fyons
truth vérité ⓕ vay·ree·tay
try essayer ay·say·yay
T-shirt T-shirt ⓜ tee·shert
tube (tyre) chambre à air ⓕ shom·brer a air
Tuesday mardi ⓜ mar·dee
tune air ⓜ air
turn tourner toor·nay
TV télé ⓕ tay·lay
TV series série ⓕ say·ree
tweezers pince à épiler ⓕ puns a ay·pee·lay
twice deux fois der fwa
twin beds lits jumeaux ⓜ pl day lee zhew·mo
twins jumeaux/jumelles ⓜ/ⓕ zhew·mo/zhew·mel
two deux der
type type ⓜ teep
typical typique tee·peek
tyre pnou ⓜ pner

U

ugly laid(e) ⓜ/ⓕ lay/led
ultrasound ultrason ⓜ ewl·tra·son
umbrella parapluie ⓜ pa·ra·plwee
uncertain incertain(e) ⓜ/ⓕ un·sair·tun/un·sair·ten
uncomfortable inconfortable ung·kon·for·ta·bler
under sous soo

understand comprendre kom·pron·drer
underwater camera appareil photo sous-marin ⓜ a·pa·ray fo·to soo·ma·run
underwear sous-vêtements ⓜ soo·vet·mon
unemployed chômeur/chômeuse ⓜ/ⓕ sho·mer/sho·merz
unemployment chômage ⓜ sho·mazh
unfair injuste un·zhewst
unfurnished non-meublé(e) ⓜ/ⓕ no·mer·blay
uniform uniforme ⓜ ew·nee·form
union union ⓕ ew·nyon
union (trade) syndicat ⓜ sun·dee·ka
universe univers ⓜ ew·nee·vair
university université ⓕ ew·nee·vair·see·tay
unleaded sans plomb son plom
unsafe dangereux/dangereuse ⓜ/ⓕ don·zhrer/don·zhrerz
until (Friday, etc) jusqu'à zhew·ska
unusual peu commun(e) ⓜ/ⓕ per ko·mun/ko·mewn
up en haut on o
uphill (to go) monter mon·tay
upstairs en haut on o
urgent urgent(e) ⓜ/ⓕ ewr·zhon(t)
us nous noo
USA les USA ⓜ lay zew·es·a
use utiliser ew·tee·lee·zay
useful utile ew·teel
usually habituellement a·bee·twel·mon

V

vacancy chambre libre ⓕ shom·brer lee·brer
vacant libre lee·brer
vacation vacances ⓕ pl va·kons
vaccination vaccination ⓕ vak·see·na·syon
vagina vagin ⓜ va·zhun
validate valider va·lee·day
valley vallée ⓕ va·lay
valuable de valeur der va·ler
value (price) valeur ⓕ va·ler
van camionnette ⓕ ka·myo·net
vegetable légume ⓜ lay·gewm
vegetarian végétarien/végétarienne ⓜ/ⓕ vay·zhay·ta·ryun/vay·zhay·ta·ryen
vehicle véhicule ⓜ vay·ee·kewl
vein veine ⓕ ven
venereal disease maladie vénérienne ⓕ ma·la·dee vay·nay·ryen
very très tray
vest maillot de corps ⓜ ma·yo der kor
via via vee·a
video camera caméra vidéo ⓕ ka·may·ra vee·day·yo
view vue ⓕ vew
village village ⓜ vee·lazh
vine vigne ⓕ vee·nyer
vineyard vignoble ⓜ vee·nyo·bler
virus virus ⓜ vee·rews
visa visa ⓜ vee·za
visit (museum etc) visiter vee·zee·tay
visit (person) aller voir a·lay vwar
visitor visiteur/visiteuse ⓜ/ⓕ vee·zee·ter/vee·zee·terz
visitor (guest) invité(e) ⓜ/ⓕ un·vee·tay
vitamin vitamine ⓕ vee·ta·meen
volume volume ⓜ vo·lewm
voluntary (not paid) bénévole bay·nay·vol
volunteer bénévole ⓜ/ⓕ bay·nay·vol
vomit vomir vo·meer
vote voter vo·tay

W

wage salaire ⓜ sa·lair
wait (for) attendre a·ton·drer
waiter serveur/serveuse ⓜ/ⓕ sair·ver/sair·verz
waiting room salle d'attente ⓕ sal da·tont

wake (someone) up réveiller ray·vay·yay
wake up se réveiller ser ray·vay·yay
walk marcher mar·shay
wall (outer) mur ⓜ mewr
want vouloir voo·lwar
war guerre ⓕ gair
wardrobe penderie ⓕ pon·dree
warm chaud(e) ⓜ/ⓕ sho(d)
warn prévenir prayv·neer
warning avertissement ⓜ a·vair·tees·mon
wash (oneself) se laver ser la·vay
wash (something) laver la·vay
washing machine machine à laver ⓕ ma·sheen a la·vay
wasp guêpe ⓕ gep
watch regarder rer·gar·day
watch montre ⓕ mon·trer
water eau ⓕ o
water bottle (hot) bouillotte ⓕ boo·yot
waterfall cascade ⓕ kas·kad
waterproof imperméable um·pair·may·abler
waterskiing ski ⓜ nautique skee no·teek
wave vague ⓕ vag
way direction ⓕ dee·rek·syon
way (manner) façon ⓕ fa·son
way (road) chemin ⓜ sher·mun
we nous noo
weak faible fay·bler
wealthy riche reesh
wear porter por·tay
weather temps ⓜ tom
weather forecast météo ⓕ may·tay·o
wedding mariage ⓜ ma·ree·azh
Wednesday mercredi ⓜ mair·krer·dee
week semaine ⓕ ser·men
weekend week-end ⓜ week·end
weigh peser per·zay
weight poids ⓜ pwa
welcome accueillir a·ker·yeer
welfare (aid) assistance publique ⓕ a·sees·tons pewb·leek
well bien byun
west ouest ⓜ west
wet mouillé(e) ⓜ/ⓕ moo·yay
what quel(le) ⓜ/ⓕ kel
wheel roue ⓕ roo
wheelchair fauteuil ⓜ roulant fo·ter·yee roo·lon
when quand kon
where où oo
which quel(le) ⓜ/ⓕ kel
which lequel/laquelle ⓜ/ⓕ ler·kel/la·kel
which qui kee
whistle siffler see·flay
white blanc/blanche ⓜ/ⓕ blong/blonsh
who qui kee
whole tout entier/toute entière ⓜ/ⓕ too ton·tyay/too ton·tyair
why pourquoi poor·kwa
wide large larzh
widow veuve ⓕ verv
widower veuf ⓜ verf
wife femme ⓕ fum
wild sauvage so·vazh
win gagner ga·nyay
wind vent ⓜ von
window fenêtre ⓕ fer·nay·trer
windscreen/windshield pare-brise ⓜ par·breez
windsurfer planche ⓕ à voile plonsh a vwal
windsurfing (to go) faire de la plancheà voile fair der la plonsh a vwal
wine vin ⓜ vun
winery cave viticole ⓕ kaav vee·tee·kol
wings ailes ⓕ el
winner gagnant(e) ⓜ/ⓕ ga·nyon(t)
winter hiver ⓜ ee·vair
wire fil de fer ⓜ feel der fair
wish souhaiter sway·tay
with avec a·vek
withdrawal retrait ⓜ rer·tray
within (an hour etc) avant a·von
without sans son
witness témoin ⓜ tay·mwun
woman femme ⓕ fum

wonderful merveilleux/ merveilleuse ⓜ/ⓕ mair·vay·yer/ mair·vay·yerz
wood bois ⓜ bwa
wool laine ⓕ len
word mot ⓜ mo
work travail ⓜ tra·vai
work travailler tra·va·yay
work experience stage en entreprise ⓜ stazh on on·trer·preez
work permit permis de travail ⓜ pair·mee der tra·vai
world monde ⓜ mond
World Cup La Coupe du Monde la koop dew mond
worms vers ⓜ vair
worried inquiet/inquiète ⓜ/ⓕ ung·kyay/ung·kyet
worry s'inquiéter sung·kyay·tay
worse pire peer
worship faire ses dévotions fair say day·vo·syon
worship (someone) adorer a·do·ray
wrist poignet ⓜ pwa·nyay
write écrire ay·kreer
writer écrivain ⓜ ay·kree·vun
wrong faux/fausse ⓜ/ⓕ fo/fos
wrong (direction) mauvais(e) ⓜ/ⓕ mo·vay(z)
wrong (to be) avoir tort a·vwar tor

Y

year année ⓜ a·nay
yellow jaune zhon
yes oui wee
yesterday hier ee·yair
yet encore ong·kor
yoga yoga ⓜ yo·ga
you vous pl/pol voo
you tu inf tew
young jeune zhern
your pol votre/vos sg/pl vo·trer/vo
your sg&inf ton/ta/tes ⓜ/ⓕ/pl ton/ ta/tay
youth hostel auberge de jeunesse ⓕ o·bairzh der zher·nes

Z

zero zéro zay·ro
zip/zipper fermeture éclair ⓕ fair·mer·tewr ay·klair
zoo zoo ⓜ zo

DICTIONARY

French to English

FRANÇAIS–ANGLAIS

Nouns have their gender indicated by ⓜ or ⓕ. You'll also see sg and pl for singular and plural nouns. Where a word that could be either a noun or a verb has no gender indicated, it's a verb.

A

à a at • to
à bord a bor aboard
à côté de a ko·tay der beside • next to
à droite a drwat right (direction)
à gauche a gosh left (direction)
à la maison a la may·zon home
à l'étranger a lay·tron·zhay abroad
à l'heure a ler on time
à peu près a per pray approximately
à plein temps a plun ton full-time
à temps partiel a tom par·syel part-time
abeille ⓕ a·bay bee
abondance ⓕ a·bon·dons plenty
abri ⓜ a·bree shelter
accepter ak·sep·tay accept
accident ⓜ ak·see·don accident • crash
accueillir a·ker·yeer welcome
accumulation ⓕ a·kew·mew·la·syon collection
acheter ash·tay buy
acte de naissance ⓜ akt der nay·sons birth certificate
acteur/actrice ⓜ/ⓕ ak·ter/ak·trees actor
actualités ak·twa·lee·tay news (on TV etc)
actuel(le) ⓜ/ⓕ ak·twel current
acupuncture ⓕ a·kew·pongk·tewr acupuncture
adaptateur ⓜ a·dap·ta·ter adaptor
addition ⓕ a·dee·syon bill • check
admettre ad·me·trer admit
administration ⓕ ad·mee·nee·stra·syon administration
admirer ad·mee·ray admire
adorer a·do·ray worship (someone)
adresse ⓕ a·dres address
adulte ⓜ/ⓕ a·dewlt adult
adversaire ⓜ/ⓕ ad·vair·sair opponent
aérobic ⓜ a·ay·ro·beek aerobics
aérogramme ⓜ a·ay·ro·gram aerogram
aéroport ⓜ a·ay·ro·por airport
affaires ⓕ a·fair business
affreux/affreuse ⓜ/ⓕ a·frer/a·frerz awful • terrible
Afrique ⓕ a·freek Africa
âge ⓜ azh age
âgé(e) ⓜ/ⓕ a·zhay elderly
agence de voyage ⓕ a·zhons der vwa·yazh travel agency

agence immobilière ⓕ a·zhons ee·mo·bee·lyair estate agency
agenda ⓜ a·zhun·da diary
agent de police ⓜ a·zhon der po·lees officer (police)
agent immobilier ⓜ a·zhon ee·mo·bee·lyay real estate agent
agiter a·zhee·tay shake (something)
agréable a·gray·a·bler nice (pleasant)
agressif/agressive ⓜ/ⓕ a·gray·seef/a·gray·seev aggressive
agriculteur/agricultrice ⓜ/ⓕ a·gree·kewl·ter/a·gree·kewl·trees farmer
agriculture ⓕ a·gree·kewl·tewr agriculture
aide ⓕ ed help
aider ay·day help
aiguille ⓕ ay·gwee·yer needle
ailes ⓕ el wings
aimant(e) ⓜ/ⓕ ay·mon(t) caring
aimer ay·may like • love
air ⓜ air air • tune
alcool ⓜ al·kol alcohol
Allemagne ⓕ al·ma·nyer Germany
aller a·lay go
aller retour ⓜ a·lay rer·toor return (ticket)
aller voir a·lay vwar visit (person)
allergie ⓕ a·lair·zhee allergy
allocation de chômage ⓕ a·lo·ka·syon der sho·mazh dole
allume-feu anti-moustiques ⓜ a·lewm·fer on·tee·moo·steek mosquito coil
allumettes ⓕ pl a·lew·met matches (for lighting)
alors a·lor then (at the time)
alpinisme ⓜ al·pee·nee·smer mountaineering
alternative ⓕ al·tair·na·teev alternative
altitude ⓕ al·tee·tewd altitude
amant(e) ⓜ/ⓕ a·mon(t) lover
amateur ⓜ a·ma·ter amateur
ambassade ⓕ om·ba·sad embassy
ambassadeur/ambassadrice ⓜ/ⓕ om·ba·sa·der/om·ba·sa·drees ambassador
ambulance ⓕ om·bew·lons ambulance
améliorer a·may·lyo·ray improve
amende ⓕ a·mond fine (penalty)
amener am·nay bring (a person)
amer/amère ⓜ/ⓕ a·mair bitter
ami/amie ⓜ/ⓕ a·mee friend
amical(e) ⓜ/ⓕ a·mee·kal friendly
amitié ⓕ a·mee·tyay friendship
amour a·moor love
ample om·pler loose (clothes)
ampoule ⓕ om·pool blister • light bulb
analgésique ⓜ a·nal·zhay·zeek painkiller
analyse de sang ⓕ a·na·leez der son blood test
anglais(e) ⓜ/ⓕ ong·glay(z) English
Angleterre ⓕ ong·gler·tair England
animal ⓜ a·nee·mal animal
animal familier ⓜ a·nee·mal fa·mee·lyay pet
anneau ⓜ a·no ring (shape)
année ⓜ a·nay year
anniversaire ⓜ a·nee·vair·sair birthday
annuaire ⓜ an·wair phone book
annuel(le) ⓜ/ⓕ a·nwel annual
annuler a·new·lay cancel
antibiotiques ⓜ on·tee·byo·teek antibiotics
anti-nucléaire on·tee·new·klay·air antinuclear
antique on·teek ancient
antiquité ⓕ on·tee·kee·tay antique
antiseptique ⓜ on·tee·sep·teek antiseptic
août ⓜ oot August
appareil acoustique ⓜ a·pa·ray a·koos·teek hearing aid
appareil de chauffage ⓜ a·pa·ray der sho·fazh heater

appareil photo ⓜ a·pa·ray fo·to camera
— jetable zhay·ta·bler disposable camera
— numérique new·may·reek digital camera
— sous-marin soo·ma·run underwater camera
appel en PCV ⓜ a·pel on pay·say·vay collect call
appeler a·play call
appendice a·pun·dees appendix
apporter a·por·tay bring (a thing)
apprendre a·pron·drer learn
après a·pray after
après-demain a·pray·der·mun day after tomorrow (the)
après-midi ⓜ a·pray·mee·dee afternoon
après-rasage ⓜ a·pray·ra·zazh aftershave
après-shampooing ⓜ a·pray·shom·pwung conditioner (hair)
araignée ⓕ a·ray·nyay spider
arbitre ⓜ ar·bee·trer referee
arbre ⓜ ar·brer tree
archéologie ⓕ ar·kay·o·lo·zhee archaeology
architecte(e) ⓜ/ⓕ ar·shee·tekt architect
architecture ar·shee·tek·tewr architecture
argent ⓜ ar·zhon cash • money • silver
arnaque ⓕ ar·nak rip-off
arrêt ⓜ a·ray stop
arrêt d'autobus ⓜ a·ray do·to·bews bus stop
arrêter a·ray·tay stop (something, someone) • arrest
arrière a·ryair rear (seat etc)
arrivées ⓕ a·ree·vay arrivals
arriver a·ree·vay arrive
art ⓜ ar art
artisanat ⓜ ar·tee·za·na crafts
artiste ⓜ/ⓕ ar·teest artist
arts martiaux ⓜ pl ar mar·syo martial arts
ascenseur ⓜ a·son·ser lift • elevator
Asie ⓕ a·zee Asia
aspirine ⓕ as·pee·reen aspirin
assez a·say enough
assiette ⓕ a·syet plate
assistance publique ⓕ a·sees·tons pewb·leek welfare (aid)
assurance ⓕ a·sew·rons insurance
assurer a·sew·ray insure
asthme ⓜ as·mer asthma
atelier ⓜ a·ter·lyay studio
athlétisme ⓜ at·lay·tees·mer athletics
atmosphère ⓕ at·mos·fair atmosphere
attaché(e) ⓜ/ⓕ a·ta·shay attached
atteindre a·tun·drer reach • wait (for)
attraper a·tra·pay catch
au coin o kwun on the corner
au revoir o rer·vwar goodbye
aube ob dawn
auberge de jeunesse ⓕ o·bairzh der zher·nes youth hostel
aucun(e) ⓜ/ⓕ o·kun/o·kewn none
au-dessus o·der·sew above
aujourd'hui o·zhoor·dwee today
aussi o·see also
Australie ⓕ o·stra·lee Australia
autel ⓜ o·tel altar
autobus ⓜ o·to·bews bus (city)
autocar ⓜ o·to·kar bus (intercity)
automatique o·to·ma·teek automatic
automne ⓜ o·ton autumn • fall
autoroute ⓕ o·to·root highway • motorway
autour o·toor around
autre o·trer other
avant a·von before
avant-hier a·von·tyair day before yesterday
avec a·vek with
avenir av·neer future
avenue ⓕ av·new avenue

avertissement ⓜ a·vair·tees·mon warning
aveugle a·ver·gler blind
avide a·veed greedy (money)
avion ⓜ a·vyon aeroplane
aviron ⓜ a·vee·ron rowing
avis ⓜ a·vee opinion
avocat(e) ⓜ/ⓕ a·vo·ka(t) lawyer
avoir a·vwar have
— besoin de ber·zwun de need
— de la chance der la shons lucky (to be)
— des hallucinations day za·lew·see·na·syon hallucinate
— faim fum hungry (to be)
— la tête qui tourne la tet kee toorn dizzy (to be dizzy)
— le mal de mer ler mal der mair seasick (to be)
— mal au ventre mal o von·trer stomachache (to have a)
— mal aux dents mal o don toothache
— raison ray·zon right (to be right)
— soif swaf thirsty (to be)
— sommeil so·may sleepy (to be sleepy)
— tort tor wrong (to be)
avortement ⓜ a·vor·ter·mon abortion
avril ⓜ a·vreel April

B

baby-sitter ⓜ&ⓕ ba·bee·see·ter babysitter
bac ⓜ bak ferry
bagages ⓜ pl ba·gazh baggage • luggage
bagarre ⓕ ba·gar fight
bague ⓕ bag ring (on finger)
baignoire ⓕ bey·nwar bath
bail ⓜ ba·yer lease
bain ⓜ bun bath (have a)
baiser bay·zay fuck
baiser ⓜ bay·zay kiss
balcon ⓜ bal·kon balcony
balle (de tennis) ⓕ bal (der tay·nees) (tennis) ball
ballet ⓜ ba·lay ballet
ballon (de football) ⓜ ba·lon (der foot·bol) football • soccer ball
bande ⓕ bond band (music)
bande dessinée ⓕ bond day·see·nay comic (magazine)
banlieue ⓕ bon·lyer suburb
banque ⓕ bonk bank
baptême ⓜ ba·tem baptism
bar ⓜ bar bar • pub
barrière ⓕ bar·yair fence • gate
bas ⓜ ba stockings
bas/basse ⓜ/ⓕ ba(s) low
baseball ⓜ bez·bol baseball
basket(ball) ⓜ bas·ket(bol) basketball
bateau ⓜ ba·to boat
bâtiment ⓜ ba·tee·mon building
batterie ⓕ bat·ree battery (car) • drums
bavarder ba·var·day chat
bavoir ⓜ ba·vwar bib
beau/belle ⓜ/ⓕ bo/bel beautiful • handsome
beaucoup (de) bo·koo (der) a lot (of) • many • plenty
beau-père ⓜ bo·pair father-in-law
bébé ⓜ bay·bay baby
belle-mère ⓕ bel·mair mother-in-law
bénéfice ⓜ bay·nay·fees profit
bénévole ⓜ/ⓕ bay·nay·vol voluntary (not paid) • volunteer
bible ⓕ bee·bler bible
bibliothèque ⓕ bee·blee·o·tek library
bien byun well
bien déterminé byun day·tair·mee·nay definite
bientôt byun·to soon
bière ⓕ byair beer
bijoux ⓜ pl bee·zhoo jewellery
billard américain ⓜ bee·yar a·may·ree·kun pool (game)
billet ⓜ bee·yay ticket
— de banque der bonk banknote
— stand-by stond·bai stand-by ticket

blanc/blanche ⓜ/ⓕ blong/blonsh white
blanchisserie ⓕ blon·shees·ree laundry (place)
blessé(e) ⓜ/ⓕ blay·say hurt • injured
blessure ⓕ blay·sewr injury
bleu ⓜ bler bruise
bleu(e) ⓜ/ⓕ bler blue
bloqué(e) ⓜ/ⓕ blo·kay blocked
bœuf ⓜ berf ox
bohémien/bohémienne ⓜ/ⓕ bo·ay·myun/bo·ay·myen Bohemian • hippie
boire bwar drink
bois ⓜ bwa wood
bois de chauffage ⓜ bwa der sho·fazh firewood
boisson ⓕ bwa·son drink
boîte ⓕ bwat box • can (tin) • carton (for ice cream) • nightclub
boîte aux lettres ⓕ bwat o lay·trer mailbox
bol ⓜ bol bowl
bon/bonne ⓜ/ⓕ bon/bon good
bon marché ⓜ bon mar·shay cheap
bonde ⓕ bond plug (bath)
bondé(e) ⓜ/ⓕ bon·day crowded
bord ⓜ bor edge
— de la mer der la mair seaside
— du trottoir dew tro·twar kerb
botte ⓕ bot boot (footwear)
bouche ⓕ boosh mouth
boucherie ⓕ boosh·ree butcher's shop
bouchon ⓜ boo·shon traffic jam
boucles d'oreille ⓕ boo·kler do·ray earrings
bouddhiste boo·deest Buddhist
boue ⓕ boo mud
bouger boo·zhay move
bougie ⓕ boo·zhee candle
bouillie ⓕ boo·yee baby food
bouillotte ⓕ boo·yot water bottle (hot)
boulangerie ⓕ boo·lon·zhree bakery
boulevard ⓜ bool·var boulevard
boussole ⓕ boo·sol compass
bout ⓜ boo end
bouteille ⓕ boo·tay bottle
bouton ⓜ boo·ton button
boxe ⓕ boks boxing
boxer-short ⓜ bok·sair·short boxer shorts
braderie ⓕ bra·dree street market
braille ⓜ bra·yer Braille
bras ⓜ bra arm
briquet ⓜ bree·kay cigarette lighter
brochure ⓕ bro·shewr brochure
broderie ⓕ bro·dree embroidery
bronchite ⓕ bron·sheet bronchitis
brosse ⓕ bros brush
— à cheveux a shver hairbrush
— à dents a don toothbrush
brûler brew·lay burn
brûlure ⓕ brew·lewr burn
brumeux/brumeuse ⓜ/ⓕ brew·mer/brew·merz foggy
brun/brune ⓜ/ⓕ brun/brewn brown
bruyant(e) ⓜ/ⓕ brew·yon(t) noisy
budget ⓜ bewd·zhay budget
buffet ⓜ bew·fay buffet
bureau ⓜ bew·ro office
— de poste der post post office
— de tabac der ta·ba tobacconist
— des objets trouvés day zob·zhay troo·vay lost property office
bus ⓜ bews bus (city)
but ⓜ bewt goal

C

cabine téléphonique ⓕ ka·been tay·lay·fo·neek telephone box
câble ⓜ ka·bler cable
cache-sexe ⓜ kash·seks G-string
cadeau ⓜ ka·do gift • present
cadenas ⓜ kad·na padlock
cafard ⓜ ka·far cockroach
café ⓜ ka·fay cafe • coffee
caisse (enregistreuse) ⓕ kes (on·rer·zhee·strerz) cash register
caissier/caissière ⓜ/ⓕ kay·syay/kay·syair cashier • teller

calculatrice ⓕ kal·kew·la·trees calculator
calendrier ⓜ ka·lon·dree·yay calendar
caméra vidéo ⓜ ka·may·ra vee·day·yo video camera
camion ⓜ ka·myon lorry • truck
camionnette ⓕ ka·myo·net van
camp ⓜ kon camp
campagne ⓕ kom·pa·nyer countryside
camping ⓜ kom·peeng camping ground
Canada ⓜ ka·na·da Canada
canard ⓜ ka·nar duck
cancer ⓜ kon·sair cancer
canif ⓜ ka·neef penknife
canot automobile ⓜ ka·no o·to·mo·beel motorboat
cape ⓕ kap cloak
capitalisme ⓜ ka·pee·ta·lees·mer capitalism
car ⓜ kar bus (intercity)
caravane ⓕ ka·ra·van caravan
carnet ⓜ kar·nay notebook
carrefour ⓜ kar·foor intersection
carrière ⓕ kar·ryair career
carte ⓕ kart menu
carte ⓕ kart map (of country)
— de crédit kart der kray·dee credit card
— d'embarquement kart dom·bar·ker·mon boarding pass
— d'identité kart dee·don·tee·tay identification card (ID)
— grise kart greez car owner's title
— postale kart pos·tal postcard
— routière kart roo·tyair road map
cartouche de gaz ⓕ kar·toosh der gaz gas cartridge
cas urgent ⓜ ka ewr·zhon emergency
cascade ⓕ kas·kad waterfall
casher ka·shair kosher
casque ⓜ kask helmet
cassé(e) ⓜ/ⓕ ka·say broken
casse-croûte ⓜ kas·kroot snack
casser ka·say break
casserole ⓕ kas·rol pan
cathédrale ⓕ ka·tay·dral cathedral
catholique ka·to·leek Catholic
cause ⓕ koz cause
CD ⓜ say·day CD
ce ⓜ ser that • this
ce soir ser swar tonight
ceci ser·see this (one)
ceinture de sécurité ⓕ sun·tewr der say·kew·ree·tay seatbelt
cela ser·la that (one)
célèbre say·leb·rer famous
célibataire say·lee·ba·tair single (person)
cendrier ⓜ son·dree·yay ashtray
cent son hundred
cent ⓜ sent cent
centimètre ⓜ son·tee·me·trer centimetre
centre ⓜ son·trer centre
centre commercial ⓜ son·trer ko·mair·syal shopping centre
centre-ville ⓜ son·trer·veel city centre
céramique ⓕ say·ra·meek ceramic
cercle ⓜ sair·kler circle
certain(e) ⓜ/ⓕ sair·tun/·ten certain
certificat ⓜ sair·tee·fee·ka certificate
cette ⓕ set that • this
chaîne ⓕ shen chain • channel
— de bicyclette der bee·see·klet bike chain
— de montagnes der mon·ta·nyer mountain range
— hi-fi ee·fee stereo (system)
chaise ⓕ shez chair
chaleur ⓕ sha·ler heat
chambre ⓕ shom·brer room
— à air a air tube (tyre)
— à coucher a koo·shay bedroom
— libre lee·brer vacancy
— pour deux personnes poor der pair·son double room
— pour une personne poor ewn pair·son single room

champ ⓜ shom field
champ de courses ⓜ shon der koors racetrack
champagne ⓜ shom·pa·nyer Champagne
championnat ⓜ shom·pyo·na championship
chance ⓕ shons luck
changer shon·zhay change
chanson ⓕ shon·son song
chanter shon·tay sing
chanteur/chanteuse ⓜ/ⓕ shon·ter/shon·terz singer
chapeau ⓜ sha·po hat
chaque shak each • every
charcuterie ⓕ shar·kew·tree delicatessen
chariot ⓜ shar·yo trolley
charmant(e) ⓜ/ⓕ shar·mon(t) charming
chasse ⓕ shas hunting
chat ⓜ sha cat
château ⓜ sha·to castle
chaton ⓜ sha·ton kitten
chaud(e) ⓜ/ⓕ sho(d) hot • warm
chauffé(e) ⓜ/ⓕ sho·fay heated
chaussettes ⓕ sho·set socks
chaussure ⓕ sho·sewr shoe
chaussures de marche ⓕ pl sho·sewr der marsh hiking boots
chef ⓜ shef leader
chef de cuisine ⓜ shef der kwee·zeen chef
chemin ⓜ shmun path • lane • way
— de fer der fair railway
— de montagne der mon·ta·nyer mountain path
chemise ⓕ sher·meez shirt
chèque ⓜ shek cheque • check (banking)
chèque de voyage ⓜ shek der vwa·yazh travellers cheque
cher/chère ⓜ/ⓕ shair expensive
chercher shair·shay look for
cheval ⓜ shval horse
cheveux ⓜ shver hair
cheville ⓕ sher·vee·yer ankle
chèvre ⓕ shev·rer goat
chien ⓜ shyun dog
chien d'aveugle ⓜ shyun da·ver·gler guide dog
chiot ⓜ shyo puppy
chocolat ⓜ sho·ko·la chocolate
choisir shwa·zeer choose
choix ⓜ shwa choice
chômage ⓜ sho·mazh unemployment
chômeur/chômeuse ⓜ/ⓕ sho·mer/sho·merz unemployed
chose ⓕ shoz thing
chrétien(ne) ⓜ/ⓕ kray·tyun/kray·tyen Christian
ciel ⓜ syel sky
cigare ⓜ see·gar cigar
cigarette ⓕ see·ga·ret cigarette
cime ⓕ seem peak
cimetière ⓜ seem·tyair cemetery
cinéma ⓜ see·nay·ma cinema
cinq sungk five
circulation ⓕ seer·kew·la·syon traffic
cirque ⓜ seerk circus
ciseaux ⓜ pl see·zo scissors
citoyen(ne) ⓜ/ⓕ see·twa·yun/see·twa·yen citizen
citoyenneté ⓕ see·twa·yen·tay citizenship
clair(e) ⓜ/ⓕ klair clear • light (of colour)
classe ⓕ klas class
— affaires klas a·fair business class
— touriste klas too·reest economy class
classique kla·seek classical
clavier ⓜ kla·vyay keyboard
clé ⓕ klay key
client(e) ⓜ/ⓕ klee·on(t) client • customer
clignotant ⓜ klee·nyo·ton indicator (on car)
climatisé kee·ma·tee·zay air-conditioned

FRENCH – ENGLISH C

clinique privée ⓕ klee·neek pree·vay private hospital
cocaïne ⓕ ko·ka·een cocaine
cochon ⓜ ko·shon pig
cocktail ⓜ kok·tel cocktail
code postal ⓜ kod pos·tal post code
cœur ⓜ ker heart
coffre-fort ⓜ kof·rer·for safe
coiffeur/coiffeuse ⓜ/ⓕ kwa·fer/kwa·ferz hairdresser
coin ⓜ kwun corner
colis ⓜ ko·lee parcel
collant ⓜ ko·lon pantyhose
colle ⓕ kol glue
collectionner ko·lek·syo·nay collect (stamps etc)
collègue ⓜ/ⓕ ko·leg colleague
collier ⓜ ko·lyay necklace
colline ⓕ ko·leen hill
colloque ⓜ ko·lok conference (small)
colonne vertébrale ⓕ ko·lon vair·tay·bral spine
combinaison ⓕ kom·bee·nay·zon combination
comédie ⓕ ko·may·dee comedy
comme kom as • like
commencement ⓜ ko·mons·mon start
commencer ko·mon·say begin • start
comment ko·mon how
commerce ⓜ ko·mairs trade
commissariat ⓜ ko·mee·sar·ya police station
commission ⓕ ko·mee·syon commission
commotion cérébrale ⓕ ko·mo·syon say·ray·bral concussion
commun(e) ⓜ/ⓕ ko·mun/ko·mewn common
communauté ⓕ ko·mew·no·tay community
communisme ⓜ ko·mew·nees·mer communism
communiste ko·mew·neest communist
compagnon/compagne ⓜ/ⓕ kom·pa·nyon/kom·pa·nyer companion
compétence ⓕ kom·pay·tons skill
compétition ⓕ kom·pay·tees·yon competition
complet/complète ⓜ/ⓕ kom·play/kom·plet booked up • no vacancy
composition directe ⓕ kom·po·zees·yon dee·rekt direct-dial
comprendre kom·pron·drer understand
compris(e) ⓜ/ⓕ kom·pree(z) included
compte ⓜ kont account
compte bancaire ⓜ kont bong·kair bank account
compter kon·tay count
compteur (de vitesse) ⓜ kon·ter (der vee·tes) speedometer
comptoir ⓜ kon·twar counter (at bar)
concert ⓜ kon·sair concert
concessionnaire ⓜ kon·say·syo·nair distributor
concevoir kon·ser·vwar design
conduire kon·dweer drive
confession ⓕ kon·fay·syon confession (religious)
confiance ⓕ kon·fyons trust
confirmer kon·feer·may confirm (a booking)
confondre kon·fon·drer mix up (confuse)
confortable kon·for·ta·bler comfortable
congrès ⓜ kong·gray conference (big)
connaître ko·nay·trer know (be familiar with)
conseil ⓜ kon·say advice
conservateur/conservatrice ⓜ/ⓕ kon·sair·va·ter/kon·sair·va·trees conservative
consigne ⓕ kon·see·nyer left luggage (office)

consigne automatique ⓕ kon·see·nyer o·to·ma·teek luggage lockers
constipation ⓕ kon·stee·pa·syon constipation
construire kon·strweer build
consulat ⓜ kon·su·la consulate
contraceptif ⓜ kon·trer·sep·teef contraceptive
contrat ⓜ kon·tra contract
contre kon·trer against
contrôle ⓜ kon·trol checkpoint
contrôleur ⓜ kon·tro·ler ticket collector
conversation ⓕ kon·vair·sa·syon conversation
coopérer ko·o·pay·ray cooperate
coq ⓜ kok rooster
coquillage ⓜ ko·kee·yazh seashell
corde ⓕ kord rope
corde à linge ⓕ kord a lunzh clothes line
corps ⓜ kor body
correct(e) ⓜ/ⓕ ko·rekt correct
corrompu(e) ⓜ/ⓕ ko·rom·pew corrupt
côté ⓜ ko·tay side
côte ⓕ kot coast
coton ⓜ ko·ton cotton
couche ⓕ koosh diaper • nappy
couche d'ozone ⓕ koosh do·zon ozone layer
coucher du soleil ⓜ koo·shay dew so·lay sunset
coudre koo·drer sew
couleur ⓕ koo·ler colour
couloir ⓜ koo·lwar aisle (on plane)
coup de soleil ⓜ koo der so·lay sunburn
coupable koo·pa·bler guilty
coupe ⓕ koop haircut
coupe-ongles ⓜ koop·ong·gler nail clippers
couper koo·pay cut
coupon ⓜ koo·pon coupon
courageux/courageuse ⓜ/ⓕ koo·ra·zher/koo·ra·zherz brave
courant ⓜ koo·ron current (electricity)
courir koo·reer run
courrier ⓜ koo·ryay mail (letters)
courroie de ventilateur ⓕ koor·wa der von·tee·la·ter fanbelt
course ⓕ koors race (sport)
court ⓜ koor court (tennis)
court(e) ⓜ/ⓕ koor(t) short (height)
court de tennis ⓜ koor der tay·nees tennis court
coût ⓜ koo cost
couteau ⓜ koo·to knife
coutume ⓕ koo·tewm custom
couvent ⓜ koo·von convent
couvert ⓜ koo·vair cover charge
couverts ⓜ koo·vair cutlery
couverture ⓕ koo·vair·tewr blanket
crayon ⓜ kray·yon pencil
crèche ⓕ kresh creche
crédit ⓜ kray·dee credit
crème ⓕ krem cream
— de bronzage der bron·zazh tanning lotion
— hydratante ee·dra·tont moisturiser
crevaison ⓕ krer·vay·zon puncture
crier kree·yay shout
crique ⓕ kreek creek
critique ⓕ kree·teek review (article)
croire krwar believe
croix ⓕ krwa cross (religious)
croyance ⓕ krwa·yons belief
cru(e) ⓜ/ⓕ krew raw
cueillette de fruits ⓕ ker·yet der frwee fruit picking
cuillère ⓕ kwee·yair spoon
cuir ⓜ kweer leather
cuire kweer cook
cuisine ⓕ kwee·zeen kitchen
cuisinier/cuisinière ⓜ/ⓕ kwee·zee·nyay/kwee·zee·nyair cook
cul ⓜ kew ass (bum)
culture ⓕ kewl·tewr crop (grown)

cure-dent ⓜ kewr·don toothpick
CV ⓜ say·vay CV • resumé
cyclisme ⓜ see·klee·smer cycling
cycliste ⓜ/ⓕ see·kleest cyclist

D

dangereux/dangereuse ⓜ/ⓕ don·zhrer/don·zhrerz dangerous
dans don in • into
danse ⓕ dons dancing
danser don·say dance
date ⓕ dat date (day)
date de naissance ⓕ dat der nay·sons date of birth
de der from
— droite drwat right-wing
— gauche gosh left-wing
— la la some
— l'autre côté de lo·trer ko·tay der across
— luxe lewks luxury
— seconde classe skond klas second class
— valeur va·ler valuable
débat ⓜ day·ba argument
déboisement ⓜ day·bwaz·mon deforestation
décalage horaire ⓜ day·ka·lazh o·rair time difference
décembre ⓜ day·som·brer December
décharge ⓕ day·sharzh rubbish dump
déchets nucléaires ⓜ day·shay new·klay·air nuclear waste
déchets toxiques ⓜ pl day·shay tok·seek toxic waste
décision ⓕ day·see·zyon decision
découvrir day·koov·reer discover
déçu(e) ⓜ/ⓕ day·sew disappointed
dedans der·don inside
défectueux/défectueuse ⓜ/ⓕ day·fek·twer/day·fek·twerz faulty
dégâts ⓜ day·ga damage
dehors der·or outside
déjà day·zha already
déjeuner ⓜ day·zher·nay lunch
délicieux/délicieuse ⓜ/ⓕ day·lees·yer/day·lees·yerz tasty
délit ⓜ day·lee crime
demain der·mun tomorrow
— après-midi a·pray·mee·dee tomorrow afternoon
— matin ma·tun tomorrow morning
— soir swar tomorrow evening
demander der·mon·day ask for (something)
démangeaison ⓕ day·mon·zhay·zon itch
demi-litre ⓜ der·mee·lee·trer half a litre
démocratie ⓕ day·mo·kra·see democracy
dent ⓕ don tooth
dentelle ⓕ don·tel lace
dentifrice ⓜ don·tee·frees toothpaste
dentiste ⓜ don·teest dentist
dents ⓕ don teeth
déodorant ⓜ day·o·do·ron deodorant
dépanneuse ⓕ day·pa·nerz tow truck
départ ⓜ day·par departure
dépendance ⓕ day·pon·dons addiction
dépenser day·pon·say spend (money)
dépôt ⓜ day·po deposit
depuis der·pwee since (May etc)
déranger day·ron·zhay disturb
dernier/dernière ⓜ/ⓕ dair·nyay/dair·nyair last (previous)
derrière dair·yair behind
des pl day some
désastre ⓜ day·zas·trer disaster
descendant(e) ⓜ/ⓕ day·son·don(t) descendant
descendre day·son·drer get off (a train, etc) • go down (stairs, etc)
désert ⓜ day·zair desert
désinfectant ⓜ day·zun·fek·ton disinfectant

dessert ⓜ day·sair dessert
dessin animé ⓜ day·sun a·nee·may cartoon
dessiner day·see·nay draw (picture)
destin ⓜ des·tun fate
destination ⓕ des·tee·na·syon destination
détail ⓜ day·tai detail
détaillé(e) ⓜ/ⓕ day·ta·yay itemised
détester day·tes·tay hate
détruire day·trweer destroy
deux der two
deux fois der fwa twice
devant der·von in front of
développement ⓜ day·vlop·mon development
devenir derv·neer become
deviner der·vee·nay guess
devoir ⓜ der·vwar duty
devoir der·vwar owe
devoirs ⓜ der·vwar homework
diabète ⓜ dya·bet diabetes
diaphragme ⓜ dya·frag·mer diaphragm
diarrhée ⓕ dya·ray diarrhoea
dictionnaire ⓜ deek·syo·nair dictionary
dieu ⓜ dyer god
différent(e) ⓜ/ⓕ dee·fay·ron(t) different
difficile dee·fee·seel difficult
dimanche ⓜ dee·monsh Sunday
dîner ⓜ dee·nay dinner
diplôme ⓜ dee·plom degree • diploma
dire deer say • tell
direct(e) ⓜ/ⓕ dee·rekt direct
directeur/directrice ⓜ/ⓕ dee·rek·ter/doo·rok·troos manager
direction ⓕ dee·rek·syon direction
diriger dee·ree·zhay manage (business)
discours ⓜ dees·koor speech
discrimination ⓕ dee·skree·mee·na·syon discrimination
discuter dee·skew·tay discuss
diseuse de bonne aventure ⓕ dee·zerz der bon a·von·tewr fortune teller
disponible dees·po·nee·bler free (available)
dispute ⓕ dees·pewt quarrel
disquaire ⓜ dee·skair music shop
distance ⓕ dees·tons distance
distributeur de tickets ⓜ dee·stree·bew·ter der tee·kay ticket machine
divorcé(e) ⓜ/ⓕ dee·vor·say divorced
dix dee(s) ten
doigt ⓜ dwa finger
dollar ⓜ do·lar dollar
donc dongk therefore
donner do·nay deal (cards) • give
dormir dor·meer sleep
dos ⓜ do back (body)
dose ⓕ doz dose
douane ⓕ dwan customs
double doo·bler double
douche ⓕ doosh shower
douleur ⓕ doo·ler ache • pain
douloureux/douloureuse ⓜ/ⓕ doo·loo·rer/doo·loo·rerz painful • sore
doux/douce ⓜ/ⓕ doo/doos soft
douzaine ⓕ doo·zen dozen
draguer dra·gay chat up
drap ⓜ dra sheet (bed)
drapeau ⓜ dra·po flag
draps ⓜ dra bed linen
drogué dro·gay addicted (to drugs)
drogue ⓕ drog drug • drugs
droit ⓜ drwa law (study, professsion)
droit(e) ⓜ/ⓕ drwa(t) straight
droite ⓜ drwa right (entitlement)
droits civils ⓜ pl drwa see·veel civil rights
droits de l'homme ⓜ pl drwa der lom human rights
drôle drol funny
du ⓜ dew some
dur(e) ⓜ/ⓕ dewr hard (not soft)

E

eau ⓕ o water
eau minérale ⓕ o mee·nay·ral mineral water
échange ⓜ ay·shonzh exchange
échanger ay·shon·zhay change (money) • exchange
échapper ay·sha·pay escape
écharpe ⓕ ay·sharp scarf
échec ⓜ ay·shek failure
échecs ⓜ ay·shek chess
échiquier ⓜ ay·shee·kyay chess board
école ⓕ ay·kol school
école professionnelle ⓕ ay·kol pro·fay·syo·nel college (vocational)
économie ⓕ ay·ko·no·mee economy
Ecosse ⓕ ay·kos Scotland
écouter ay·koo·tay listen (to)
écran ⓜ ay·kron screen
— solaire so·lair sunscreen
— solaire total so·lair to·tal sunblock
écrire ay·kreer write
écrivain ⓜ ay·kree·vun writer
ecstasy ⓜ ek·sta·zee ecstasy (drug)
eczéma ⓜ eg·zay·ma eczema
éducation ⓕ ay·dew·ka·syon education
effet ⓜ ay·fay effect
effrayé(e) ⓜ/ⓕ ay·fray·yay scared
égale ay·gal equal
égalité ⓕ ay·ga·lee·tay equality
égalité des chances ⓕ ay·ga·lee·tay day shons equal opportunity
église ⓕ ay·gleez church
égoïste ay·go·eest selfish
élection ⓕ ay·lek·syon election
électricité ⓕ ay·lek·tree·see·tay electricity
elle ⓕ el she
elles ⓕ pl el they (women)
éloigné(e) ⓜ/ⓕ ay·lwa·nyay remote
e-mail ⓜ ay·mel email
embrasser om·bra·say kiss
embrayage om·bray·yazh clutch
empêcher om·pay·shay prevent
employé/employée ⓜ/ⓕ om·plwa·yay/om·plwa·yay employee
employé(e) de bureau ⓜ/ⓕ om·plwa·yay der bew·ro office worker
employeur ⓜ om·plwa·yer employer
emprunter om·prun·tay borrow
en on made of (cotton, wood etc)
— avant a·von ahead
— bas ba down
— désordre day·zor·drer messy
— face de fas der opposite
— grève grev on strike
— haut o up • upstairs
— panne pan broken down
— recommandé rer·ko·mon·day r egistered mail/post (by)
— retard rer·tar late
encaisser ong·kay·say cash (a cheque)
enceinte on·sunt pregnant
encore ong·kor again • yet
endroit ⓜ on·drwa spot (place)
énergie ⓕ ay·nair·zhee energy
énergie nucléaire ⓕ ay·nair·zhee new·klay·air nuclear energy
enfant ⓜ&ⓕ on·fon child
enfants ⓜ&ⓕ pl on·fon children
ennuyeux/ennuyeuse ⓜ/ⓕ on·nwee·yer/on·nwee·yerz boring
énorme ay·norm huge
enregistrement on·rer·zhee·strer·mon check-in (desk)
enregistrer on·rer·zhees·tray record
ensemble on·som·bler together
ensoleillé(e) ⓜ/ⓕ on·so·lay·yay sunny
entendre on·ton·drer hear
enterrement ⓜ on·tair·mon funeral
enthousiaste on·tooz·yast enthusiastic
entorse ⓕ on·tors sprain
entracte ⓜ on·trakt intermission
entraîneur ⓜ on·tray·ner coach
entre on·trer between
entrée ⓕ on·tray entry
entreprise ⓕ on·trer·preez company

entrer on·tray enter
entrevue ⓕ on·trer·vew interview
enveloppe ⓕ on·vlop envelope
envers on·vair toward (feelings)
environ on·vee·ron about
environnement ⓜ on·vee·ron·mon environment
envoyer on·vwa·yay send
épais/épaisse ⓜ/ⓕ ay·pay/ay·pes thick
épaule ⓕ ay·pol shoulder
épicé(e) ⓜ/ⓕ ay·pee·say spicy
épicerie ⓕ ay·pee·sree grocery
épilepsie ⓕ ay·pee·lep·see epilepsy
épingle ⓕ ay·pung·gler pin
épouser ay·poo·zay marry
épuisé(e) ⓜ/ⓕ ay·pwee·zay exhausted
équipe ⓕ ay·keep team
équipement ⓜ ay·keep·mon equipment
équipement de plongée ⓜ ay·keep·mon der plon·zhay diving equipment
équitation ⓕ ay·kee·ta·syon horse riding
erreur ⓕ ay·rer mistake
escalier ⓜ es·ka·lyay stairway
escalier roulant ⓜ es·ka·lyay roo·lon escalator
escargot ⓜ es·kar·go snail
escrime ⓕ es·kreem fencing
espace ⓜ es·pas space
Espagne ⓕ es·pa·nyer Spain
espèce menacée de disparition ⓕ es·pes mer·na·say der dees·pa·rees·yon endangered species
espérer es·pay·ray hope
espoir ⓜ es·pwar hope
esprit ⓜ ay·spree mind • spirit
essai ⓜ ay·say test
essayer ay·say·yay try
essence ⓕ ay·sons petrol • gas
est ⓜ est east
estomac ⓜ es·to·ma stomach
et ay and
établissement d'enseignement secondaire ⓜ ay·ta·blees·mon don·say·nyer·mon zgon·dair high school
étage ⓜ ay·tazh floor (storey)
étagère ⓕ ay·ta·zhair shelf
étang ⓜ ay·tong pond
été ⓜ ay·tay summer
étiquette ⓕ ay·tee·ket luggage tag
étoiles ⓕ ay·twal stars
étrange ay·tronzh strange
étranger/étrangère ⓜ/ⓕ ay·tron·zhay/ay·tron·zhair foreign • stranger
être e·trer be
être d'accord e·trer da·kor agree
être enrhumé e·trer on·rew·may have a cold
étroit(e) ⓜ/ⓕ ay·trwa(t) tight
étudiant(e) ⓜ/ⓕ ay·tew·dyon(t) student
étudier ay·tew·dyay study
euro ⓜ er·ro euro
Europe ⓕ er·rop Europe
euthanasie ⓕ er·ta·na·zee euthanasia
événement ⓜ ay·ven·mon event
évident(e) ⓜ/ⓕ ay·vee·don(t) obvious
exactement eg·zak·ter·mon exactly
examen ⓜ eg·za·mun exam
excédent ek·say·don excess (baggage)
excellent(e) ⓜ/ⓕ ek·say·lon excellent
exemple ⓜ eg·zom·pler example
exercice ⓜ eg·zair·sees exercise
exiger eg·zee·zhay demand
expérience ⓕ eks·pair·yons experience
expliquer eks·plee·kay explain
exploitation ⓕ eks·plwa·ta·syon exploitation
exporter eks·por·tay export

exposé ⓜ eks·po·zay talk (lecture)
exposition ⓕ ek·spo·zee·syon exhibition
exprès eks·pres express (mail)
expression ⓕ ek·spray·syon phrase
extraordinaire eks·tra·or·dee·nair extraordinary

F

fâché(e) ⓜ/ⓕ fa·shay angry
facile fa·seel easy
facilement ému fa·seel·mon ay·mew emotional (person)
façon ⓕ fa·son way (manner)
facteur ⓜ fak·ter postman
faible fay·bler weak
faire fair do • make
— attention a·ton·syon look out
— confiance à kon·fyons a trust
— de la planche à voile der la plonsh a vwal windsurfing (to go)
— des courses day koors shop
— du lèche-vitrines dew lesh·vee·treen go window-shopping
— du stop dew stop hitchhike
— du vélo dew vay·lo cycle
— frire freer fry
— la randonnée la ron·do·nay hike
— les courses lay koors go shopping
— semblant som·blon pretend
— ses dévotions say day·vo·syon worship
— une fausse couche ewn fos koosh miscarriage (to have a)
fait ⓜ fet fact
fait/faite à le main ⓜ/ⓕ fay/fet a la mun handmade
falaise ⓕ fa·lez cliff
famille ⓕ fa·mee family
fan ⓜ/ⓕ fan fan (of person)
fasciste fa·sheest fascist
fatigué(e) fa·tee·gay tired
faute ⓕ fot foul (football) • fault
fauteuil ⓜ fo·ter·yee armchair
fauteuil roulant ⓜ fo·ter·yee roo·lon wheelchair
faux/fausse ⓜ/ⓕ fo/fos false • wrong
fax ⓜ faks fax machine
félicitations fay·lee·see·ta·syon congratulations
femelle fer·mel female
femme ⓕ fum wife • woman
— au foyer o fwa·yay homemaker
— d'affaires da·fair business woman
fenêtre ⓕ fer·nay·trer window
fer à repasser ⓜ fair a rer·pa·say iron (for clothes)
ferme ⓕ ferm farm
fermé(e) ⓜ/ⓕ fair·may closed
fermé(e) à clé ⓜ/ⓕ fair·may a klay locked
fermer fair·may close
fermer à clé fair·may a klay lock
fermeture éclair ⓕ fair·mer·tewr ay·klair zip • zipper
fête ⓕ fet celebration • festival
feu ⓜ fer fire
feuille ⓕ fer·yee leaf • sheet (of paper)
feux ⓜ fer traffic lights
février ⓜ fayv·ree·yay February
fiançailles ⓕ fyon·sai engagement
fiancé ⓜ fyon·say fiancé
fiancé(e) ⓜ/ⓕ fyon·say engaged
fiancée ⓕ fyon·say fiancée
ficelle ⓕ fee·sel string
fiction ⓕ feek·syon fiction
fièvre ⓕ fyev·rer fever
fil de fer ⓜ feel der fair wire
fil dentaire ⓜ feel don·tair dental floss
filet ⓜ fee·lay net
fille ⓕ fee·yer daughter • girl
film ⓜ feelm film (cinema) • movie
fils ⓜ fees son
fines herbes ⓕ feen zairb herbs
fini(e) ⓜ/ⓕ fee·nee over (finished)
finir fee·neer end • finish
fleur ⓕ fler flower
fleuriste ⓜ&ⓕ fler·reest florist
flic ⓜ fleek cop

foi ⓕ fwa faith
foie ⓜ fwa liver
foncé(e) ⓜ/ⓕ fon·say dark (of colour)
fondamental fon·da·mon·tal basic
foot(ball) ⓜ foot(bol) football • soccer
forêt ⓕ fo·ray forest
forme ⓕ form shape
fort(e) ⓜ/ⓕ for(t) loud • strong
fortune ⓕ for·tewn fortune (money)
fou/folle ⓜ/ⓕ foo/fol crazy
foule ⓕ fool crowd
four ⓜ foor oven
four à micro-ondes ⓜ foor a mee·kro·ond microwave (oven)
fourchette ⓕ foor·shet fork
fourmi ⓕ foor·mee ant
fragile fra·zheel fragile
frais/fraîche ⓜ/ⓕ fray/fresh cool • fresh
franchise ⓕ fron·sheez baggage allowance
freins ⓜ frun brakes
fréquent(e) ⓜ/ⓕ fray·kon(t) frequent
frère ⓜ frair brother
froid(e) ⓜ/ⓕ frwa(d) cold
frontière ⓕ fron·tyair border
frottis ⓜ fro·tee pap smear
fruit ⓜ frwee fruit
fumée ⓕ few·may smoke
fumer few·may smoke

G

gagnant(e) ⓜ/ⓕ ga·nyon(t) winner
gagner ga·nyay earn • win
galerie ⓕ gal·ree art gallery (private)
gamin/gamine ⓜ/ⓕ ga·mun/ga·meen kid (boy or girl)
gant de toilette ⓜ gon der twa·let face cloth
gants ⓜ pl gon gloves
garage ⓜ ga·razh garage
garanti(e) ⓜ/ⓕ ga·ron·tee guaranteed
garçon ⓜ gar·son boy
garde-fou ⓜ gard·foo rail
garderie ⓕ gard·ree childminding
gardien de but ⓜ gar·dyun der bewt goalkeeper
gare ⓕ gar train station
gare routière ⓕ gar roo·tyair bus station
garer (une voiture) ga·ray (ewn vwa·tewr) park (a car)
gas-oil ⓜ gaz·wal diesel
gastro-entérite ⓕ gastro·on·tay·reet gastroenteritis
gaz ⓜ gaz gas (for cooking)
gazon ⓜ ga·zon grass (lawn)
gel ⓜ zhel frost
gelé(e) ⓜ/ⓕ zher·lay frozen
geler zher·lay freeze
gênant(e) ⓜ/ⓕ zhay·non(t) embarrassing
gendarme ⓜ zhon·darm police officer (in country)
gêné(e) ⓜ/ⓕ zhay·nay embarrassed
gêner zhay·nay embarrass
général(e) ⓜ/ⓕ zhay·nay·ral general
généreux/généreuse ⓜ/ⓕ zhay·nay·rer/zhay·nay·rerz generous
génial(e) ⓜ/ⓕ zhay·nyal brilliant
genou ⓜ zhnoo knee
genre ⓜ zhon·rer kind (type)
gens ⓜ pl zhon people
gentil/gentile ⓜ/ⓕ zhon·tee kind • nice
gérant(e) ⓜ/ⓕ zhay·ron(t) manager (restaurant, hotel)
gilet de sauvetage ⓜ zhee·lay der sov·tazh life jacket
glace ⓕ glas ice • ice cream
gorge ⓕ gorzh throat
gourmand(e) ⓜ/ⓕ goor·mon(d) greedy (food)
goût ⓜ goo flavour
gouvernement ⓜ goo·vair·ner·mon government
grâce ⓕ gras blessing
gramme ⓜ gram gram
grand lit ⓜ gron lee double bed

grand magasin ⓜ gron ma·ga·zun department store
grand(e) ⓜ/ⓕ gron(d) big • large • tall
grande route ⓕ grond root main road
grand-mère ⓕ grom·mair grandmother
grand-père ⓜ grom·pair grandfather
grands-parents ⓜ pl grom·pa·ron grandparents
gras/grasse ⓜ/ⓕ gra/gras fat
gratuit(e) ⓜ/ⓕ gra·twee(t) free (gratis)
grenouille ⓕ grer·noo·yer frog
grille-pain ⓜ greey·pun toaster
grippe ⓕ greep flu
gris(e) ⓜ/ⓕ gree(z) grey • gray
grosseur ⓕ gro·ser lump
grotte ⓕ grot cave
groupe ⓜ **de rock** groop der rok rock group
groupe ⓜ **sanguin** groop song·gun blood group
guêpe ⓕ gep wasp
guerre ⓕ gair war
guichet ⓜ gee·shay ticket office
guichet automatique de banque (GAB) ⓜ gee·shay o·to·ma·teek der bonk automatic teller machine (ATM)
guide ⓜ geed guide (person) • guidebook
guidon ⓜ gee·don handlebars
guitare ⓕ gee·tar guitar
gym ⓕ zheem gym (activity)
gymnase ⓜ zheem·naz gym (place)
gym(nastique) ⓕ zheem(na·steek) gymnastics
gynécologue ⓜ/ⓕ zhee·nay·ko·log gynaecologist

H

habiter a·bee·tay live (in a place)
habitude ⓕ a·bee·tewd habit
habituellement a·bee·twel·mon usually
halal a·lal Halal
hall ⓜ ol foyer (of cinema)
hamac ⓜ a·mak hammock
handicapé(e) ⓜ/ⓕ on·dee·ka·pay disabled
harcèlement ⓜ ar·sel·mon harassment
hasard ⓜ a·zar chance
haut(e) ⓜ/ⓕ o(t) high
hauteur ⓕ o·ter height
hémisphère nord ⓜ ay·mees·fair nor northern hemisphere
hémisphère sud ⓜ ay·mees·fair sewd southern hemisphere
hépatite ⓕ ay·pa·teet hepatitis
herbe ⓕ airb grass (marijuana)
herboriste ⓜ/ⓕ air·bo·reest herbalist
héroïne ⓕ ay·ro·een heroin
heure ⓕ er hour • time
heures d'ouverture ⓕ pl lay zer doo·vair·tewr opening hours
heureux/heureuse ⓜ/ⓕ er·rer/er·rerz happy
hier ee·yair yesterday
hindou(e) ⓜ/ⓕ un·doo Hindu
histoire ⓕ ees·twar history • story
historique ees·to·reek historical
hiver ⓜ ee·vair winter
hockey ⓜ o·kay hockey
hockey sur glace ⓜ o·kay sewr glas ice hockey
homme ⓜ om man
homme d'affaires ⓜ om da·fair business man
homme/femme politique ⓜ/ⓕ om/fum po·lee·teek politician
homosexuel(le) ⓜ/ⓕ o·mo·sek·swel gay • homosexual
honnête o·net honest
hôpital ⓜ o·pee·tal hospital
horaire ⓜ o·rair timetable
horoscope ⓜ o·ro·skop horoscope
hors jeu or·zher offside (sport)
hors service or sair·vees out of order
hospitalité ⓕ os·pee·ta·lee·tay hospitality
hôtel ⓜ o·tel hotel

huile (f) weel oil
huit weet eight
humain (m) ew·mun human
humour (m) ew·moor humour

I

ici ee·see here
idée (f) ee·day idea
idiot(e) (m)/(f) ee·dyo(t) idiot
ignorant(e) (m)/(f) ee·nyo·ron(t) ignorant
il eel he
île (f) eel island
illégal(e) (m)/(f) ee·lay·gal illegal
ils (m) eel they (men)
image (f) ee·mazh picture
imagination (f) ee·ma·zhee·na·syon imagination
immatriculation ee·ma·tree·kew·la·syon car registration
immédiatement ee·may·dyat·mon immediately/right now
immigration (f) ee·mee·gra·syon immigration
imperméable um·pair·may·abler raincoat • waterproof
impoli(e) (m)/(f) um·po·lee rude • impolite
important(e) (m)/(f) um·por·ton(t) important
importer um·por·tay import
impossible um·po·see·bler impossible
impôt sur le revenu (m) um·po sewr ler rerv·new income tax
imprimante (f) um·pree·mont printer (computer)
incertain(e) (m)/(f) un·sair·tun/ un·sair·ten uncertain
inconfortable ung·kon·for·ta·bler uncomfortable
Inde (f) und India
indépendant(e) (m)/(f) un·day·pon·don(t) independent • self-employed
indigestion (f) un·dee·zhes·tyon indigestion
indiquer un·dee·kay point
individu (m) un·dee·vee·dew individual
industrie (f) un·dews·tree industry
industriel/industrielle (m)/(f) un·dews·tree·el industrial
infection (f) un·fek·syon infection
infirmier/infirmière (m)/(f) un·feer·myay/un·feer·myair nurse
inflammation (f) un·fla·ma·syon inflammation
influence (f) un·flew·ons influence
informatique (f) un·for·ma·teek IT
ingénierie un·zhay·nee·ree engineering
ingénieur (m) un·zhay·nyer engineer
ingrédient (m) ung·gray·dyon ingredient
injecter un·zhek·tay inject
injuste un·zhewst unfair
innocent(e) (m)/(f) ee·no·son(t) innocent
inondation (f) ee·non·da·syon flood
inopportun(e) (m)/(f) ee·no·por·tun/ ee·no·po·tewn inconvenient
inquiet/inquiète (m)/(f) ung·kyay/ ung·kyet worried
insecte (m) un·sekt bug • insect
institut universitaire (m) un·stee·tew ew·nee·vair·see·tair college
intelligent(e) (m)/(f) un·tay·lee·zhon(t) intelligent
intéressant(e) (m)/(f) un·tay·ray·son(t) interesting
international(e) (m)/(f) un·tair·na·syo·nal international
internet (m) un·tair·net internet
interprète (m)/(f) un·tair·pret interpreter
intime un·teem intimate
invité(e) (m)/(f) un·vee·tay visitor (guest)
inviter un·vee·tay invite
Irlande (f) eer·lond Ireland

itinéraire ⓜ ee·tee·nay·rair itinerary • route
itinéraire de randonnée ⓜ ee·tee·nay·rair der ron·do·nay hiking route
ivre ee·vrer drunk

J

jaloux/jalouse ⓜ/ⓕ zha·loo/zha·looz jealous
jamais zha·may never
jambe ⓕ zhomb leg
jambon ⓜ zhom·bon ham
janvier ⓜ zhon·vyay January
Japon ⓜ zha·pon Japan
jardin ⓜ zhar·dun garden
— botanique bo·ta·neek botanic garden
— d'enfants don·fon kindergarten
jardinage ⓜ zhar·dee·nazh gardening
jaune zhon yellow
je zher I
jean ⓜ zheen jeans
jeep ⓕ zheep jeep
jeter zher·tay throw
jeu ⓜ zher game
jeu électronique ⓜ zher ay·lek·tro·neek computer game
jeudi ⓜ zher·dee Thursday
jeune zhern young
jockey ⓜ zho·kay jockey
jogging ⓜ zho·geeng jogging
joie ⓕ zhwa joy
joindre zhwun·drer join
joli(e) ⓜ/ⓕ zho·lee pretty
jouer zhoo·ay act • play
jouet ⓜ zhway toy
jour ⓜ zhoor day
— de l'An der lon New Year's Day
— de Noël der no·el Christmas Day
journal ⓜ zhoor·nal newspaper
journaliste ⓜ/ⓕ zhoor·na·leest journalist
juge ⓜ zhewzh judge
juif/juive ⓜ/ⓕ zhweef/zhweev Jewish
juillet ⓜ zhwee·yay July
juin ⓜ zhwun June
jumeaux/jumelles ⓜ/ⓕ pl zhew·mo/zhew·mel twins
jupe ⓕ zhewp skirt
jusqu'à zhew·ska until (Friday, etc)
justice ⓕ zhew·stees justice

K

kascher ka·shair kosher
kilo ⓜ kee·lo kilo
kilogramme ⓜ kee·lo·gram kilogram
kilomètre ⓜ kee·lo·may·trer kilometre
kinésithérapeute ⓜ/ⓕ kee·nay·zee·tay·ra·pert physiotherapist
kinésithérapie ⓕ kee·nay·zee·tay·ra·pee physiotherapy
kiosque ⓜ kyosk kiosk

L

là la there
lac ⓜ lak lake
laid(e) ⓜ/ⓕ lay/led ugly
laine ⓕ len wool
laisser lay·say leave (something)
laisser tomber lay·say tom·bay drop
lait ⓜ lay milk
lame de rasoir ⓕ lam der ra·zwar razor blade
lampe ⓕ lomp lamp
— de poche der posh torch (flashlight)
langue ⓕ long language
lapin ⓜ la·pun rabbit
large larzh wide
laver la·vay wash (something)
laverie ⓕ lav·ree launderette
laxatif ⓜ lak·sa·teef laxative
le/la plus grand(e) ⓜ/ⓕ ler/la plew gron(d) biggest
le plus petit/la plus petite ⓜ/ⓕ ler plew per·tee/la plew per·teet smallest
le/la plus proche ⓜ/ⓕ ler/la plew prosh nearest

le/la meilleur(e) ⓜ/ⓕ ler/la may·yer best
légal(e) ⓜ/ⓕ lay·gal legal
léger/légère ⓜ/ⓕ lay·zhay/lay·zhair light (not heavy)
législation ⓕ lay·zhee·sla·syon legislation
légume ⓜ lay·gewm vegetable
lent(e) ⓜ/ⓕ lon(t) slow
lentement lon·ter·mon slowly
lequel/laquelle ⓜ/ⓕ ler·kel/la·kel which
Les Jeux Olympiques lay zher zo·lum·peek Olympic Games
lesbienne ⓕ les·byen lesbian
lettre ⓕ lay·trer letter
lettres classiques ⓕ pl le·trer kla·seek humanities
leur/leurs sg/pl ler their
lever ler·vay lift (arm)
lever du soleil ⓜ ler·vay dew so·lay sunrise
lèvre ⓕ lay·vrer lip
lézard ⓜ lay·zar lizard
liaison ⓕ lyay·zon affair
liberté ⓕ lee·bair·tay freedom
librairie ⓕ lee·bray·ree bookshop
libre lee·brer free (at liberty) • vacant
libre-service ⓜ lee·brer·sair·vees self service
lieu ⓜ lyer place
— de naissance der nay·sons place of birth
— saint sun shrine
lièvre ⓜ lyev·rer hare
ligne ⓕ lee·nyer line
ligne aérienne ⓕ lee·nyer a·ay·ryen airline
limitation de vitesse ⓕ lee·mee·ta·syon der vee·tes speed limit
lin ⓜ lun linen (material)
linge ⓜ lunzh laundry (clothes) • linen
lingerie ⓕ lun·zhree lingerie
lire leer read
lit ⓜ lee bed
literie ⓕ leet·ree bedding
lits jumeaux ⓜ pl day lee zhew·mo twin beds
livre ⓜ leev·rer book
livre ⓕ leev·rer pound (money, weight)
livrer leev·ray deliver
local(e) ⓜ/ⓕ lo·kal local
locataire ⓜ/ⓕ lo·ka·tair tenant
location de voitures ⓕ lo·ka·syon der vwa·tewr car hire
logement ⓜ lozh·mon accommodation
logiciel ⓜ lo·zhee·syel software
loi ⓕ lwa law
lointain(e) ⓜ/ⓕ lwun·tun/·ten far
long ⓜ long long
long-courrier long·koo·ryay long-distance (flight)
longue ⓕ long long
longueur ⓕ long·ger length
louer loo·ay hire • rent
louer à bail loo·way a ba·yer lease
lourd(e) ⓜ/ⓕ loor(d) heavy
loyal(e) ⓜ/ⓕ lwa·yal loyal
lubrifiant ⓜ lew·bree·fyon lubricant
lumière ⓕ lew·myair light
lundi ⓜ lun·dee Monday
lune de miel ⓕ lewn der myel honeymoon
lunettes ⓕ pl lew·net glasses (spectacles) • goggles (skiing)
— de soleil der so·lay sunglasses
luxe ⓜ lewks luxury

M

ma ⓕ ma my
machine ⓕ ma·sheen machine
machine à laver ⓕ ma·sheen a la·vay washing machine
mâchoire ⓕ ma·shwar jaw
Madame ma·dam Mrs • Ms
Mademoiselle mad·mwa·zel Miss

magasin ⓜ ma·ga·zun shop
— de chaussures der sho·sewr shoe shop
— de souvenirs der soov·neer souvenir shop
— de sports der spor sports store/shop
— de vêtements der vet·mon clothing store
— de vins et spiritueux der vun ay spee·ree·twer liquor store
— pour équipement de camping poor ay·keep·mon der kom·peeng camping store
— qui vend des appareils électriques kee von day za·pa·ray ay·lek·treek electrical store
magazine ⓜ ma·ga·zeen magazine
magicien/magicienne ⓜ/ⓕ ma·zhee·syun/ma·zhees·yen magician
mai ⓜ may May
maigre may·grer thin
maillot de bain ⓜ may·yo der bun bathing suit
maillot de corps ⓜ ma·yo der kor singlet • vest
main ⓕ mun hand
maintenant mun·ter·non now
maire ⓜ mair mayor
mairie ⓕ may·ree city hall
mais may but
maison ⓕ may·zon house
majorité ⓕ ma·zho·ree·tay majority
mal à la tête ⓜ mal a la tet headache
mal des transports ⓜ mal day trons·por travel sickness
malade ma·lad ill • sick
maladie ⓕ ma·la·dee disease • sickness
— de cœur der ker heart condition
— vénérienne vay·nay·ryen venereal disease
malhonnête mal·o·net dishonest
maman ⓕ ma·mon mum
mammographie ⓕ ma·mo·gra·fee mammogram
manger mon·zhay eat
manif(estation) ⓕ ma·neef(ay·sta·syon) protest
manifester ma·nee·fay·stay protest
manoeuvre ⓜ ma·ner·vrer labourer
manque ⓜ mongk shortage
manquer mong·kay miss
manquer de mong·kay der run out of
manteau ⓜ mon·to coat
maquillage ⓜ ma·kee·yazh make-up
marchand ⓜ mar·shon shopkeeper
— de journaux mar·shon der zhoor·no newsagent
— de légumes mar·shon der lay·gewm greengrocer
marche ⓕ marsh step
marché ⓜ mar·shay market
marché aux puces ⓜ mar·shay o pews flea market
marcher mar·shay walk
mardi ⓜ mar·dee Tuesday
marée ⓕ ma·ray tide
mari ⓜ ma·ree husband
mariage ⓜ ma·ryazh marriage • wedding
marié(e) ⓜ/ⓕ ma·ryay married
marihuana ⓕ ma·ree·wa·na marijuana
mars ⓜ mars March
marteau ⓜ mar·to hammer
massage ⓜ ma·sazh massage
masser ma·say massage
masseur/masseuse ⓜ/ⓕ ma·ser/ma·serz masseur/masseuse
match ⓜ matsh game (sports)
match nul ⓜ matsh newl tie (draw)
matelas ⓜ mat·la mattress
matériel ⓜ ma·tay·ryel material
matin ⓜ ma·tun morning
mauvais(e) ⓜ/ⓕ mo·vay(z) bad • off (meat) • wrong (direction)
mécanicien/mécanicienne ⓜ/ⓕ may·ka·nee·syun/may·ka·nee·syen mechanic

médecin ⓜ mayd·sun doctor
médecine ⓕ med·seen medicine
médias ⓜ pl may·dya media
médicament ⓜ may·dee·ka·mon medicine (medication)
méditation ⓕ may·dee·ta·syon meditation
meilleur(e) ⓜ/ⓕ may·yer better
mélanger may·lon·zhay mix
membre ⓜ mom·brer member
même mem same
mémoire ⓕ may·mwar memory (ability to remember)
ménage ⓜ may·nazh housework
mensonge ⓜ mon·sonzh lie
menstruation ⓕ mon·strew·a·syon menstruation
menteur/menteuse ⓜ/ⓕ mon·ter/mon·terz liar
mentir mon·teer lie (tell lies)
menuisier ⓜ mer·nwee·zyay carpenter
mer ⓕ mair sea
mercredi ⓜ mair·krer·dee Wednesday
mère ⓕ mair mother
merveilleux/merveilleuse ⓜ/ⓕ mair·vay·yer/mair·vay·yerz wonderful
mes pl may my
message ⓜ may·sazh message
messe ⓕ mes mass (Catholic)
métal ⓜ may·tal metal
météo ⓕ may·tay·o weather forecast
mètre ⓜ may·trer metre
métro ⓜ may·tro subway
mettre may·trer put
meublé(e) ⓜ/ⓕ mer·blay furnished
meubles ⓜ mer·bler furniture
midi mee·dee midday • noon
mignon/mignonne ⓜ/ⓕ mee·nyon/mee·nyon cute
migraine ⓕ mee·gren migraine
militaire mee·lee·tair military
militant/militante ⓜ/ⓕ mee·lee·ton(t) activist
millénaire ⓜ mee·lay·nair millennium
millimètre ⓜ mee·lee·may·trer millimetre
million ⓜ mee·lyon million
minorité ⓕ mee·no·ree·tay minority
minuit mee·nwee midnight
minuscule mee·new·skewl tiny
minute ⓕ mee·newt minute
miroir ⓜ mee·rwar mirror
mode ⓕ mod fashion
modem ⓜ mo·dem modem
moderne mo·dairn modern
moi mwa me
moins ⓜ mwun least
moins de mwun der less
mois ⓜ mwa month
moitié ⓕ mwa·tyay half
mon ⓜ mon my
monarchie ⓕ mo·nar·shee monarchy
monastère ⓜ mo·na·stair monastery
monde ⓜ mond world
monnaie ⓕ mo·nay change (coins)
mononucléose infectieuse ⓕ mo·no·new·klay·oz un·fek·syerz glandular fever
Monsieur mer·syer Mr
montagne ⓕ mon·ta·nyer mountain
monter mon·tay climb
— à bord de a bor der board (a plane, ship)
— à (cheval) a (shval) ride (horse)
montre ⓕ mon·trer watch
montrer mon·tray show
monument ⓜ mo·new·mon monument
morceau ⓜ mor·so piece
mordre mor·drer bite
morsure ⓕ mor·sewr bite (dog)
mort ⓕ mor death
mort(e) ⓜ/ⓕ mor(t) dead
mosquée ⓕ mo·skay mosque
mot ⓜ mo word
motel ⓜ mo·tel motel
moteur ⓜ mo·ter engine
moto ⓕ mo·to motorcycle
mouche ⓕ moosh fly

mouchoir ⓜ moo·shwar handkerchief
mouchoirs en papier ⓜ pl moo·shwar om pa·pyay tissues
mouillé(e) ⓜ/ⓕ moo·yay wet
mourir moo·reer die
mousse à raser ⓕ moos a ra·zay shaving cream
moustiquaire ⓕ moo·stee·kair mosquito net
moustique ⓜ moo·steek mosquito
mouton ⓜ moo·ton sheep
muguet ⓜ mew·gay thrush (illness)
mur ⓜ mewr wall (outer)
muscle ⓜ mews·kler muscle
musée ⓜ mew·zay museum • art gallery (state)
musicien/musicienne ⓜ/ⓕ mew·zees·yun/mew·zees·yen musician
musicien(ne) des rues ⓜ/ⓕ mew·zee·syun/mew·zee·syen day rew busker
musique ⓕ mew·zeek music
musulman(e) ⓜ/ⓕ mew·zewl·mon/mew·zewl·man Muslim

N

nager na·zhay swim
nager avec un tuba na·zhay a·vek un tew·ba snorkel
nappe ⓕ nap tablecloth
nationalité ⓕ na·syo·na·lee·tay nationality
nature ⓕ na·tewr nature
naturopathe ⓜ&ⓕ na·tew·ro·pat naturopath
nausée ⓕ no·zay nausea
nausées matinales ⓕ pl no·zay ma·tee·nal morning sickness
navire ⓜ na·veer ship
né(e) ⓜ/ⓕ nay born
nécessaire nay·say·sair necessary
neige ⓕ nezh snow
neiger nay·zhay snow
nettoyage ⓜ net·wa·yazh cleaning
nettoyer net·wa·yay clean
neuf nerf nine
nez ⓜ nay nose
ni nee neither
nier nee·ay deny
n'importe où num·port oo anywhere
n'importe quel/quelle ⓜ/ⓕ num·port kel any
n'importe qui num·port kee anyone
n'importe quoi num·port kwa anything
niveau ⓜ nee·vo level (tier, height)
Noël ⓜ no·el Christmas
noir(e) ⓜ/ⓕ nwar black
noir et blanc nwar ay blong B&W (film)
nom ⓜ nom name
— de famille der fa·mee family name • surname
non non no
non-direct non·dee·rekt nondirect
non-fumeur non·few·mer nonsmoking
non-meublé(e) ⓜ/ⓕ no·mer·blay unfurnished
nord ⓜ nor north
normal(e) ⓜ/ⓕ nor·mal regular
nostalgique nos·tal·zheek homesick
notre no·trer our
nourrir noo·reer feed
nourriture ⓕ noo·ree·tewr food
nous noo us • we
nouveau/nouvelle ⓜ/ⓕ noo·vo/noo·vel new
Nouvelle-Zélande ⓕ noo·vel·zay·lond New Zealand
nuage ⓜ nwazh cloud
nuageux/nuageuse ⓜ/ⓕ nwa·zher/nwa·zherz cloudy
nuit ⓕ nwee night
numéro ⓜ new·may·ro number
— de chambre der shom·brer room number
— de passeport der pas·por passport number

O

objectif ⓜ ob·zhek·teef lens
objet ⓜ ob·zhay purpose
objets artisanaux ⓜ pl ob·zhay ar·tee·za·no handicrafts
obscur(e) ⓜ/ⓕ ob·skewr dark
obtenir op·ter·neer obtain
occasion ⓕ o·ka·zyon opportunity
occupation ⓕ o·kew·pa·syon occupation
occupé(e) ⓜ/ⓕ o·kew·pay busy
océan ⓜ o·say·on ocean
odeur ⓕ o·der smell
œil ⓜ er·yee eye
office de tourisme ⓜ o·fees·der too·rees·mer tourist office
officier ⓜ o·fees·yay officer
oiseau ⓜ wa·zo bird
ombre ⓕ om·brer shade • shadow
opéra ⓜ o·pay·ra opera
opérateur/opératrice ⓜ/ⓕ o·pay·ra·ter/o·pay·ra·trees operator
opération ⓕ o·pay·ra·syon operation
or ⓜ or gold
orage ⓜ o·razh storm
orange o·ronzh orange (colour)
ordinaire or·dee·nair ordinary
ordinateur ⓜ or·dee·na·ter computer
ordinateur portable ⓜ or·dee·na·ter por·ta·bler laptop
ordonnance ⓕ or·do·nons prescription
ordonner or·do·nay order
ordre ⓜ or·drer order
ordures ⓕ pl or·dewr rubbish • garbage
oreille ⓕ o·ray ear
oreiller ⓜ o·ray·yay pillow
organisation ⓕ or·ga·nee·za·syon organisation
organiser or·ga·nee·zay organise
orgasme ⓜ or·gas·mer orgasm
original(e) ⓜ/ⓕ o·ree·zhee·nal original
orteil ⓜ or·tay toe
os ⓜ os bone
ou oo or
où oo where
ouate de coton ⓕ wat der ko·ton cotton balls
oublier oo·blee·yay forget
ouest ⓜ west west
oui wee yes
outre-mer oo·trer·mair overseas
ouvert(e) ⓜ/ⓕ oo·vair(t) open
ouvre-boîte ⓜ oo·vrer·bwat can/tin opener
ouvre-bouteille ⓜ oo·vrer·boo·tay bottle opener
ouvrier/ouvrière ⓜ/ⓕ oo·vree·yay/oo·vree·yair manual worker
ouvrier d'usine ⓜ oo·vree·yay dew·zeen factory worker
ouvrière d'usine ⓕ oo·vree·yair dew·zeen factory worker
ouvrir oo·vreer open
overdose ⓕ o·vair·doz overdose
oxygène ⓜ ok·see·zhen oxygen

P

pacemaker ⓜ pes·may·ker pacemaker
page ⓕ pazh page
paiement ⓜ pay·mon payment
pain ⓜ pun bread
pain grillé ⓜ pung gree·yay toast
paire ⓕ pair pair (couple)
paix ⓕ pay peace
palais ⓜ pa·lay palace
panier ⓜ pan·yay basket
panne pan break down
pansement ⓜ pons·mon bandage
pantalon ⓜ pon·ta·lon trousers • pants
papa ⓜ pa·pa dad
paperasserie ⓕ pa·pras·ree paperwork
papeterie ⓕ pa·pet·ree stationer's (shop)
papier ⓜ pa·pyay paper

papier hygiénique ⓜ pa·pyay ee·zhyay·neek toilet paper
papillon ⓜ pa·pee·yon butterfly
Pâques pak Easter
paquet ⓜ pa·kay package • packet
par par by • per (day)
— avion a·vyon airmail
— exprès eks·pres express mail (by)
— voie de terre vwa der tair surface mail (by land)
— voie maritime vwa ma·ree·teem surface mail (by sea)
parade ⓕ pa·rad parade (ceremony)
paraplégique pa·ra·play·zheek paraplegic
parapluie ⓜ pa·ra·plwee umbrella
parc ⓜ park park
parc national ⓜ park na·syo·nal national park
parce que pars ker because
par-dessus par·der·sew over (above)
pardonner par·do·nay forgive
pare-brise ⓜ par·breez windscreen • windshield
parents ⓜ pl pa·ron parents
paresseux/paresseuse ⓜ/ⓕ pa·ray·ser/pa·ray·serz lazy
parfait(e) ⓜ/ⓕ par·fay(t) perfect
parfum ⓜ par·fum perfume
pari ⓜ pa·ree bet
parier par·yay bet
parking ⓜ par·keeng car park/ parking lot
parler par·lay speak • talk
parmi par·mee among
partager par·ta·zhay share
parti ⓜ par·tee party (politics)
participer par·tee·see·pay participate
particulier/particulière ⓜ/ⓕ par·tee·kew·lyay/par·tee·kew·lyair particular
partie ⓕ par·tee part
partir par·teer depart • leave
pas compris pa kom·pree excluded
pas encore pa zong·kor not yet
pas frais/fraîche ⓜ/ⓕ pa fray/fresh stale
pas mal pa mal not bad
passe ⓕ pas pass (football)
passé ⓜ pa·say past
passeport ⓜ pas·por passport
passer pa·say pass • spend (time)
passe-temps ⓜ pas·ton hobby
pâtisserie ⓕ pa·tees·ree cake shop
pauvre po·vrer poor
pauvreté ⓕ po·vrer·tay poverty
payer pay·yay pay
pays ⓜ pay·ee country
paysage ⓜ pay·yee·zazh scenery
Pays-Bas ⓜ pl pay·ee·ba Netherlands
peau ⓕ po skin
pêche ⓕ pesh fishing
pédale ⓕ pay·dal pedal
peigne ⓜ pe·nyer comb
peine ⓕ pen trouble
peintre ⓜ pun·trer painter
peinture ⓕ pun·tewr painting (the art)
pellicule ⓕ pay·lee·kewl film (for camera)
pendant pon·don during
pendant la nuit pon·don la nwee overnight
penderie ⓕ pon·dree wardrobe
pendule ⓕ pon·dewl clock
pénicilline ⓕ pay·nee·see·leen penicillin
pénis ⓜ pay·nees penis
penser pon·say think
pension ⓕ pon·syon boarding house
pension (de famille) ⓕ pon·syon (der fa·mee) guesthouse
perdant(e) ⓜ/ⓕ pair·don(t) loser
perdre pair·drer lose
perdu(e) ⓜ/ⓕ pair·dew lost
père ⓜ pair father
permanent(e) ⓜ/ⓕ pair·ma·non(t) permanent
permettre pair·me·trer allow
permis ⓜ pair·mee permit

— de conduire der kon·dweer driver's licence
— de travail der tra·vai work permit
permission ⓕ pair·mee·syon permission
personnalité ⓕ pair·so·na·lee·tay personality
personne ⓕ pair·son person
personnel(le) ⓜ/ⓕ pair·so·nel personal
perte ⓕ pairt loss
pertinent(e) ⓜ/ⓕ pair·tee·non(t) relevant
peser per·zay weigh
petit(e) ⓜ/ⓕ per·tee(t) little • small
— ami ⓜ per·tee ta·mee boyfriend
— amie ⓕ per·teet a·mee girlfriend
— cuillère ⓕ per·teet kwee·yair teaspoon
— déjeuner ⓜ per·tee day·zher·nay breakfast
— monnaie ⓕ per·teet mo·nay loose change
— tapis ⓜ per·tee ta·pee mat
petite-fille ⓕ per·teet fee·yer granddaughter
petit-fils ⓜ per·tee fees grandson
pétition ⓕ pay·tees·yon petition
pétrole ⓜ pay·trol oil (petrol)
peu ⓜ per little bit
— commun(e) ⓜ/ⓕ ko·mun/ko·mewn unusual
— profond(e) ⓜ/ⓕ pro·fon(d) shallow
peur ⓕ per fear
peut-être per·tay·trer maybe
phares ⓜ pl far headlights
pharmacie ⓕ far·ma·see chemist • pharmacy
pharmacien(ne) ⓜ/ⓕ far·ma·syun/far·ma·syen chemist (person)
photo ⓕ fo·to photo
photographe ⓜ/ⓕ fo·to·graf photographer
photographie ⓕ fo·to·gra·fee photography

pièce (de théâtre) ⓕ pyes (der tay·a·trer) play (theatre)
pièce d'identité ⓕ pyes dee·don·tee·tay identification
pièces ⓕ pyes coins
pied ⓜ pyay foot
pierre ⓕ pyair stone
piéton ⓜ pyay·ton pedestrian
pile ⓕ peel battery
pilule ⓕ pee·lewl pill
pince à épiler ⓕ puns a ay·pee·lay tweezers
pipe ⓕ peep pipe
pique-nique ⓜ peek·neek picnic
piquets de tente ⓜ pee·kay der tont tent pegs
piqûre ⓕ pee·kewr bite (insect) • injection
pire peer worse
piscine ⓕ pee·seen swimming pool
piste ⓕ peest track (sports) • trail
piste cyclable ⓕ peest see·kla·bler bike path
pistolet ⓜ pees·to·lay gun
placard ⓜ pla·kar cupboard
place ⓕ plas seat (place) • square (town)
place centrale ⓕ plas son·tral main square
plage ⓕ plazh beach
plainte ⓕ plunt complaint
plaisanterie ⓕ play·zon·tree joke
plan ⓜ plon map (of town)
planche à voile ⓕ plonsh a vwal windsurfer
planche de surf ⓕ plonsh der serf surfboard
plancher ⓜ plon·shay floor
planète ⓕ pla·net planet
plaque d'immatriculation ⓕ plak dee·ma· tree·kew·la·syon licence plate number
plastique ⓜ plas·teek plastic
plat ⓜ pla dish
plat(e) ⓜ/ⓕ pla(t) flat

FRENCH – ENGLISH P

plein(e) ⓜ/ⓕ plun/plen full
pleurer pler·ray cry
pleuvoir pler·vwar rain
plongée (sous-marine) ⓕ plon·zhay (soo·ma·reen) diving
plonger plon·zhay dive
pluie ⓕ plwee rain
plus ⓜ plews most
plus de plews der more
plus grand(e) ⓜ/ⓕ plew gron(d) bigger
plus petit(e) ⓜ/ⓕ plew per·tee/·teet smaller
plus tard plew·tar later
plusieurs plew·zyer several
pneu ⓜ pner tyre • tire
poche ⓕ posh pocket
poêle ⓕ pwal frying pan
poésie ⓕ po·ay·zee poetry
poids ⓜ pwa weight
poignet ⓜ pwa·nyay wrist
pointe ⓕ pwunt point
poisson ⓜ pwa·son fish
poissonnerie ⓕ pwa·son·ree fish shop
poitrine ⓕ pwa·treen chest
police ⓕ po·lees police
policier ⓜ po·lee·syay police officer (in city)
politique ⓕ po·lee·teek policy • politics
pollen ⓜ po·len pollen
pollution ⓕ po·lew·syon pollution
pommade pour les lèvres ⓕ po·mad poor lay lay·vrer lip balm
pompe ⓕ pomp pump
pont ⓜ pon bridge
populaire po·pew·lair popular
port ⓜ por harbour • port
portable ⓜ por·ta·bler mobile/cell phone
porte ⓕ port door
porte-monnaie ⓜ port·mo·nay purse
porter por·tay carry • wear
posemètre ⓜ poz·may·trer light meter
poser po·zay ask (a question)
positif/positive ⓜ/ⓕ po·zee·teef/po·zee·teev positive
possible po·see·bler possible
poste ⓕ post mail (postal system)
pot ⓜ po carton • jar • pot
pot d'échappement ⓜ po day·shap·mon exhaust (car)
pot-de-vin ⓜ po·der·vun bribe
poterie ⓕ po·tree pottery
poubelle ⓕ poo·bel rubbish bin/garbage can
poulet ⓜ poo·lay chicken
poumon ⓜ poo·mon lung
poupée ⓕ poo·pay doll
pour poor for
— cent son percent
pourboire ⓜ poor·bwar tip (gratuity)
pourquoi poor·kwa why
pousser poo·say grow • push
poussette ⓕ poo·set pushchair • stroller
poussière ⓕ poo·syair dust
pouvoir poo·vwar can (be able or have permission)
pouvoir ⓜ poo·vwar power
poux ⓜ pl poo lice
pratique pra·teek practical
pratiquer pra·tee·kay practise
précédent(e) ⓜ/ⓕ pray·say·don(t) previous
préférer pray·fay·ray prefer
premier/première ⓜ/ⓕ prer·myay/prer·myair first
premier ministre ⓜ prer·myay mee·nee·strer prime minister
première classe ⓕ prer·myair klas first class
prendre pron·drer take
prendre en photo pron·drer on fo·to take a photo of (someone)
prénom ⓜ pray·non first/given name
préparer pray·pa·ray prepare
près de pray der near
présent ⓜ pray·zon present (time)

présenter pray·zon·tay introduce (people)

préservatif ⓜ pray·zair·va·teef condom

président ⓜ pray·zee·don president

presque pres·ker almost

pressé(e) ⓜ/ⓕ pray·say in a hurry

pression ⓕ pray·syon pressure

prêt(e) ⓜ/ⓕ pray/pret ready

prêtre ⓜ pray·trer priest

prévenir prayv·neer warn

prévision ⓕ pray·vee·zyon forecast

prévoir pray·vwar forecast

prière ⓕ pree·yair prayer

principal(e) ⓜ/ⓕ prun·see·pal main

printemps ⓜ prun·tom spring (season)

prise ⓕ preez plug (electricity)

prison ⓕ pree·zon jail • prison

prisonnier/prisonnière ⓜ/ⓕ pree·zo·nyay/pree·zo·nyair prisoner

privé(e) ⓜ/ⓕ pree·vay private

prix ⓜ pree price

prix d'entrée ⓜ pree don·tray admission (price)

probable pro·ba·bler probable

problème ⓜ pro·blem problem

prochain(e) ⓜ/ⓕ pro·shun/pro·shen next (month)

proche prosh close

produire pro·dweer produce

professeur ⓜ pro·fay·ser teacher

professeur (à l'université) ⓜ pro·fay·ser (a lew·nee·vair·see·tay) lecturer

professionnel(le) ⓜ/ⓕ pro·fay·syo·nel professional

profond(e) ⓜ/ⓕ pro·fon(d) deep

programme ⓜ pro·gram programme

programme des spectacles ⓜ pro·gram day spek·tak·ler entertainment guide

projecteur ⓜ pro·zhek·ter projector

prolongation ⓕ pro·long·ga·syon extension (visa)

promenade ⓕ prom·nad ride

promesse ⓕ pro·mes promise

promettre pro·may·trer promise

promouvoir pro·moo·vwar promote

propre pro·prer clean

propriétaire ⓜ&ⓕ pro·pree·ay·tair landlady • landlord • owner

prostituée ⓕ pro·stee·tway prostitute

protection ⓕ pro·tek·syon protection

protégé(e) ⓜ/ⓕ pro·tay·zhay protected (species)

protéger pro·tay·zhay protect

protège-slips ⓜ pl pro·tezh·sleep panty liners

provisions ⓕ pl pro·vee·zyon food supplies • provisions

prudence ⓕ prew·dons caution

psychothérapie ⓕ psee·ko·tay·ra·pee psychotherapy

public ⓜ pewb·leek public

publicité ⓕ pewb·lee·see·tay advertisement

puce ⓕ pews flea

puis pwee then (next)

puissance nucléaire ⓕ pwee·sons new·klay·air nuclear power

pull ⓜ pewl jumper • sweater

punir pew·neer punish

pur(e) ⓜ/ⓕ pewr pure

Q

quai ⓜ kay platform

qualification ⓕ ka·lee·fee·ka·syon qualification

qualité ⓕ ka·lee·tay quality

quand kon when

quantité ⓕ kon·tee·tay quantity

quarantaine ⓕ ka·ron·ten quarantine

quart ⓜ kar quarter

quatre ka·trer four

quel/quelle ⓜ/ⓕ kel what • which

quelque chose kel·ker shoz something

quelquefois kel·ker·fwa sometimes

quelques kel·ker some
quelqu'un kel·kun someone
question ⓕ kay·styon question
queue ⓕ ker queue • tail
qui kee which • who
quincaillerie ⓕ kung·kay·ree hardware store
quitter kee·tay quit
quotidien(ne) ⓜ/ⓕ ko·tee·dyun/ko·tee·dyen daily

R

race ⓕ ras race
racisme ⓜ ra·sees·mer racism
raconter ra·kon·tay tell (a story)
radiateur ⓜ ra·dya·ter radiator
radical(e) ⓜ/ⓕ ra·dee·kal radical
radio ⓕ ra·dyo radio
raide red steep
raison ⓕ ray·zon reason
raisonnable ray·zo·na·bler sensible
ramasser ra·ma·say pick up (something)
randonnée ⓕ ron·do·nay hiking
rapide ra·peed fast • quick
rapport ⓜ ra·por connection
rapports sexuels protégés ⓜ pl ra·por seks·wel pro·tay·zhay safe sex
raquette ⓕ ra·ket racquet
rare rar rare
rasoir ⓜ ra·zwar razor
rassis(e) ⓜ/ⓕ ra·see(z) stale (bread)
rat ⓜ ra rat
rave ⓕ raiv rave
réalisateur/réalisatrice ⓜ/ⓕ ray·a·lee·za·ter/ray·a·lee·za·trees director (film)
réaliser ray·a·lee·zay direct (a film)
réaliste ray·a·leest realistic
réalité ⓕ ray·a·lee·tay reality
rebord ⓜ rer·bor ledge
récemment ray·sa·mon recently
receveur ⓜ rer·ser·ver conductor (bus)
recevoir rer·ser·vwar receive
réchaud ⓜ ray·sho stove
recherches ⓕ pl rer·shairsh research
récolte ⓕ ray·kolt crop (gathered)
recommander rer·ko·mon·day recommend
reconnaissant(e) ⓜ/ⓕ rer·ko·nay·son(t) grateful
reconnaître rer·ko·nay·trer recognise
reçu ⓜ rer·sew receipt
recueil d'expressions ⓜ rer·ker·yer dek·spray·syon phrasebook
recyclable rer·see·kla·bler recyclable
recyclage ⓜ rer·see·klazh recycling
recycler rer·see·klay recycle
rédacteur/rédactrice ⓜ/ⓕ ray·dak·ter/ray·dak·trees editor
réduire ray·dweer reduce
référence ⓕ ray·fay·rons reference
réfrigérateur ⓜ ray·free·zhay·ra·ter refrigerator
réfugié(e) ⓜ/ⓕ ray·few·zhyay refugee
refuser rer·few·zay refuse
regarder rer·gar·day look • look at • watch
régime ⓜ ray·zheem diet
région ⓕ ray·zhyon region
règles ⓕ ray·gler rules
règles douloureuses ⓕ pl ray·gler doo·loo·rerz period pain
reine ⓕ ren queen
relation ⓕ rer·la·syon relationship
religieuse ⓕ rer·lee·zhyerz nun
religieux/religieuse ⓜ/ⓕ rer·lee·zhyer/rer·lee·zhyerz religious
religion ⓕ rer·lee·zhyon religion
remboursement ⓜ rom·boor·ser·mon refund
remercier rer·mair·syay thank
remise ⓕ rer·meez discount
remplir rom·pleer fill
rencontrer ron·kon·tray meet
rendez-vous ⓜ ron·day·voo appointment • date
renseignements ⓜ pl ron·sen·yer·mon information
réparer ray·pa·ray repair
repas ⓜ rer·pa meal

repasser rer·pa·say iron (clothes)
répondre ray·pon·drer answer • reply
réponse ⓕ ray·pons answer • response
repos ⓜ rer·po rest
représenter rer·pray·zon·tay represent
république ⓕ ray·pewb·leek republic
réseau ⓜ ray·zo network
réservation ⓕ ray·zair·va·syon reservation
réserver ray·zair·vay book (make a booking)
respirer res·pee·ray breathe
ressort ⓜ rer·sor spring (coil)
restaurant ⓜ res·to·ron restaurant
rester res·tay stay
retard ⓜ rer·tard delay
retrait ⓜ rer·tray withdrawal
retrait des bagages ⓜ rer·tray day ba·gazh baggage claim
retraité(e) ⓜ/ⓕ rer·tray·tay pensioner • retired
réussite ⓕ ray·ew·seet achievement
réveil ⓜ ray·vay alarm clock
réveiller ray·vay·yay wake (someone) up
revenir rerv·neer return
revenus ⓜ pl rerv·new income
rêver ray·vay dream
révolution ⓕ ray·vo·lew·syon revolution
rhume ⓜ **des foins** rewm day fwun hay fever
riche reesh rich • wealthy
rien ryun nothing
rire reer laugh
risque ⓜ reesk risk
rivière ⓕ ree·vyair river
riz ⓜ ree rice
robe ⓕ rob dress
robinet ⓜ ro·bee·nay tap • faucet
rocher ⓜ ro·shay rock
rock ⓜ rok rock (music)
roi ⓜ rwa king
roller ⓜ ro·lair rollerblading
roman ⓜ ro·mon novel
romantique ro·mon·teek romantic
rond(e) ⓜ/ⓕ ron(d) round
rond-point ⓜ rom·pwun roundabout (traffic)
rose roz pink
roue ⓕ roo wheel
rouge roozh red
rouge à lèvres ⓜ roozh a lay·vrer lipstick
rougeole ⓕ roo·zhol measles
rougeur ⓕ roo·zher rash
route ⓕ root road
royaume ⓜ rwa·yom kingdom
rue ⓕ rew street
ruelle ⓕ rwel lane (city)
rugby ⓜ rewg·bee rugby
ruines ⓕ pl rween ruins
ruisseau ⓜ rwee·so stream
ruse ⓕ rewz trick
rythme ⓜ reet·mer rhythm

S

sa ⓕ sa her • his
sabbat ⓜ sa·ba Sabbath
sable ⓜ sa·bler sand
sac ⓜ sak bag
— à dos a do backpack
— à main a mun handbag
— de couchage der koo·shazh sleeping bag
saint(e) ⓜ/ⓕ sun(t) saint
Saint-Sylvestre ⓕ sun·seel·ves·trer New Year's Eve
saison ⓕ say·zon season
salaire ⓜ sa·lair salary • wage
salaud ⓜ sa·lo bastard
sale sal dirty
salle ⓕ sal room
— d'attente sal da·tont waiting room
— de bain sal der bun bathroom
— de transit sal der tron·zeet transit lounge
salon de beauté ⓜ sa·lon der bo·tay beauty salon
s'allonger sa·lon·zhay lie (not stand)
salope ⓕ sa·lop bitch

S FRENCH – ENGLISH

samedi ⓜ sam·dee Saturday
s'amuser sa·mew·zay enjoy (oneself)• fun (have fun)
sandales ⓕ son·dal sandals
sang ⓜ son blood
sans son without
sans plomb son plom unleaded
sans-abri son·za·bree homeless
santé ⓕ son·tay health
s'arrêter sa·ray·tay stop (doing)
s'asseoir sa·swar sit
satisfait(e) ⓜ/ⓕ sa·tees·fay/sa·tees·fet satisfied
sauf sof except
sauna ⓜ so·na sauna
sauter so·tay jump
sauvage so·vazh wild
sauver so·vay save
savoir sa·vwar know
savon ⓜ sa·von soap
scénario ⓜ say·na·ryo script
scénariste ⓜ/ⓕ say·na·reest scriptwriter
scène ⓕ sen stage
science ⓕ syons science
science-fiction ⓕ syons·feek·syon science fiction
scientifique ⓜ&ⓕ syon·tee·feek scientist
score ⓜ skor score
sculpture ⓕ skewl·tewr sculpture
se coucher ser koo·shay go to bed
se décider ser day·see·day decide
se disputer ser dees·pew·tay argue
se laver ser la·vay wash (oneself)
se mettre à genoux ser may·trer a zher·noo kneel
se mettre en grève ser may·trer ong grev strike (go on strike)
se plaindre ser plun·drer complain
se raser ser ra·zay shave
se rendre compte de ser ron·drer kont der realise
se reposer ser rer·po·zay relax (rest)
se réveiller ser ray·vay·yay wake up
se souvenir ser soo·ver·neer remember
seau ⓜ so bucket
sec/sèche ⓜ/ⓕ sek/sesh dry
sécher say·shay dry (clothes)
second(e) ⓜ/ⓕ skon/skond second
seconde ⓕ skond second (clock)
secret ⓜ ser·kray secret
secrétaire ⓜ/ⓕ ser·kray·tair secretary
sécurité ⓕ say·kew·ree·tay safety • security
sécurité sociale ⓕ say·kew·ree·tay so·syal social welfare
sein ⓜ sun breast
sel ⓜ sel salt
selle ⓕ sel saddle
semaine ⓕ ser·men week
semblable som·bla·bler similar
séminaire ⓜ say·mee·nair seminar
s'ennuyer son·nwee·yay bored (be)
sensation ⓕ son·sa·syon feeling (physical)
sensuel(le) ⓜ/ⓕ son·swel sensual
sentier ⓜ son·tyay footpath
sentiment ⓜ son·tee·mon feeling (emotion)
sentir son·teer smell
séparé(e) ⓜ/ⓕ say·pa·ray separate
sept set seven
septembre ⓜ sep·tom·brer September
série ⓕ say·ree series
sérieux/sérieuse ⓜ/ⓕ say·ree·yer/say·ree·yerz serious
seringue ⓕ ser·rung syringe
séropositif/séropositive ⓜ/ⓕ say·ro·po·zee·teef/say·ro·po·zee·teev HIV positive
serpent ⓜ sair·pon snake
serrer dans ses bras say·ray don say bra hug
serrure ⓕ say·rewr lock
serveur/serveuse ⓜ/ⓕ sair·ver/sair·verz waiter

service ⓜ sair·vees service • service charge
service militaire ⓜ sair·vees mee·lee·tair military service
serviette ⓕ sair·vyet briefcase • napkin • towel
serviette hygiénique ⓕ sair·vyet ee·zhyay·neek sanitary napkin
ses pl say her • his
seul(e) ⓜ/ⓕ serl only
sexe ⓜ seks sex
sexisme ⓜ sek·see·smer sexism
sexiste sek·seest sexist
sexy sek·see sexy
s'habiller sa·bee·yay dress (oneself)
shampooing ⓜ shom·pwung shampoo
short ⓜ short shorts
si see if
SIDA ⓜ see·da AIDS
siège pour enfant ⓜ syezh poor on·fon child seat
siffler see·flay whistle
signature ⓕ see·nya·tewr signature
signe ⓜ see·nyer sign
simple sum·pler simple
Singapour sung·ga·poor Singapore
singe ⓜ sunzh monkey
s'inquiéter sung·kyay·tay worry
situation ⓕ see·twa·syon situation
situation ⓕ **familiale** see·twa·syon fa·mee·lyal marital status
six sees six
skateboard ⓜ sket·bord skate-boarding
ski ⓜ skee skiing
ski nautique ⓜ skee no·teek waterskiing
skier skee·yay ski
skis ⓜ skee skis
slip ⓜ sleep panties • underpants
s'occuper de so·kew·pay der look after
socialisme ⓜ so·sya·lees·mer socialism
socialiste so·sya·leest socialist
societé ⓕ so·syay·tay society
sœur ⓕ ser sister
soie ⓕ swa silk
soigner swa·nyay care for (someone)
soigneux/soigneuse ⓜ/ⓕ swa·nyer/swa·nyerz careful
soir ⓜ swar evening
soirée ⓕ swa·ray night out • party
soldat ⓜ sol·da soldier
solde ⓜ sold balance (account)
soleil ⓜ so·lay sun
solide so·leed solid
somme ⓕ som amount (money)
sommeil ⓜ so·may sleep
somnifère ⓜ som·nee·fair sleeping pill
son ⓜ son her • his
sonner so·nay ring (of phone)
sortie ⓕ sor·tee exit
sortir sor·teer go out
sortir avec sor·teer a·vek date (go out with)
souffrir soo·freer suffer
souhaiter sway·tay wish
soulever sool·vay lift • raise
sourd(e) ⓜ/ⓕ soor(d) deaf
sourire soo·reer smile
sourire ⓜ soo·reer smile
souris ⓕ soo·ree mouse
sous soo below • under
sous-titres ⓜ soo·tee·trer subtitles
sous-vêtements ⓜ soo·vet·mon underwear
soutien-gorge ⓜ soo·tyung·gorzh bra
souvenir ⓜ soov·neer memory (recollection) • souvenir
souvent soo·von often
sparadrap ⓜ spa·ra·dra plaster • Band-Aid
spécial(e) ⓜ/ⓕ spay·syal special
spécialiste ⓜ/ⓕ spay·sya·leest specialist
spectacle ⓜ spek·ta·kler performance • show
sport ⓜ spor sport

sportif/sportive ⓜ/ⓕ spor·teef/spor·teev sportsperson
stade ⓜ stad stadium
stage en entreprise ⓜ stazh on on·trer·preez work experience
station de métro ⓕ sta·syon der may·tro metro station
station de taxi ⓕ sta·syon der tak·see taxi stand
station-service ⓕ sta·syon·sair·vees petrol station
stérilet ⓜ stay·ree·lay IUD
stupéfiant ⓜ stew·pay·fyon narcotic
stupéfiant(e) ⓜ/ⓕ stew·pay·fyon(t) amazing
stupide stew·peed stupid
style ⓜ steel style
stylo ⓜ stee·lo pen (ballpoint)
suborner sew·bor·nay bribe
sucré(e) ⓜ/ⓕ sew·kray sweet
sud ⓜ sewd south
suivre swee·vrer follow
supérette de quartier ⓕ sew·pay·ret der kar·tyay convenience store
supermarché ⓜ sew·pair·mar·shay supermarket
superstition ⓕ sew·pair·stee·syon superstition
supplémentaire sew·play·mon·tair additional • extra
supporter sew·por·tay support
sur sewr on
sûr(e) ⓜ/ⓕ sewr sure
surf (des neiges) ⓜ serf (day nezh) snowboarding
surfer ser·fay surf
surnom ⓜ sewr·nom nickname
surprise ⓕ sewr·preez surprise
survivre sewr·vee·vrer survive
synagogue ⓕ see·na·gog synagogue
syndicat ⓜ sun·dee·ka union (trade)
syndrome prémenstruel ⓜ sun·drom pray·mon·strwel premenstrual tension
synthétique sun·tay·teek synthetic
syrop contre la toux ⓜ see·ro kon·trer la too cough medicine

T

ta ⓕ sg inf ta your
tabac ⓜ ta·ba tobacco
table ⓕ ta·bler table
tableau ⓜ ta·blo painting (a work)
tableau d'affichage ⓜ ta·blo da·fee·shazh scoreboard
taie d'oreiller ⓕ tay do·ray·yay pillowcase
taille ⓕ tai size (general)
tailleur ⓜ ta·yer tailor
talc ⓜ talk baby powder
tambour ⓜ tom·boor drum
tampon hygiénique ⓜ tom·pon ee·zhyay·neek tampon
tante ⓕ tont aunt
tapis ⓜ ta·pee rug
tarif ⓜ ta·reef fare
tarifs postaux ⓜ pl ta·reef pos·to postage
tasse ⓕ tas cup
taux de change ⓜ to der shonzh currency exchange • exchange rate
taxe ⓕ taks tax
— à la vente a la vont sales tax
— d'aéroport da·ay·ro·por airport tax
taxi ⓜ tak·see taxi
technique ⓕ tek·neek technique
télé ⓕ tay·lay TV
télécarte ⓕ tay·lay·kart phone card
télécommande ⓕ tay·lay·ko·mond remote control
télégramme ⓜ tay·lay·gram telegram
téléphérique ⓜ tay·lay·fay·reek cable car
téléphone ⓜ tay·lay·fon telephone
téléphone public ⓜ tay·lay·fon pewb·leek public telephone
téléphoner tay·lay·fo·nay telephone
télescope ⓜ tay·lay·skop telescope

télésiège ⓜ tay·lay·syezh chairlift (skiing)
télévision ⓕ tay·la·vee·zyon television
témoin ⓜ tay·mwun witness
température ⓕ tom·pay·ra·tewr temperature
temple ⓜ tom·pler temple
temps ⓜ tom time (general) • weather
tennis ⓜ tay·nees tennis
tennis de table ⓜ tay·nees der ta·bler table tennis
tension artérielle ⓕ ton·syon ar·tay·ryel blood pressure
tente ⓕ tont tent
terrain ⓜ tay·rung ground
— de camping der kom·peeng campsite
— de golf der golf golf course
— de jeux der zher playground
— de sport der spor sports ground
Terre ⓕ tair Earth
terre ⓕ tair earth • land
terrorisme ⓜ tay·ro·rees·mer terrorism
tes pl inf tay your
test de grossesse ⓜ test der gro·ses pregnancy test kit
tête ⓕ tet head
tétine ⓕ tay·teen dummy • pacifier
teush ⓜ tersh hash
théâtre ⓜ tay·a·trer drama (theatre)
timbre ⓜ tum·brer stamp
timide tee·meed shy
tire-bouchon ⓜ teer·boo·shon corkscrew
tirer tee·ray pull • shoot
tissu ⓜ tee·sew fabric
toilettes ⓕ pl twa·let public toilet
toit ⓜ twa roof
tombe ⓕ tomb grave
tomber tom·bay fall
ton ⓜ sg inf ton your
tonalité ⓕ to·na·lee·tay dial tone
tôt to early
toucher too·shay feel • touch
toujours too·zhoor always
tour ⓕ toor tower
touriste ⓜ&ⓕ too·reest tourist
tourner toor·nay turn
tournoi ⓜ toor·nwa tournament
tous les deux too lay der both
tous les jours too lay zhoor every day
tout too all • everything
— droit drwa straight ahead
— le monde ler mond everyone
— près pray nearby
tout(e) seul(e) ⓜ/ⓕ too(t) serl alone
toux ⓕ too cough
toxicomanie ⓕ tok·see·ko·ma·nee drug addiction
traduire tra·dweer translate
trafiquant de drogue ⓜ tra·fee·kon der drog drug dealer
train ⓜ trun train
traite bancaire ⓕ tret bong·kair bank draft
traitement ⓜ tret·mon treatment
tranchant(e) ⓜ/ⓕ tron·shon(t) sharp (blade, etc)
tranche ⓕ tronsh slice
tranquille trong·keel quiet
transfert ⓜ trons·fair transfer
transport ⓜ trons·por transport
travail ⓜ tra·vai job • work
— dans un bar don zun bar bar work
— intermittent un·tair·mee·ton casual work
travailler tra·va·yay work
traverser tra·vair·say cross
tremblement de terre ⓜ trom·bler·mon der tair earthquake
très tray very
tribunal ⓜ tree·bew·nal court (legal)
tricheur/tricheuse ⓜ/ⓕ tree·sher/tree·sherz cheat
tricot ⓜ tree·ko knitting
triste treest sad
trois trwa three
troisième trwa·zyem third
tromper trom·pay trick
trop tro too (expensive etc)

trop de tro der too much (rain etc) • too many (people etc)
trou ⓜ troo hole
trousse à pharmacie ⓕ troos a far·ma·see first-aid kit
trouver troo·vay find
T-shirt ⓜ tee·shert T-shirt
tu inf tew you
tuer tew·way kill
type ⓜ teep type
typique tee·peek typical

U

ultrason ⓜ ewl·tra·son ultrasound
un peu ⓜ um per a little
un(e) ⓜ/ⓕ un/ewn a/an • one
une fois ewn fwa once
uniforme ⓜ ew·nee·form uniform
union ⓕ ew·nyon union
univers ⓜ ew·nee·vair universe
université ⓕ ew·nee·vair·see·tay university
urgent(e) ⓜ/ⓕ ewr·zhon(t) urgent
usine ⓕ ew·zeen factory
utile ew·teel useful
utiliser ew·tee·lee·zay use

V

vacances ⓕ pl va·kons holidays • vacation
vaccination ⓕ vak·see·na·syon vaccination
vache ⓕ vash cow
vagin ⓜ va·zhun vagina
vague ⓕ vag wave
valeur ⓕ va·ler value (price)
valider va·lee·day validate
valise ⓕ va·leez suitcase
vallée ⓕ va·lay valley
varappe ⓕ va·rap rock climbing
végétarien/végétarienne ⓜ/ⓕ vay·zhay·ta·ryun/vay·zhay·ta·ryen vegetarian
véhicule ⓜ vay·ee·kewl vehicle
veine ⓕ ven vein
vélo ⓜ vay·lo bicycle
vélo tout terrain (VTT) ⓜ vay·lo too tay·run (vay·tay·tay) mountain bike
vendre von·drer sell
vendredi von·drer·dee Friday
venimeux/venimeuse ⓜ/ⓕ ver·nee·mer/ver·nee·merz poisonous
venir ver·neer come
vent ⓜ von wind
vente ⓕ vont sale
vente aux enchères ⓕ vont o zon·shair auction
ventilateur ⓜ von·tee·la·ter fan (machine)
vérifier vay·ree·fyay check
vérité ⓕ vay·ree·tay truth
verre ⓜ vair drink (alcoholic) • glass
verres de contact ⓜ vair der kon·takt contact lenses
vers vair toward (direction)
vers ⓜ vair worms
vert(e) ⓜ/ⓕ vair(t) green
veste ⓕ vest jacket
vestiaire ⓜ vays·tyair cloakroom
vêtements ⓜ vet·mon clothing
veuf ⓜ verf widower
veuve ⓕ verv widow
via vee·a via
viande ⓕ vyond meat
vide veed empty
vie ⓕ vee life
vieux/vieille ⓜ/ⓕ vyer/vyay old
vigne ⓕ vee·nyer vine
vignoble ⓜ vee·nyo·bler vineyard
VIH (virus immunodéficitaire humain) ⓜ vay·ee·ash (vee·rews ee·mew·no·day·fee·see·tair ew·mun) HIV
village ⓜ vee·lazh village
ville ⓕ veel city • town
vin ⓜ vun wine
violer vyo·lay rape
violet(te) ⓜ/ⓕ vyo·lay/vyo·let purple
virus ⓜ vee·rews virus

visa ⓜ vee·za visa
visage ⓜ vee·zazh face
visite guidée ⓕ vee·zeet gee·day guided tour
visiter vee·zee·tay visit (museum etc)
visiteur/visiteuse ⓜ/ⓕ vee·zee·ter/vee·zee·terz visitor
vitamine ⓕ vee·ta·meen vitamin
vitesse ⓕ vee·tes speed
vivant(e) ⓜ/ⓕ vee·von(t) alive
vivre vee·vrer live
voile ⓕ vwal sail • sailing
voir vwar see
voiture ⓕ vwa·tewr car
voiture de police ⓕ vwa·tewr der po·lees police car
vol ⓜ vol flight • robbery
volé(e) ⓜ/ⓕ vo·lay stolen
voler vo·lay fly • rob • steal
voleur/voleuse ⓜ/ⓕ vo·ler/vo·lerz thief
volume ⓜ vo·lewm volume
vomir vo·meer vomit
vos pl/pol vo your
voter vo·tay vote
votre sg pol vo·trer/vo your
vouloir voo·lwar want
vous pl pol voo you
voyage ⓜ vwa·yazh journey • tour • trip
voyage d'affaires ⓜ vwa·yazh da·fair business trip
voyager vwa·ya·zhay travel
voyageur/voyageuse ⓜ/ⓕ vwa·ya·zher/vwa·ya·zherz passenger
vrai(e) ⓜ/ⓕ vray real • true
vraiment vray·mon really
vue ⓕ vew view

W

wagon-lit ⓜ va·gon·lee sleeping car
wagon-restaurant ⓜ va·gon·res·to·ron dining car
week-end ⓜ week·end weekend

Y

yeux ⓜ yer eyes
yoga ⓜ yo·ga yoga

Z

zéro zay·ro zero
zoo ⓜ zo zoo

INDEX

L'INDICE

For topics that are covered in several sections of this book, we've indicated the most relevant page number in bold.

A

B

C

D

E

F

G

H

I

Q

R

S

T

V

W

10 Ways TO START A SENTENCE

At what time is (the next train)?	À quelle heure part (le prochain train)?	a kel er par (ler pro·shun trun)
Where's (the station)?	Où est (la gare)?	oo ay (la gar)
Where can I (buy a ticket)?	Où est-ce que je peux (acheter un billet)?	oo es ker zher per (ash·tay um bee·yay)
Do you have (a map)?	Avez-vous (une carte)?	a·vay·voo (ewn kart)
Is there (a toilet)?	Y a-t-il (des toilettes)?	ya·teel (day twa·let)
I'd like (a coffee).	Je voudrais (un café).	zher voo·dray (ung ka·fay)
I'd like to (hire a car).	Je voudrais (louer une voiture).	zher voo·dray (loo·ay ewn vwa·tewr)
Can I (enter)?	Puis-je (entrer)?	pweezh (on·tray)
Could you please (help me)?	Pouvez-vous (m'aider), s'il vous plaît?	poo·vay·voo (may·day) seel voo play
Do I have to (book a seat)?	Faut-il (réserver une place)?	fo·teel (ray·zair·vay ewn plas)